CAPTAIN OF WALES

By
WALLEY BARNES

GCR BOOKS
www.gcrbooks.co.uk

First Published in Great Britain 1953 by Stanley Paul

This edition published 2012 by GCR Books Ltd - www.gcrbooks.co.uk
ISBN 978-0-9559211-86

Copyright © Walley Barnes 1953

Cover image courtesy of Mirrorpix
Cover design by GCR Books Ltd
Editing by Greg Adams

Printed and bound in Great Britain by Lonsdale Print Solutions, Wellingborough

The Arsenal Classic Collection

from

GCRBOOKS

CLASSIC FOOTBALL BOOKS - REPUBLISHED

Vol. 1 – *The Arsenal Stadium Mystery*

Vol. 2 – *Forward, Arsenal!*

Vol. 3 – *Football Ambassador*

Vol. 4 – *Herbert Chapman on Football*

Vol. 5 – *Cliff Bastin Remembers*

Vol. 6 – *Over the Bar*

Vol. 7 – *Arsenal Football Club*

Vol. 8 – *Captain of Wales*

How many do *you* have?

Visit **www.gcrbooks.co.uk** for details.

With thanks to
Andrew and Chrissie Tooze
for their generosity and kind cooperation in the
republication of this book.

AUTHOR'S NOTE

Before the end of the memorable 1951/52 soccer season – during which I enjoyed the supreme honour of leading Wales to success in the international championship – the suggestion was made that I should write a book. I gave the matter deep consideration, and decided that my story was worth telling. Indeed, there were many things that I was anxious to see set down on paper as a result of my wide experience in first-class football.

But how to set about it? I was a professional footballer, not a trained writer. Although I had written a number of short press articles, and I was fairly experienced at giving talks and lectures, the thought of setting down 75,000 words to be printed in a book was enough to give me a severe headache.

So what I did was to ask the advice of my friend Ken Wheeler, who is a professional sports writer, and he at once offered to help. But what he said was this:

"You've got an interesting story to tell, Walley, and it would be easy enough for me to "ghost" if for you. But I'm not going to do that, because I believe that you are quite capable of telling your own story in a bright and interesting way with a little help of the right kind. What I suggest is that you should tell your story to me. I'll put it down on paper as you say it, polishing a word here and a phrase there to conform to professional standards. But you must do all the creative work, and you must read and approve every word that I put down to make sure that the sense of all you say is fully interpreted."

And that's what we did. Ken and I met two or three times a week for the next few months, in a corner of the Arsenal dressing-room, at my office or at his, until my hoarse voice and his aching wrist told us that we were getting to the end of the road.

At this stage I read the statement of a prominent F.A. official reported in the *Daily Express*.

"One of these days a footballer will write his own book," this official was reported to have said. "The public is being fooled – it's time they were told that not one footballer in a thousand is capable of writing a chapter let alone a whole book.

Whether there is any truth in this statement I cannot say. I can't answer for all the other footballers whose names have appeared on books. But this I can say: *Captain of Wales*, by Walley Barnes, is what it says it is. Every account and every opinion expressed in it is mine: every word has been approved by me. I am deeply grateful to Ken Wheeler for his invaluable help and advice, without which this book could not have been written, but he is as anxious as I am that the public should know that this is *my* book, and not his under my name. We are not attempting to fool the public in any way, and that is why I have explained exactly how this book was written.

Chapter One

I knocked on the ever-open door of the manager's office at Highbury, and at once heard Tom Whittaker's cheery "Come right in!"

There was a moment's hesitation on my part. I had been "sent for", and although a member of the "senior class" I was nevertheless very much the guilty schoolboy, summoned to the Headmaster's study.

What was it I had done wrong? We'd given the Wolves a good licking on Saturday. I'd done a good morning's training. I was feeling as fit as a fiddle, playing on top form; and I'd already been told that I had been selected to play for Wales against Ireland on Wednesday – indeed, I had prepared to leave for Wrexham that very afternoon.

"Oh well – let's face it, whatever it is," I told myself, and I went in.

"Hello, Walley," the boss greeted my quietly. "I'll get straight to the point," he said. "You made one or two slips on Saturday, so let's have a chat and see if we can put them right..."

The boss then proceeded to tear me off a strip for several errors of judgement that unsuspectingly I had made against the Wolves. As he made each point I had to confess that his criticism was justified, and truly I was glad to listen and to learn.

When things are going well, there is always the danger that a player will get cocky, and careless in his play, and many an Arsenal player, like me, has had good reason to be grateful for Mr. Whittaker's wise intervention before the rot sets in. Undoubtedly, his wigging did me the world of good.

"Well, now that we've ironed that out there's another matter to concern you," said Tom, looking at me over the top of his horn-rimmed spectacles. "According to a message I've just received, Ronnie Burgess has to play for his club in the Cup semi-final replay on Wednesday and so he won't be available for the International.

"Under the circumstances," Tom continued, the suggestion of a twinkle in his eyes betraying the gravity of his expression, "the Football Association of Wales has decided to honour *you*. You are to captain the Welsh international team against Ireland."

It was the biggest and pleasantest surprise I ever had.

Of course, I had realised that Ronnie Burgess might not be available for this match, but in his absence I had assumed that one of the more experienced internationals, like Tom Jones, would take charge.

But there it was – I was to be the lucky one, and actually it was Tom Jones who was the first member of the team to congratulate me when I arrived at our Wrexham hotel ready for the game on March 10th, 1948.

I was very proud, and just a little nervous. You see, I'd never been asked to captain *any* team before in my life.

Looking back now, I suppose that "fruity" interview with Mr. Whittaker, in which I started by receiving a raspberry and finished with a plum, was the first of a series of significant events in my footballing lifetime. Soon I was helping my club to win the League title, then the Cup. I became established as Captain of Wales, and had the honour of leading my country to success in the international championship.

No professional footballer could wish for more.

Except this: to see his name appear on the list for his team's next match.

I speak with the experience of a footballer who has a "knee". A serious cartilage injury, sustained in the 1952 Cup Final, kept me out of action for a whole year. It stopped me from playing for my country at Wembley; it prevented me from sharing in my club's seventh League Championship success and, if I'm honest with myself, I know that there is a chance the injury has shortened my first-class playing career.

But I'm hoping that my knee will allow me another three of four years in the red shirt of Arsenal and Wales. I've recovered from serious injury before, and I'm determined to make this "come back" successful too.

To be put out of action for a full season is serious to any player, and particularly so at my age (I'm thirty-three). I know it well. That's why I'm working and training and worrying harder than ever before. It's not just a matter of coming back – now I've come back I want to make quite sure that I can stay.

But sooner or later I shall have to face the inevitable end of my playing days. Then my hope will be that there is still a corner of the game left for me to fill. It isn't that I'm worried about making a living – I've taken good care to build for the future – it's just that the idea of leaving football altogether fills me with an indescribable emptiness and despair. As long as I can be of use to the game – in any capacity – I'll be first man on parade. I'm a sucker for soccer, and that's all there is to it.

Both my parents were born within a hefty kick of Arsenal Stadium. But my soldier-father happened to be stationed in Brecon on January 16th, 1920, when I was born, so my place of birth gives me a different nationality from that of all other members of the family.

According to F.A. rules I am a Welshman. Yet I only lived in Brecon long enough to cut my milk teeth, and to acquire that curious Christian name of mine.

This is how I got my name.

As my father's third son I represented a good omen, and my birth was the excuse for hearty celebrations by the sergeants of the South Wales Borderers. Everybody wanted to treat my dad.

Under such circumstances the practical task of giving me a name caused last-moment consternation. Voices were raised in argument, and brows were furrowed in perplexity at the registry office, as Dad and his Army mates gave their consideration to the problem. After the assembled company had gone through the alphabet volunteering random suggestions, my father finally decided, "We'll call it Wally!"

By then, not surprisingly, the registrar was in such a state of confusion that in completing the birth certificate he made a slight spelling mistake, adding the letter "e" to my name and thus committing me to a lifetime of pedantic explanation.

When I was four years of age my mother, my elder brothers Ted and John, and myself, left Brecon to join Dad in India, where his regiment was posted. We spent four years abroad: the rest of my boyhood, and most of my Army service was spent in Southern England. It was with Arsenal, of course, that I became a professional footballer.

Not until I was twenty-four years of age did I return to the land of my birth, and then it was to play football for Wales against England.

What sort of Welshman does that make me?

My father joined the South Wales Borderers in the mistaken belief that it was a horsed regiment. But he stayed with them because of the affection and regard he formed for Taffy.

I, too, have formed a deep attachment for the Welsh people. Unlike many members of the international team I can claim no roots or traditional ties: but Mother Wales has shown no discrimination on that account, and I know that I have found a real home with compatriots eager to accept me as one of themselves.

Wales was the first team I ever captained, but I had no hesitation in accepting the job. Indeed, I jumped at it, recognizing a great opportunity.

With the officials of the Football Association of Wales and with my fellow-players, I shared a conviction that our team, modest though resources were from which it must be drawn, could combine intelligent tactics with the national fervour that had always characterized its displays and thus become a great match-winning combination.

4

I was anxious to put into practice ideas about tactics and leadership that I had formed in the Army, and at Arsenal, and I was given a free hand to do so.

And, because each individual has dedicated his every thought and action to the one ideal, I believe our team of today is one that Mother Wales can claim with pride.

Ted Robbins used to say, "Welsh football begins on the hearth." The greatest man in Welsh football history appealed to the players through their mam and their dad, inspiring them to fight against odds, and beyond normal ability; not as individuals, but as a team for the honour and glory of our little country.

It was a magic formula to inspire, and often to bring success to Welsh teams during the thirty-six years in which Ted Robbins ruled.

But, without his personal inspiration, the national fervour stirred up by Ted Robbins could have become wasted effort, unless backed by a solid foundation of up-to-date soccer tactics. In consultation with Mr. Herbert Powell, other officials and fellow players, it has been my task to direct that do-or-die spirit to advantage.

The Welsh Honorary Medical Officer, Doc Hughes, and Trainer Walter Robbins always sit-in at our team talks and their help is invaluable. No one knows more about Welsh football than the doctor, and when he quietly intervenes in the discussion it is always to make some shrewd, farsighted point that would not have occurred to the rest of us. As for Walter Robbins, he is far more than just a good trainer. He doesn't have a great deal to say, but when he does express an opinion it is as firm and penetrating as was his style of play when he dominated the Welsh left wing in the thirties.

Ronnie, Trevor and all the other members of the team also make their contributions to the discussion. No plan is made hard and fast unless everybody agrees that it is a good one from the team's point of view.

5

Of course, plans do not always come off. The ball has not always run kindly for us. Sometimes the weight of talent ranged against us has been too great, as in the 1952/53 tournament: or else we tried *too* hard.

But in 1951/52, our 75th anniversary season, we were on top of the tree. What a wonderful year it was for Welsh sport! Not only did our little country produce Olympic Games' heroes like Harry Llewellyn and John Disley, and earn further individual sporting honours through Dai Rees and Tommy Farr: not only did Wales win Rugby's Triple Crown: but Cardiff City won promotion to the First Division of the Football League, Wales beat the combined might of England, Scotland and Ireland at Cardiff and went on to share the International soccer championship. Surely that constitutes a unique record?

In my opinion, that international side which I was so proud to lead to championship honours was the finest *team* ever to represent our country. Fortunately its nucleus remains today, and there are many talented young players who will soon be ready to infuse new blood when it becomes necessary.

I can see that I may already have started an argument: no doubt I shall start many more before I have finished. But in order to substantiate my claim, let's take a look at the eleven men with whom I had the honour to play in 1951/52.

Take Billy Shortt, to start with. It may be contended that several of his predecessors were better goalkeepers, and I'll not enter the argument; but tell me of a better *team* man and I'll argue Billy's qualities until the cows come home.

Bill and I usually "room" together before international matches, and I think I know him pretty well. In my opinion Wales could not have wished for a more loyal, more reliable custodian in her year of triumph.

On the short side for a goalkeeper (and no pun is intended), Billy puts on weight all too easily, so he trains and diets harder than most of us. But this does not affect his cheerful demeanour,

6

nor his agility and shrewd judgement. Like me, he was born just inside the border.

He's a Wrexham man who settled down at Plymouth after a spell with Chester. In 1946, the same year that he joined Argyle, he was selected for a Victory international, and he gained his first full cap against Ireland the following season.

I've always been lucky in my partner at full-back – who could have wished for a better mate than Laurie Scott, Lionel Smith, Ray Lambert or Alf Sherwood? In playing ability the Cardiff skipper compares very favourably with any of the others, and I do not know of a defender with more fighting spirit and guts.

Born at Aberaman, Alf has the unusual distinction of having played for Welsh schoolboy international teams at both soccer and cricket in the same year – 1938. He gained his first full cap in 1946, and if anyone is going to challenge the record of the incomparable Billy Meredith, who was capped fifty-one times, Alf is the player most likely to do it. During my absence from the side through injury, Alf was partnered at full-back by Ron Stitfall, his Cardiff colleague, and Wales thus had the opportunity of fielding one of the best club pairs in the First Division.

A footballer's footballer, as well as a crowd favourite, is Ronnie Burgess, captain of the Spurs and my predecessor as Welsh skipper. Born at Ebbw Vale, Ronnie learnt his soccer at the pit-head, and polished it at the Tottenham "Academy" which he joined at the age of seventeen. A footballer from the top of his head to the tip of his toes, Ronnie is the hardest worker I've ever known on the field, and it is no exaggeration to say that he does the work of two men. No one ever gave more for his country on the field of sport.

Taking over the captaincy from an established player who is still a valued member of the team is a task that no one would relish. But Ronnie made it easier for me by backing me up with all his authority, guiding and helping discreetly in the many problems of international captaincy in which he was experienced. I shall always be grateful to him for that, and no less for the way he has undertaken the lion's share of the left-flank work on the field of play.

To find a successor to Tommy Jones was no easy matter, and it says much for my former Arsenal colleague, Ray Daniel (now with Sunderland), that he has filled the breach so competently. The former Swansea amateur, who gained his first cap when still an Arsenal reserve, gets better with every game, and he is still young enough to reach the Tommy Jones standard – which, in my opinion, is the highest class in centre-half play.

What a fine, strong player Roy Paul, the wartime Royal Marine, who was first discovered by a Swansea scout while playing with George Lowrie for Ton Pentre Boys' Club. The touch and artistry with which he decorates his honest labour makes him one of the most pleasing as well as valuable wing half-backs in the game, and he has also proved his versatility by playing both at centre-half and inside-forward for Wales.

1951-52 was the first season for some time that Wales were able to establish a regular forward line, and it was led with rare dash and fire by rumbustious Trevor Ford, the man who, after failing to impress Cardiff as a left-back, was converted by Swansea into the most striking centre-forward of our day.

What a man to have on your side! Trevor, to my mind, is the complete centre-forward, blending natural skill and maximum effort into a vivid combination. Tough as teak on the field, yet gentle of speech and manner in mufti, Trevor is worth at least a goal start to Wales.

Like Alf Sherwood, Trevor played cricket as well as soccer for Wales as a schoolboy.

What a versatile bunch of sportsmen these Sons of Wales are! Roy Clarke, the hawk-like left-winger with a sudden powerful shot, has not only earned many soccer caps for Wales, he also played for his country against England at baseball!

Born at Newport, one of the mining family, Roy first joined Cardiff City as an inside-forward. In 1946-47 he helped Cardiff City to win promotion to the 2nd Division, but after playing for the Welsh club in their last League Three game he was transferred to Manchester City. He played one match for Manchester City that season, their last in Division Two for they also won promotion. So the next match in which Roy played, the first of the following season, was a League One fixture. I the space of three matches he had played a game in each division of the league!

I don't think that cheery, likeable Billy Foulkes, our right-winger, will forget season 1951-52 in a hurry. Not only did he make a sensational international debut, scoring a goal with his first kick, but joining Newcastle United from Chester at the beginning of the year he quickly helped himself to a Cup-winners' medal at Wembley – at Arsenal's expense. He has already done much to make Merthyr Vale proud of him, and has the ability to go on to still greater deeds.

I still don't think we've seen the best of young Noel Kinsey either. Originally a right-half, this little chap from Treorchy has the makings of a sound international class inside-forward, but was not ready in our championship year to replace wee Billy Morris, the tidy Burnley craftsman from North Wales, who proved a decided asset to our attack.

As for Ivor Allchurch, the tall, golden-haired inside-left of Swansea, who made such an impressive debut against England in 1950, he is already in the top class and young and promising enough to earn the stamp of greatness. Ivor is a natural player and, with John Charles, must go down as the outstanding discovery in Welsh football since the war.

But Ivor is not the only discovery – we've got plenty more up our sleeves like Jack Kelsey and Dave Bowen (of Arsenal). As for John Charles (of Leeds United) he made a splendid international debut at centre-half when he was only eighteen, and now he has become a champion goal-scoring centre-forward for his club and Wales, and an international inside-forward as well. He's jack-of-all-trades and master of all!

So you see, 1951-52 was not only our championship year, it marked the beginning of a new era in Welsh football. True, results were disappointing in 1952-53, but I think this was merely a temporary setback. As long as Wales can go on producing fine young players at the rate they are doing at present, and as long as the red jersey continues to inspire its wearers to play up to, and even above their best form, the outlook is rosy.

Now you might like to make a note of these names: B. Thomas (Swansea); R. Smith (Merthyr); R. Harris (Cardiff); T. Arnold (Swansea); B. Hughes (Rhyl); M. Nurse (Swansea); C. Court (Ebbw Vale); J. Miller (Cardiff); M. Hughes (Ebbw Vale); H. Davies (Merthyr) and Willie Rees (Swansea).

Who are they? The gallant Welsh schoolboy team which drew 3-3 with the English schoolboys at Wembley in 1953. Among them, I should say, there are more than a few senior internationals of tomorrow.

Chapter Two

"Well done, young Tich! You saved a certain goal!"

With the other Borderers' supporters, my Dad was enjoying a good laugh. But I was nearer to tears; I felt as if I had stopped a cannon ball.

The smallest boy in the school at Lebong, an Army hill station near Darjeeling, on the lower slopes of the Himalayas, I was proud of my job as mascot to the regimental football team, which permitted me to dress-up in the miniature football kit made for me by the local tradesmen, and to kick-off for our team. After kicking-off, of course, I was expected to run off the field, leaving the grown-ups to get on with the game.

On this particular occasion, however before I could reach the touchline I got tangled-up with the play. So quickly were the visitors off the mark that I was still in the vicinity of our goal when the centre-forward let drive. The ball, unerringly despatched in the direction of the goal though it had been, never reached its mark; instead, it struck me on the backside and bowled me over.

Thus at the tender age of five, I gained something of a reputation as a defender.

Lebong was a most attractive station. We lived in married quarters, our house being one in a block of four; all around the flowers and trees grew in profusion, delighting us with their colour and rich perfume. Magnolias and rhododendrons bloomed as big as horse chestnuts, and luscious fruit came readily to our hands. It was perpetual summer yet, in contrast, amid the clouds we could see the twin snow-capped peaks of Kunchinjunga above, part of the great mountain wall which shuts India off from the rest of Asia.

Under such celestial conditions we kids might have been expected to behave like angels. But we didn't. Indeed our gang, led by the Briggs brothers, sons of the regimental butcher, and including brother John and myself, its smallest member, got into more trouble than did the harum-scarum kids of Casey's Court.

One of my earliest memories concerns a very hot afternoon in June when we were on our way home from school. Because of the heat, lessons had finished at midday, but the idea of taking a siesta, which we had been advised to do, held no appeal.

The elder Briggs pulled a tennis ball from his pocket and started to dribble down the road. His brother went to tackle him and a game of football began.

Obeying local orders, we all wore topees to begin with but when I found that mine stopped me from heading the ball I gladly offered it as a means of marking one of the goal posts.

I didn't realize the strength of the afternoon sun that was beating down on my bare head but, after a while, I began to feel sick and giddy.

"What's up, Tich?" asked Bill Gibbs, when I made no attempt to gather his pass. The other boys gathered round, and I started to shiver violently. "It's sunstroke," decided the elder Briggs. "Come on, blokes, we must get him to hospital straight away!"

Sunstroke it was, and I spent two unpleasant weeks in bed, learning a little more respect for orders.

Meantime, at the very moment of my entry into hospital, John was falling head-first from the roof of our house on to the concrete yard twelve feet below.

Brother John was tougher than I, however; Mum got home and found him sitting at the table, tucking-in to a good tea. She bandaged the gash in his head; then she attacked another portion of his anatomy, to such good effect that John literally ached from top to bottom.

It was Mum who administered the corporal punishment in our family, and for this reason we were far more frightened of her than ever we were of Dad. It only needed one of us to commit a misdemeanour and we *all* got a thrashing with the thick box-strap reserved for the purpose. Such was Mum's method of dispensing justice, and no doubt John and I deserved all that we got. All the same, it did seem hard on our eldest brother, Ted, who was the quiet and studious type, seldom getting into trouble.

Mum's reputation for administering a thrashing was confined to the household, but Dad, fighting as Sergeant Teddy Barnes, used to top the bill at Liverpool. During the First World War he fought exhibition bouts against "Peerless Jim" Driscoll, Jimmy Wilde and Johnny Basham.

Dad might have made an even greater name for himself in sport had he not damaged his knee on a vaulting-horse in the gym at Aldershot. By a strange coincidence I was to suffer a similar accident there in years to come, as I shall be telling you.

Dad was still a P.T. instructor and a leading figure in regimental sport, however, and he saw to it that his sons did not lack in instruction. As for us, naturally enough, we were sport crazy.

Our particular idol was the Borderers' strong and pugnacious centre-forward Frank ("Bonzo") Newton who was later bought out of the Army and became a leading goal-scorer with Stockport County, Fulham and Reading.

As a boy Frank had run away to sea. When he was old enough he joined the Army and, during his service, represented them at soccer, rugby and hockey. He was also a good light-heavyweight boxer and, to cap it all, an excellent performer on the cornet.

It was as a marksman, however, that Frank Newton impressed me most. In Lebong I saw him take a penalty and break the net with the force of his shot.

In October, after the monsoon, we moved down to the plains, not far from the picturesque city of Agra. There, beside the still waters of the River Jumna rose the famous Taj Mahal, majestic in its beauty against the blue skies and green trees.

In Agra the open park where we played bordered on the jungle, which John and I lost no time in exploring. One day we managed to stun a small snake. We were carrying it home on a green stick to add it to our collection when a well-dressed Indian, surprising us by speaking with a cultured Oxford accent, politely stopped to warn us that, although insignificant in appearance, the reptile that we carried so carelessly was actually a deadly poisonous crate; that its black stripes, which had led us to christen the snake "Newcastle United", actually denoted the number of victims it was capable of killing with its deadly fangs.

We were impressed, but not daunted, determined now to have this great prize in our collection. But as we continued our journey, rather more gingerly, one look at the snake which John held at the end of the green stick was enough to remind every native in the vicinity or urgent business elsewhere. Indeed, as we entered the front door of our house the cook and bearer went out the back, imploring us to: "Throw it away!"

I held up a wide-necked pickle jar containing methylated spirit while John shook the snake off the stick and let it slither in. All at once the snake began to take an interest in what was going on.

"It's alive!" exclaimed John. "Put the lid on the jar quickly, Tich!"

With trembling hands I rammed home the stopper. Fascinated with terror we watched our pet snake rear up and thump its head against the top and sides of the jar. It took fully ten minutes to die.

Another hobby of ours in Agra was keeping pigeons. This kept us out of trouble until one evening, after holding a check parade, we found that two of our pigeons were missing.

"Tell you what," said John, "they must have got into the regimental police loft by mistake."

So we went down to the barracks, climbed the roof of the police hut without disturbing its occupants, liberated a couple of pigeons not unlike those of ours that were missing, and took them home with us.

"Are you sure they are ours?" I asked innocently.

"'Course they're ours," said John. "We're two short, aren't we?"

That seemed logical enough to me, but John had second thoughts. "Better not put 'em in the loft right away," he decided. "Let's hide 'em under the fire-grate until we're sure it's all right." So that's what we did.

Just before bedtime two burly regimental policemen came to report to Dad that two pigeons were missing. We returned Dad's suspicious glance with injured innocence.

"Have a good look round to see if they're here," Dad invited the policemen. "I wouldn't put anything past these rascals of mine." Their search failed to reveal the pigeons, however, and thus our innocence was established, at least to Dad's satisfaction. The next morning we retrieved the unfortunate birds from under the fire-grate and set them free. Eventually they flew back to their original loft, where they were accepted as wild recruits!

Those pigeons had a lucky escape from the birds of prey, quite numerous in this area. One morning, on the way to school, a vulture swooped down and snatched from my hand a sandwich I had been munching. It was a terrifying experience.

When the time came to move up to the hills again our destination was Kalani, a refuge from the summer heat and monsoon.

What interested us about our new quarters was that they were staggered in blocks down a steep cud which led to the Army barracks at the bottom. The first few mornings, on our way to school, we merely noted that the dustbins, standing like giant sentries outside each house were the biggest we had ever seen. Then Bill Gibbs, of a scientific turn of mind, set us wondering what sort of speed one of these magnificent receptacles would achieve if upended and rolled down the cud.

"I bet it would travel at well over a hundred miles an hour," he claimed, so before long we put his theory to the test.

That dustbin certainly rolled beautifully. It crashed down the hill, gathering speed all the time, until at tremendous velocity it launched itself into the air to smash through the roof of the nearest barrack-room like a block-buster through straw. Fortunately, the three soldiers whose beds were mangled as a result of this playful escapade, were taking tea in the mess hut at the time.

Pleased with the success of our experiment we went home singing, but Dad, who was the Regimental Police Sergeant, was not in a good humour when he arrived home that evening.

"Someone has pushed a dustbin down the cud," he announced angrily. "It did a lot of damage; in fact it might have killed someone."

I knew by the tone of his voice that this time he wasn't going to see the joke, and I was right. No sooner had we owned up than he double-marched us down the hill and handed us over to the police to be locked in the cells!

The disgrace was bad enough but, worse, we hadn't had any supper.

Just before dusk John heard the cry of the char-wallah. "Nip up on my shoulders, Tich," he said, "you might be able to see him through the window."

Quick as a wink I acted, shinning up his back on to his shoulders. From this position, through the narrow aperture which served as a window, I could see the char-wallah, a big tea-urn in one hand, the other balancing a plate of cakes on his head. By a great piece of luck he stopped right underneath our window, probably in order to change his grip on the tea-urn. Anyway, it gave me the opportunity to reach through the window and swipe a big handful of "wads" from his plate.

So we didn't starve, and we didn't fail to get a good night's sleep either, despite the hardness of the beds. Next morning the Provost Corporal made us wash behind the ears and sent us straight off to school without breakfast.

"That's that!" said John cheerfully. "At least in the Army you only get punished once for the same crime."

So he thought, but Mum had different ideas. "All right, my lads – into the bedroom!" were the words she used in greeting that evening. When she reached for the bow-strap we knew what was coming.

"You too!" she said, turning to Ted.

Ted looked up from doing his homework. "Me?" he protested. "But I wasn't with them when they rolled the dustbin down the hill!"

"Well you should have been," said Mother, unimpressed by his excuse. "It's your job to keep the kids out of mischief."

With a look of deep resignation on his face, poor Ted followed us into the bedroom.

Looking through an old family album, I see a picture of my mother and father, a horrified expression on their faces as they regard what appear to be three completely bald little boys. Thereby hangs the tale of the annual family photograph.

"All three of you must put on your best clothes and then go down to the village and get your hair cut," Mum told us on this occasion. "After the photo's been taken, if you've been good boys you can go out and play football."

As good as gold we got spruced up and then walked down to the barber's shop. It was full of native troops, but knowing our Dad was the "dandy-wallah", or Police Sergeant, the barber left everyone else to attend to us.

"How do you want your hair cut?" he asked, anxious to please.

"Like the footballers!" we declared. That meant, of course, fairly short in front so that we could head the ball better.

The barber misunderstood and shaved our heads practically bare. That was how native footballers had their hair cut!

Needless to say, Mum was shocked, and you can guess the consequences: no football for us that day.

I must tell you next about Ginney, a large monkey we kept in addition to our dogs, Mutton, Jeff and Cutlet.

The Indians swear that monkeys are so intelligent that there is no doubt that, if they wanted to, they could talk. But, they say, they're also artful, and know that if they did talk they would be made to work. I'm sure that's right, and you'd agree if you had met Ginney.

When Mum took Pearl, our baby sister born in Lebong, out in the pram, Ginney would walk beside it, in an upright position, and help to push. If a man approached the pram Ginney would jump on his shoulder and make a fuss of him, but let a woman try to inspect the baby and Ginney would fly into a rage, preventing her from getting near.

One Sunday, in Kalani, the family were all indoors, with Ginney taking a nap at the end of her twenty-foot chain. Looking out of the window, Ted noticed that Pearl had climbed the trellis railing on the verandah and had got her feet trapped so that she was in danger of falling onto the concrete below, a sheer drop of thirty feet.

What could we do? We dared not shout a warning, for that would only have frightened baby and placed her in even greater danger.

Ginney had summed up the situation, however, and it was she who acted. Picking up her own chain so that it would not rattle, the monkey crept stealthily across the room, on to the verandah and behind the baby. Reaching out her long arms, swiftly and surely she grabbed Pearl and pulled her back to safety. Mum went rushing out, but Ginney would not allow Mum near the child until she had herself cuffed Pearl for being naughty. Once that job was completed Ginney stood back and let Mum take over.

To our distress, we had to leave our monkey in the zoo at Aden when we started our journey back to England. There, without human company, I'm afraid she went mad and had to be destroyed.

"Fatty" was yet another of our animals. He was a small hill pony, presented to Pearl on her third birthday. The poor animal was so weak and so small at first that all the kids took pity on it and spent their spare time collecting fresh grass for its nourishment. Soon the pony got as fat as a barrel and we were able to use it for rodeo rides round the football pitch. The idea was to gallop "Fatty" through the goalposts, grab the crossbar, swing out of the saddle and back into it again cowboy-fashion. Great fun, too, until Dad caught us at it and reported us to Mum.

Practically our last fling in India was at a regimental Cup Final. This took place on the parade ground at Kalani, which was separated from the jungle by wire netting forty feet high. A brand new ball was in use for this game, and play had not been in progress more than a few seconds when the full-back took a belt at the ball and whammed it straight over the netting into the jungle.

Another ball was produced, but we kids weren't there to see it. We were down into the jungle, looking for the new ball which we found and took home to play our own Cup Final.

"Did you find the ball?" Dad asked us when he came home, accompanied by the sports officer. "No, Dad," we declared innocently, and were minding our own business when Pearl walked into the room with the ball under her arm. You can guess what happened next!

Soon after, we said our reluctant farewells, and no doubt the mystic East breathed a sigh of relief as we set sail for England. Our arrival in Lichfield Barracks coincided with the 1928 F.A. Cup Final, and I remember sitting under the open window of the officers' mess with John in order to listen to the radio commentary. Blackburn Rovers were John's pet team, and you may remember that in the match they created a first-class sensation by beating Huddersfield 3-1.

Thus began a new chapter in our lives; promising new but not less, adventure in Lichfield, Portsmouth, Crofton and Stubbington, where we lived before finding a permanent home at Gosport in 1932.

Chapter Three

In 1929, after twenty-two years' service, Dad retired from the Army to become P.T. instructor for a New Zealand shipping company. While he was away, Mum was left with the task of bringing us up. It wasn't easy for her because money was short, meaning that a good deal of pinching and scraping was necessary in order that we three growing lads should be adequately fed and clothed.

Like the others, I mucked-in to try and earn a few coppers where I could, picking fruit, collecting eggs and doing odd jobs during the school holidays. At Lichfield Golf Club I tried a bit of caddying, and my first guv'nor was the famous left-handed amateur champion from Durham, Dr. William Tweddell. The good doctor paid me a shilling for eighteen holes, which was generous because there were times when he had to carry the bag in order to give me a rest; it was almost as big as I was.

Out of the bob, I spent four-pence on ice cream, and got a hiding for my extravagance.

Once John, a pal of his called Nobby Clark, and I, were given the job of collecting eggs from about two hundred chickens. I was about to put an egg into the basket when Clark said: "We don't want that one . It's a china egg."

I examined it closely. "It looks a real one to me," I protested.

But John and Nobby insisted that I had got hold of a china egg. "Throw it up in the air, Tich, and see if it breaks," said John. I did so; it didn't break. "There you are," said John. He picked up the egg and put it in his pocket. When we got home, I was just going through the gate when John threw something at me. "Catch!" he called, but too late. The object hit me square in the middle of the forehead. It was the egg. As I had thought in the first place, it was not made of china.

What a sight I must have looked. At the time I had no teeth in front; I was crying, and my tears, mingling with the contents of the egg, dripped steadily off the end of my nose.

While we were living at Crofton, in the mews of a country mansion, we boys had to get to Stubbington Council School five miles away as best we could, using one bicycle between the three of us.

On Saturdays, after collecting our three-pence pocket money, John would take me to Fareham on the handlebars of the bike for our weekly treat – a cowboy film!

Another highlight was to make the bus ride to Gosport, and then cross the water by ferry to Southsea where we could play on the beach.

John and I were always together in those days, thanks to Mother. Sometimes my brother would try to sneak off on his own, but Mum would call him back. "Take Tich with you!" she would demand, and that was that.

We were both choir-boys. As a matter of fact, John has always had a very good voice. He was soloist in the Garrison Church at Portsmouth. The rest of the family wanted him to take up singing seriously, and recently I arranged for him to have a BBC audition, but he didn't turn up. "No one wants to listed to my croaking!" he said.

But sport was still our great passion. All three of us were in the Stubbington school football team, John at centre-forward, Ted outside-left and I inside-left. Often I played for the juniors in the morning, and the seniors in the afternoon, and you didn't find me complaining about "too much football"!

We all did well in the school sports, too, especially Ted, who later became an extremely good distance runner and represented the Army as a miler.

Ted had actually begun his training in the Army Technical College when John and I, aged twelve and ten respectively, took part in a big annual athletics meeting at Sir Montague Foster's College grounds. We finished first and second in the high jump, sprint, triple-jump and three-legged races, while John also won the slow cycling race. Keep it dark, but for each success we received a substantial money prize! This virtually turned us into professionals, although we didn't realize that at the time.

In 1932 Dad came home to take up an appointment as P.T. instructor at Price's College, Fareham and we moved to Gosport to live in a flat over a grocer's shop in the High Street. It was John's turn to leave school and find a job, while it was arranged that I should attend school at Clarence Square. I was delighted, for the Clarence Square record in sport was second to none; in the previous year they had annexed every sports trophy in the town.

In my first year I managed to get a place in the school team at inside-left. My masters, Mr. Keep, Mr. Civil and Mr. (Bogey) Bennett gave me every encouragement to develop my ability as a footballer and to this day I am grateful for their helpful interest.

Before the season's end we won our way into the Russell Coates' Junior Cup Final. In the last ten minutes of the match I went into a tackle and couldn't get up. I had broken my leg.

Long weeks of inactivity followed, although fortunately my bedroom overlooked the park and I was able to watch the cricket. Later in the summer my mates were allowed to take me out in a wheel-chair, and this became a fine new game for them. Split into teams, they competed against each other to see who could wheel me the fastest. It was a wonder that my other leg wasn't broken as a result.

My next game of football was the Gosport Schools Trial at the beginning of the following season. I didn't have a very good first half; frankly, I was scared to test my newly-mended leg too severely.

Then, during the interval, I overheard a snatch of conversation between two masters. "I agree with you, Sherwood," Mr. Small was saying. "If Barnes continues to shirk a tackle he must be dropped from the team."

22

That was enough for me! During the second half I forgot all about my injured leg and "got stuck in" as if my life depended on it. I was afterwards congratulated on my display, kept my place in the team and later in the season gained my place in representative games for Hampshire against Middlesex and Somerset.

I was also very interested in boxing at that time and, because there was no boxing at school, my Cub master, Doug Keating, encouraged me to join the Gosport Boys' Club run by Bert Middleton.

I had had my first fight in the shadows of "The Ladies of the Vale" at Lichfield, where I tackled a boy older and heavier than myself and beat him. After that I always fancied my chance, and when I was thirteen, fighting at 5 stone 7 pounds, I won the County Boxing championships. At the Royal Naval Barracks, Portsmouth, I had two fights each evening on three successive days and won them all on points. The strong left-arm punching, which Dad had taught me, was my greatest asset.

Incidentally, I continued to box for the club after leaving school, only giving it up at the age of twenty-two, when it began to interfere with football. In all, I have had about sixty bouts in the ring, and have only twice been beaten.

The hardest fight I ever had was in a special Services' Charity Show in Blandford in 1942. On this occasion I was chief whip for the boxers, who included Freddie Mills, and I was a competitor as well. My opponent, a former RAF champion, weighed nearly a stone more than I did, and he nearly knocked me out at the end of the second round. I recovered, however, and the fight went the full distance. By "using my loaf" I managed to win a points decision as well as the prize for the best fight of the evening.

As a youngster I always had to be playing something. I even played water polo for Gosport second team on Sunday mornings.

A significant day in my school life was when the games master took us to Fratton Park to see Portsmouth meet Arsenal in the fifth round of the FA Cup.

It was the one and only professional match I was to see before playing in top-class football myself. Little did I realize that my name would one day figure on the books of both these mighty clubs.

I remember standing behind the Milton-end goal, eating sandwiches and drinking from a bottle of milk while men swept snow off the pitch to enable play to begin. You'll see from that how bitterly cold it was.

But what a grand game! I was tremendously impressed with Arsenal, who were well-placed in the league, and had won a previous cup-tie, against Darwen, by eleven goals to one.

Fine goals by Cliff Bastin, later to captain an Arsenal team for which I played, and Joe Hulme, helped to knock Pompey out of the cup. And whereas I was chiefly interested in the tactics of inside forwards Alex James and Jackie Smith, I did not fail to note the timely interceptions in defence by Arsenal captain Tom Parker, another character destined to play a major part in my future career.

Events which followed in that 1931-32 season have a curious significance now. Just like the 1951-52 Arsenal team, of which I was a member, Tom Parker's boys threatened to achieve the "double" but fell between two stalls, finishing runners-up in both league and cup. To complete the coincidence, it was Newcastle United who beat them in the Cup Final.

When, at the age of fourteen, the time came for me to leave school, I had made up my mind that I wanted to follow in Ted's footsteps and join the Army; so I sat for the Army Tradesmen examination. For this I had to take five subjects, and it was necessary to get at least forty marks in each of them in order to pass.

Although I wasn't one of the brightest pupils at school, shining only in the subject of football, I wasn't too bad in most subjects. My great worry was whether I could scrape through in maths.

"Barnes," my schoolmaster used to say, "you're the strongest boy in my maths class, because you're always at the bottom holding everyone else up!" And that's about how it was.

In fact it was the inability to do sums that changed the whole course of my life. In the Army examination, believe it or not, I got 99½ marks for general knowledge, more than anyone else has achieved before or since, and over seventy for English, history and geography: but in maths my marks numbered only thirty-nine, and that meant that I had failed the entire examination!

If the Army didn't want me I had to find someone else who did – and pretty soon. Luckily Doug Keating stepped in and found me a job in Gosport as a butcher's boy.

I didn't realize it at the time, of course, but by starting to earn a living in this way I was not only following in the footsteps of Mr. Aneurin Bevan, but such now-famous footballers as Jack Froggatt, Tommy Briggs, Peter Goring and Jack Vernon, to name but a few.

I don't know how the others fared, but I was paid ten bob a week to start and nine bob of that went to Mum.

I was so small that I had to have blocks built on the delivery bike, to enable me to reach the pedals. But the job itself helped to build up my stature, and I used to eat two ounces of raw meat every day; it was unpleasant, but I believe that it helped to make me stronger.

The first time I went to the slaughterhouse, a hindquarter of beef, weighing 168 lb, was slung across the carrier on the front handlebars of my bike.

"What am I supposed to do with that?" I asked the tough character who had put it there.

"Drop it in Portsmouth Harbour if you like," he grinned.

And that's what I nearly did with it. After wavering drunkenly on two wheels behind Portsmouth Town Hall, and negotiating the tramlines with more luck than judgement, I managed to get as far as the ferry point in safety. But when I started down the steep slope of the pontoon leading to the ferry, my feet barely able to reach the pedals, I lost control. In the end I had to step off the bike and let it run down by itself.

The bike skipped to a standstill right at the water's edge. It took four strong men to help me pick up the meat and restore it to the carrier.

Another time I actually did lose a freshly slaughtered calf; it went into the water at the entrance to Portsmouth Harbour and a number of families went without their weekend joint as a result. But Nobby Nobes, my boss, was very understanding.

I owe a great deal to Nobby who was, fortunately enough, a sports fan, and used to let me get away early on Wednesday afternoon in order to play football. Whenever I am in Gosport nowadays we have a half-pint together and talk over old times.

John's firm ran a team known as Pink's Athletic. He was the centre-forward and in due course he wangled places in the forward line for both Dad and myself. We gained quite a local reputation as a goal-scoring trio.

Soon after my seventeenth birthday a pal of mine, named Bert Warner, and myself joined the Territorial Army as gunners in the 215 Battery of the 17th Heavy Anti-Aircraft Regiment, Royal Artillery. Now I wanted Saturday afternoons off as well as Wednesdays, in order to play football for the battery, and once more Nobby Nobes was sporting enough to let me go as soon as my deliveries were completed.

It was a direct result of one of these Saturday afternoon games that I was first "spotted" by a professional football team.

The author leads the Welsh team on to the field at Villa Park for the 1948 International against England. He is followed by Ford, Aubrey Powell and Sherwood.

Flying visit to Europe by an F.A. Services XI in 1944. The
author is second from the left of the picture.

Combined Services XI versus Ireland at Windsor Park in 1944.
Top row (l-r): Rowe, Mullen, Busby, Edelston, Carter, Swift,
Macaulay, Barnes, Mortensen, Welsh and Scott. *Bottom row:*
Matthews, Squadron-Leader Jewell, Joy, Colonel Hartley, Lawton
and Major Sloan.

28

Chapter Four

"No more football for me today!" decided Portsmouth scout, Jack Fleming, one fine Saturday afternoon in 1937. He fastened on his cycle-clips and set out on his bike to enjoy a ride through the Hampshire countryside.

But it proved to be hard going against the wind, and after completing a few miles, Mr. Flemming took a well-earned rest at the roadside. He propped his bike against a hedge, on the other side of which I happened to be playing in an inter-battery football match.

"Might have known it would turn out to be a busman's holiday," Mr. Flemming sighed to himself, and automatically he started to "study form".

He must have been impressed by my display at inside-left, because after the game he came across to congratulate me. I gave him my name and address, and thought no more about it.

Next evening, however, he called at our Gosport home to talk to me about my future.

"Have you ever thought of becoming a professional footballer?" he asked me.

I was genuinely surprised by the question, and when I did think about it I wasn't very enthusiastic, as Mr. Flemming soon realized.

"Never mind," he said, "you're young enough to have second thoughts. In the meantime, how would you like us to fix you up with a better job? We've managed to find positions for several of our players, and I think we could fix you up with the Gas Company. Your pay would be better than it is now, and you would have the opportunity of playing in better-class football. At the same time we would keep an eye on your progress.

The suggestion was generous and, after talking it over with Mr. Nobby Nobes and my parents, I decided to accept.

So for the next eighteen months I worked for the Portsmouth Gas Company stores department. My new job involved crossing the water four times a day, carrying the daily record books between the Gosport branch and head office in Portsmouth, and before long, thanks to the instruction of engine-room hand Ernie Warner, I learned enough about the handling of the ferry to be able to take it backwards and forwards on my own should the need ever arise.

On Saturdays I played football for the company, progressing from the third to the first team in successive weeks. Before long John also got a position with the company, so he and I were soon lining-up side by side in the Hampshire County League team.

That year we did well in the Russell Coates' Senior Cup Competition, and after playing against Bournemouth Gasworks in a semi-final tie, I was approached by a representative of Southampton F.C. who invited me to sign amateur forms for his club. I thanked him, but explained that I was under an obligation to the Portsmouth Club.

"Have they offered you terms?" the Saints scout wanted to know.

I told him "No."

"Well, there's nothing to stop you having a trial with us. Why not come along next Wednesday?" he asked.

He was persuasive. "O.K.," I agreed at length, "on condition that my brother is allowed to play as well."

The scout laughed. "Bring anyone you like," he said; "but you're the one we're interested in."

So the following Wednesday, John and I went along to the Southampton ground and, to tell the truth, neither of us was particularly worried about the outcome of the trial. As often happens on such occasions, however, we were both in tremendous form and John actually scored five smashing goals off his own bat.

After the game, Tom Parker, then manager of the Southampton team, with whom he had started his distinguished career, offered attractive terms to both John and me. We refused because we still didn't want to turn pro. What was more, we had already made up our minds to sign amateur forms for Portsmouth if they asked us. They did ask us, within the week as it happened, so John and I became amateur members of that famous First Division club in 1938.

During the 1938-39 season we continued to play for the Gasworks, who finished runners-up in no less than four cup finals. The same year I was selected for a senior county match for Hampshire against Sussex, and incidentally, the opposing centre-half on this occasion was John Langridge, the famous county cricketer.

We also played one match for Portsmouth "A" team. It was against a Scottish Central League side, and John and I scored the two goals that gave us victory.

I believe I have already indicated that my brother John was a footballer of considerable promise, and you may have wondered why his name has not become better known in football circles.

The fact is that John suffered a serious leg injury while playing for the Royal Engineers during the war, which made him give up the idea of making football his career. Otherwise I am sure that John would have made a name for himself as a centre-forward. In fact he and I might easily have found ourselves on opposing sides when England met Wales in International Championship matches. What a sensation that would have caused!

Incidentally, my elder brother Ted was also a better than average player. He had successful trials for Aldershot on the wing, and they wanted him to "sign pro", but since that meant his leaving the Army, Ted wasn't having any. He concentrated instead on athletics. At the annual R.A.O.C. meeting in 1938, I watched him win the half-mile, one-mile and three mile events and then help to win the relay, all in the same afternoon. Ted is now a warrant officer in the R.E.M.E., and apparently well satisfied with his choice of career.

31

It was at a party on Christmas Eve, 1938, that I first met Joan – the future Mrs. Walley Barnes. I thought at once that I had found the ideal partner, and our twelve years of happily married life have more than confirmed that impression.

Joan was a county athlete who specialized in netball and the high and long-jump. At that time she was getting more "press notices" than I was but she had never seen a game of football in her life until, after Christmas, I persuaded her to accompany the Gasworks team to Winchester, where she watched me score the winning goal against Ted Drake's old team. She has been a "fan" ever since.

Life in the summer of 1939 seemed pretty good to yours truly, and I had great plans for the future. Then in August 1939 I put on Army uniform for what I, and thousands of other young men, fondly imagined was going to be a pleasant fortnight's training at a T.A. camp: but it turned out to be an eight-year sentence.

War broke out in September, while we were at Weybourne. We moved to the Isle of Wight for fourteen days' operational training, and then my battery took up its war station. I was gun-layer in Sergeant Charlie Acton's team, manning a heavy anti-aircraft gun at Gosport; later we moved to a sight on Southsea Common.

Soon we were in action against enemy aircraft. One night we sighted an enemy plane like a sitting duck in the moonlight and shot it down. By February 1940 our regiment were credited with the greatest number of kills in the whole Anti-Aircraft Command.

But for every period of exciting action there were hours of boredom at the gun-site and I was glad of the break in routine when, in March, I was sent on a short P.T. course. When I returned I was made battery P.T. instructor.

Later that year the powers-that-be realized the vital importance of physical recreation for those confined to the often dull and lonely work at the gun-sites, and I was sent to Aldershot for a course in leadership, agility and battle training, with a view to my becoming Sergeant Instructor for the whole regiment.

The first person I met on this course was a quiet pleasantly-spoken young Scot with auburn hair, already a favourite with British football fans, and later to become a colleague of mine at Arsenal. Archie Macaulay was his name.

There were also three other blokes named Barnes on our course, but I stood out as the good-looking one!

On quite the coldest day of December someone had the bright idea that we should start our swimming instruction, and after shivering in the swimming bath for an hour we were called into a warm classroom to be given a lecture on "Mobility and Dexterity" which we had all heard before.

I made a dash for a seat near the radiator, and found it so warm and pleasant that I began to doze. The lecturer caught me at it, and forced me to sit in front of the class as a horrible example. Although I deserved such notoriety, there were others behaving even worse. Some chaps were actually snoring.

The lecturer asked me afterwards the reason for my inattention, so I told him that we had come straight into his warm classroom after swimming. As a direct result of this, no doubt, the next time we attended this classroom all the radiators were turned off and the place was even colder than the swimming bath. This time the whole class remained wide awake and glowering – in my direction. I wasn't awfully popular with the lads for some time after that.

They worked us really hard at Aldershot, but I enjoyed the training and its proud result, for when I reported back to my Regimental Headquarters, now at Cosham, I had three brand new stripes on my arm. My job then became the supervision of physical training in all the batteries, and this meant continual travelling between Portsmouth, Hayling Island, Gosport and the Isle of Wight.

About this time I was tickled to hear the news from home that Mum had joined the Wrens. She was acting as a messenger in the Naval Commander's office at St. Vincent.

"I'd hate to be in Hitler's shoes if Mum ever lays hands on him," was John's comment.

In 1941, without any fuss, Joan and I were married. Shortly afterwards my regiment moved to Cobham. I had to learn to ride a motorcycle in order to visit batteries as far afield as Woking and Manston, and during the next few months some of the close shaves I had on my machine would make Geoff Duke's hair stand on end!

Before long the regiment had a further move – to Blandford for final training before proceeding overseas. I was appointed to the gymnasium staff, where one of my assistant instructors was none other than (Bombardier) Willie Watson, the famous soccer and cricket international.

At Blandford this bold bombardier was known as "Weary Willie", because he never appeared to do any work. Appearances were deceptive, however. Willie did more than his share: he just looked lazy, as he often does on the field of play. Watch him carefully, however, and you'll see that in reality he works twice as hard as anyone else, without making a fuss about it.

At this time Willie Watson was playing for Bournemouth, and one Saturday he suggested that I should accompany him to a match. "I'll introduce you to the manager. Perhaps he'll arrange for you to have a match with us," he said.

I gladly agreed. "Where do we get the bus?" I asked, for Bournemouth was a good thirty miles away.

"Don't worry about that," replied Willy casually. "The club will send a car."

I thought he was joking, but sure enough, at one o'clock, a six-seater taxi was driven into the garrison by a smartly-uniformed chauffeur whose instructions were to collect Willie and deliver him at the Bournemouth ground in good time for the kick-off.

No doubt about it, Bombardier Watson had got this football business really well organized!

I didn't have any luck with the Bournemouth manager. That happy man had a full team, and he'd never heard of Walley Barnes, which wasn't surprising, of course. But as I left his office, who should I bump into but Tom Parker.

"Remember me?" I asked Mr. Parker.

"Why, yes!" smiled Tom. "You're the youngster who didn't want to play for Southampton. I must admit I had to look twice. Army training has turned you into quite a hefty chap." (That was quite true, of course. By now I was about 5 feet 10 inches in height, and weighed over 11 stone, though the family still called me "Tich"!)

I took the plunge and asked the Southampton manager whether he could forget my "past" and find me a place in his team.

"Of course," said the amiable Tom. "I'd be glad to. There's no place for you today, but I'll get in touch with you soon."

He took a note of my address. Feeling happier, I stayed to watch the match, saw that Willie didn't forget to collect his thirty-bob match fee and travelled back to Blandford with him in his private taxi.

A fortnight later, true to his word, Tom Parker wrote to ask if I could play for Southampton in a friendly match at Bristol the following week. My C.O. gave me the necessary permission, and later I received instructions to meet the rest of the team at Salisbury.

After my experience with Willie Watson I quite expected to have a taxi to myself for the trip to Bristol, but I had to be content to share a Rolls-Royce car with three other players.

Thus I played for Southampton after all, and had to go cap in hand to them in order to do so. The game at Bristol wasn't particularly noteworthy, but it was the forerunner of further friendly matches that season and it led to a regular place for me in league football later.

During the summer of 1942, I was posted to Lyme Regis for three months as stand-in for the P.T. instructor of a Territorial regiment from Brecknock. I took the opportunity of taking sixty soldiers down to the beach and teaching them to swim, first on dry land and then in the water.

Vastly entertained by this spectacle, local inhabitants passed the opinion that my instruction only succeeded because those Welshmen were more frightened of me than they were of drowning, but I'm sure that couldn't be true. Anyway, it wasn't a bad effort, was it?

Shortly after this my own regiment moved overseas, and I was posted to the Southern Command P.T. School at Winterbourne, Dauntsey.

This posting meant a great deal to me, for Southampton had just entered the wartime Southern Football League and Cup competition and, thanks to the cooperation of the Army authorities who gave their permission, I was able to assist the Saints throughout the 1942-43 season which followed.

Chapter Five

Talk about baptism by fire!

I played my first-ever league game at the beginning of the 1942-43 season at inside-left for Southampton at Aldershot. The result? We lost by seven clear goals, and we were lucky the score against did not run into double figures.

You see, while the Saints relied mostly on young "unknowns" like myself, Aldershot were able to cal upon a great wealth of talent from Army units stationed nearby. We found such international stars as Cliff Britton, Stan Cullis, Joe Mercer, Jimmy Hagan and Tommy Lawton opposing us. Britton, Cullis and Mercer, incidentally, formed England's wartime half-back line, one that has never been bettered, in my opinion.

Later our team was strengthened and from time to time we were able to call upon such well-known players as Charlie Mitten (of Manchester United, and later Bogota and Fulham fame), big Jack Stamps (Derby County), Peter Buchanan (Chelsea and Scotland), George Tweedy (Grimsby and England) and, on one occasion, the great Tom Finney (Preston North End).

Our skipper was John Harris (later to captain Chelsea and play for Scotland), and other regular members of the team were Tommy Hassell, Eddie Bates (that ideal club-man who became Southampton's captain after the war), Billie Stroud (of Newport County), Alf Whittingham (of Bradford City) and Bert Tann (of Charlton Athletic). Bert was the thoughtful, constructive, full-back of the whimsical sense of humour, who now lends his expert knowledge to the job of managing Bristol Rovers.

At the end of November we played a memorable return league match against the star-studded Aldershot team – and this time we beat them!

As I was on a refresher course at Aldershot at the time, arrangements were made for me to travel to Southampton in our opponents' coach. As it happened, however, I did not finish work in time to get to the appointed meeting-place, so I decided to make my own way by buses, trains and taxis.

Travelling in wartime was a slow and hazardous business. Yet on one particular stage of my journey – from Alton to Fareham – the train started late and arrived ten minutes early! I was so delighted that I gave the driver and the guard five bob each.

Six minutes before kick-off time I was hailing a taxi outside Southampton station. Under normal circumstances I would have been too late to play, but, just as my taxi turned the corner past the school, I noticed the Aldershot coach just ahead of us. The visiting team were late, too. I learned afterwards that they had been delayed in searching for a goalkeeper, since Frank Swift was not available. They had been lucky enough to find such a good substitute as Denis Herod, of Stoke City.

I raced into the dressing-room and found my stand-in, young Don Roper, already changed. "I'm glad you made it after all," Don told me sportingly, for he was obviously itching to play. He stripped and handed over the number ten jersey to me.

I still have the programme for this game in my possession, and you may be interested to read how the teams lined up:

SOUTHAMPTON: Tweedy (Grimsby); Tann (Charlton); Roles; Pond; Harris (Wolves); Stroud; Bevis; Bates; Whittingham (Bradford City); Barnes; and Mitten (Manchester United).

ALDERSHOT: Herod (Stoke City); Marsden (Bournemouth); Royston (Portsmouth); Britton (Everton and England); Halton (Derby County); Gallacher (Bournemouth); Raynor; Hagan (Sheffield United and England); Lawton (Everton and England); McCulloch (Derby County and Scotland); and Cunliffe (Blackburn Rovers and England).

Despite the late start, the game that followed was a ninety-minute thriller that more than consoled the 6,000 spectators for their patience. From the first whistle we peppered the visitors' goal. Billy Bevis, on leave from the Navy, soon found his land-legs and was unlucky not to score for us with a low cross-shot, while Alf Whittingham, Ted Bates and myself also put in shots that would have defeated a goalkeeper in less brilliant form than was Denis Herod. Meantime, Aldershot's international forwards could make little headway against our sturdy defence.

It was Billy Stroud, advancing with the forwards, who gave us the lead after about twenty minutes' play. He took a shot on the run and placed it perfectly in the far corner of the net.

Aldershot piled on the pressure. Cliff Britton hit the post with a free-kick, and Jimmy Hagan cast magic spells all over the field with his twinkling toes, but we counter-attacked and Mitten, Bates and Bevis – in that order – came close to scoring number two.

Then, just before the interval, Tommy Lawton scored a fine equalizer. He took the ball in his stride, crashed through the defence and hammered the ball past Tweedy.

From that moment I began to understand why Tommy's reputation was so high. Reputations alone have never interested me. "Prove to me that you're a good player and then I'll believe it," was my attitude towards opponents with big names, even in those days. Well, Tommy Lawton has proved it over and over again to my dismay, and to my satisfaction when I've been on his side.

Despite this set-back we were determined to keep a grip on the game somehow, and soon after the interval Eddie Bates gave us the lead, a lead that we maintained to the end.

"It was a great game," said Don Roper afterwards, a little sadly because he would dearly have liked to have played himself. "Never mind," I told him, "your chance will come," and indeed it did. Don made great strides in the next few seasons and eight years later, when I was injured in the Cup Final, it was he who took over my job at full-back and gave a sterling display.

Our win against Aldershot was just the tonic we needed to set us up for our forthcoming encounter with the Arsenal.

I can well understand the attitude of grim determination that all teams adopt when Arsenal visits them because, when I was in Southampton colours, I wanted to help bring about their downfall more than anything.

In a letter he wrote to Tom Parker before the match, George Allison promised to bring his strongest possible team, despite the fact that former Southampton stars, Ted Drake and Alf Kirchen, would unfortunately be absent on R.A.F. duty, as would Eddie Hapgood, while George Swindin and Bryn Jones were required by the Army.

Mr. Allison was as good as his word, and the Arsenal team that opposed us was strongly representative. It read as follows: Kelly (Aberdeen); Scott; Young; Johnstone (Hearts); Fields; Male; Nelson; Bastin; Lewis; Morgan and Denis Compton.

There were two changes in our line-up. Rigg (of Middlesbrough) replaced Tweedy in goal, while no less a personality than Tom Finney took over the outside-right position.

It was a grand first-half, and the 11,000 spectators, constituting a record crowd at the Dell, were given plenty to cheer about.

There was Cliff Bastin splaying accurate passes among his forwards, and a spry young Denis Compton making the most of every opportunity, while Tom Finney hit up a grand partnership with Eddie Bates on our right. Fine football.

Reg Lewis scored first for Arsenal, and impressed me by the way he turned-on-a-sixpence to make his shot. Reg is one of the very few players I know who, no matter how it comes to him, hits the ball *naturally* with his instep.

Shortly after this I had a chance of scoring, but my shot hit the crossbar. That great opportunist Alf Whittingham followed-up, however, and put the ball into the net from the rebound to equal the score.

After sixty minutes' play the score was still one-all, and I think we were actually beginning to get on top when Billy Stroud, who had been playing a grand game at right-half, met with an unfortunate accident and had to leave the field with a cut eye.

With only ten men, we were unable to keep our end up for the last half-hour. Reg Lewis scored a second goal for Arsenal and, right at the end, Morgan headed in a third goal from Bastin's corner.

Still, it was a tip-top game, and we were more than satisfied with the show we had put up against such famous opponents.

Arsenal ran away with League honours that season and we finished fifth, which wasn't bad after our shaky start. I managed to score twelve of our 114 goals.

It was after Christmas that we hit the kind of form that sent us rocketing up the league table. First we beat Spurs 2-1 at the Dell. Two weeks later Luton Town visited us and ran into an avalanche.

For the first thirty minutes there was no score. Then we rattled home five goals before the interval, four of them being scored by Alf Whittingham. In the second half we scored another six, and Whittingham brought his individual total for the match to eight goals, beating Albert Brown's record of seven in one match for the Saints, made forty years previously. After the game we all autographed the ball and presented it to Alf as a souvenir of his great performance.

Incidentally, our 11-0 victory equalled the club's highest, which had been made against Northampton in 1905.

A fluke? No! And we proved it by going to Craven Cottage and beating Fulham by eight goals to two in our next away game.

Encouraged by our run of success in the league, we had great hopes of making a name for ourselves in the cup competition which followed.

At this time the cup was not run on familiar knock-out lines. Southern teams were divided into four groups of four to play home and away games against each other on the league

41

points system. The four winners of the league groups then played off home and away semi-final ties to decide the finalists.

Meantime, Northern clubs held their own competition on similar lines. Eventually the Southern champions met the Northern champions in a Grand Final.

We were placed in group two with Brentford, Leyton Orient and Queen's Park Rangers. We started with a fixture against Orient at the Dell.

For this match I was moved to outside-left to accommodate Tomlinson, the former Southampton centre-forward, who had leave from police duty: we were without several regulars. Orient, too, had their troubles. Two of their players had failed to catch the train at Waterloo, so Tom Parker provided them with substitutes in Young, an inside-forward who Tom Parker had just signed from Bournemouth, and Jack Scott, who was formerly Southampton coach.

The game hadn't been in progress more than a few minutes when Jack Scott, playing at centre-forward for Orient, collided with Bert Tann, our right-back, and as a result Bert was carried off the field suffering from concussion.

John Harris took a quick look around the field. His eye rested on me. "Like to have a shot at playing right-back, Walley? He asked.

I'd never played in defence before, but "I'll try!" I told him and moved back to partner Roles.

For twenty minutes I enjoyed myself, booting the ball lustily up-field whenever it came within range. Then Bert Tann returned to the field.

We scraped home to a 1-0 victory, thanks to a headed goal by Eddie Bates.

Next we went to Brentford, and pulled off a fine 6-1 win, and it was evident that either Queen's Park Rangers or ourselves were going to head the group. Unfortunately we ran into a spot of bad luck with injuries before our return against Leyton Orient. Then, instead of bringing in reserves to fill the gaps, as Tom

Parker advised, a Southampton director ordered wholesale positional changes. It was this incident which caused Tom Parker to fall out with this official and to leave the club at the end of the season.

For most of the match at Leyton we were at sixes and sevens, trying to strike up some sort of understanding with each other, and in the end we lost by one goal.

Things looked pretty hopeless after that, but the following Saturday Queen's Park Rangers visited the Dell and we beat them 4-1, thus returning a slight hope of reaching the semi-finals. We were one point behind the Rangers, who were still at the head of the group, and we had a better goal average, so that if we beat Brentford the following week and if Rangers failed to beat Orient, we were there!

Brentford visited the Dell with seven members of their London Cup-winning team of 1941-42 on view – full-backs Brown and Poyser, half-backs McKenzie and James and forwards Hopkins, Smith and Hunt. They gave us a stiff fight, and in the end it was only John Harris's penalty goal that gave us a 2-1 victory.

John actually hit the ball straight at Saphin, who half-saved it and then let the ball spin out of his grasp and screw over the line.

We rushed back to the dressing-room to find out how Rangers had fared. A London phone call brought shattering news. "Queen's Park Rangers SEVEN, Orient one," was a result to end our fondest hopes.

After our last home game of the season, Tom Parker called the regular players to his office one by one, to tell us that, owing to a difference of opinion, he was ending his contract with Southampton. Tom wanted to know from each player whether he wanted to stay with Southampton or to go to another club. Most of the "guest" professionals elected to move, and Tom fixed them all up with other teams eventually.

I was the last one to enter his office.

"I'm not asking you where you want to go, Walley, I'm telling you!" said Tom. "You're going to Arsenal."

I was surprised. "Do you think I'm good enough?" I asked.

"Of course," said Tom "I certainly wouldn't recommend you to my old club if you weren't."

"By the way," he added, "I'm sending you as a left-back."

Now I was more than surprised – I was flabbergasted. I had played one match as a full-back in my life – and then only for twenty minutes as a deputy RIGHT-back.

"Oh well," I thought; "Tom of all people must know what he's talking about." If he said I was a left-back, then I would be a left-back, even if I have to convince the most famous club in the country that I could do the job.

The summer proceeded fairly quietly. I was busy with Army duties, and whenever I was free I played hockey to keep myself fit. It was in early June 1943 when I received a letter from Tom Parker to say that he had been in touch with Arsenal about me, and the very next day I received another letter, this time from George Allison, which confirmed that Arsenal would be pleased to sign me as a pro on Tom's recommendation. Before they did so, however, I had to get Portsmouth to rescind the amateur form I had signed for them before the war. This proved difficult. When Portsmouth discovered that Arsenal were after me, they tried everything they could think of to make me change my mind and stay with them.

I was adamant, however, and got my own way in the end. So, in August 1943, at the age of twenty-three, I signed professional forms for Arsenal.

Because it was wartime, much of the glamour was missing. In many ways it was a "utility" Arsenal that I joined. The Gunners were not even operating at their own stadium, for that had become an A.R.P. headquarters; home games were played at White Hart Lane. Then nearly all the Arsenal players were, like myself, in the services so there was no organized training and players met on match days only. I didn't even receive the normal £10 signing-on fee at the time!

However, utility model in a utility team though I might be, I was still "Arsenal", and that meant a great deal. My future career was there for the making, and I resolved that I would spare no effort to get to the top and to justify Tom Parker's faith in my ability.

My chance was to come sooner than I dared hope.

Chapter Six

I played my first game for Arsenal, and my first full ninety-minutes as a left-back, at Brighton on September 25th, 1943, partnering George Male in the absence of Laurie Scott, who was playing for England against Wales at Wembley.

The result was a 1-1 draw, Cliff Bastin scoring for us fifteen minutes from the end, with a penalty that entered the net on its third bounce!

I had the unenviable task of marking George Eastham, the brilliant Bolton forward who was "guesting" for Brighton. I don't think I did too badly, although I did get a ticking-off from trainer Billy Milne at half-time. That was because I started to nibble a juicy apple I had brought with me. Billy used some Scotch language at me, and of course he was right – an apple is quite the wrong thing to eat at half-time. Nowadays I suck a lemon or take a cup of tea, like the others.

Apart from that, however, I made no serious mistakes, and since Laurie Scott was likely to be absent again the following week I thought there was a good chance of retaining my place in the team at Fulham. On the Wednesday I telephoned Mr. George Allison to see how I stood.

He soon upset my hopes. "You can't expect to walk straight into a permanent place in the Arsenal team, sonny," his deep voice boomed over the telephone line. "But come along and watch the game, by all means. I'd like you to meet Tom Whittaker, and I'd like to have a word with you myself since I was unable to get to Brighton last week."

I said I would be glad to come and, since the October 1st and 2nd weekend marked Joan's birthday and our wedding anniversary as well, I arranged that she and her brother should accompany me to the game as part of a modest celebration that we planned.

There was also a dance in the Mess on the Friday, and I thought I might do a little celebrating on my own account. Before I did so, however, I phoned the club once more to make certain that I would not be required to play the following day, and I received confirmation that Ernie Collett would be playing at left-back.

There was nothing to stop me from enjoying myself then, so I entered into the party spirit with gusto. It was in the early hours of Saturday that I finally got to bed, and only slept for a few hours because I had to catch the nine o'clock train for London. The train was packed to overflowing, and I had to stand in the corridor for the whole of the one-hundred-mile journey to Waterloo.

"You don't look at all well," said Joan when she saw me. I didn't feel it, but I was determined not to spoil our little celebration, so I took her and her brother to a restaurant where we had a four-course luncheon and a glass of shandy as it was such a hot day. Then we took the tube to Hammersmith Broadway and walked round the shops until Joan found a pair of shoes she wanted me to buy for her birthday present. Finally, feeling a little leg weary and with an aching head, I called a taxi. This delivered us at the Fulham ground with twenty minutes to spare before the game started.

I was first out of the taxi, but as I held the door for Joan to descend someone grabbed me by the arm. It was trainer Billy Milne.

"Come on, lad!" he said excitedly. "We've been waiting for you. Collett can't play, so you're in the team!"

"But – I haven't got any boots," I protested, saying the first thing that came into my head.

"That's all right," said Billy, almost dragging me through the players' entrance. "We'll fix you up." And he whisked me away to the dressing-room, leaving Joan and her brother to pay for the taxi and to fend for themselves.

In the dressing-room Billy Milne went straight to the skip and pulled out a spare pair of boots. "These look about right," he said. "Sit down and try them for size."

As if in a dream I sat on the bench, acknowledging the greetings of other players with vague monosyllables as I struggled into the boots. They were obviously too small, but I crammed my feet into them somehow. As I was tying the laces, George Allison, accompanied by a broad-shouldered R.A.F. officer, entered the small Fulham dressing-room and came straight over to my corner. I sprang to attention and said "Good afternoon, sir" to the officer.

"When we're in the dressing-room my name is Tom," said Squadron Leader Whittaker, smiling pleasantly. Then he shook me by the hand. "Good luck this afternoon," he said. That was my first meeting with the Boss.

A few minutes later I walked out on to the Craven Cottage pitch with the other players, not knowing if I was on my head or my heels.

It was quite an exciting game, which we won by four goals to three. Fortunately our half-backs, Male, Joy and Crayston, were so much in control that I hardly saw the ball. When I did, I somehow managed to do the right thing, which was just as well with Messrs. Allison and Whittaker watching me play for the first time. But, to be quite, truthful, that was one game that I didn't thoroughly enjoy; it taught me that hitting the high-spots and league football just don't mix, and that a footballer should always be prepared to play even if his name is not on the sheet.

I remember that Ronnie Rooke scored twice for Fulham, and Denis Compton, who was then the recognized outside-left in England's team, score a hat-trick for us.

I was hobbling badly as we returned to the dressing-room and I couldn't wait to get my boots off. When I did so, I saw that all ten of my toes were skinned and bleeding. "Whose boots have I been wearing?" I asked Billy Milne.

Billy examined them. "This pair belongs to Bryn Jones," he told me.

"He must be a blinking pygmy!" I said. I found out later that Bryn took size six. I took seven and a half at that time!

Laurie Scott took my place for the next game at Leyton and I was a spectator. I remember this game particularly, because in the second half a buzz-bomb cut-out directly over the ground. The ball was left on the turf while the players stood still and, as slickly as a well-practiced drill-squad, the spectators on the terraces about-turned in unison as the bomb crashed to earth and exploded a few hundred yards away. Seconds later, play restarted and the spectators turned to face the pitch again just as if nothing has happened.

During that 1943-44 season I played in most league and cup games for Arsenal and in every position except centre-half and centre-forward.

Usually I partnered Sergeant Laurie Scott, the immaculate England right-back of the day, with Sergeant George Marks behind us in goal. George was a brilliant goalkeeper, better even than George Swindin I think, until he suffered an eye injury against Wales in 1943, his eighth wartime international match for England. Not only was he an exceptionally strong kicker, but his anticipation was remarkably good.

Sergeant George Male, Flight Lieutenant Bernard Joy and Ernie Collett, of the fabulously long-throw, were the regular half-backs, and the tall graceful Flying Officer Jack Crayston took up the right-half position when R.A.F. duties allowed him to do so.

Among the forwards who were usually available were Corporal Jimmy Briscoe, Lance Bombardier Reg Lewis, Cliff Bastin, Sergeant Denis Compton, Flying Officer Ted Drake, Sergeant Nelson and Marine Cumner.

For the most part, however, manager George Allison was uncertain about the composition of his team until the very last moment.

On December 11th, for instance, we were due to play West Ham at Tottenham and the same morning Mr. Allison learned that Reg Lewis was in hospital with tonsillitis, Ted Drake's knee was badly swollen and Norman Bowden was down with flu in an R.A.F. hospital. In desperation, Mr. Allison telephoned Jack Peart, the Fulham manager, and asked him if he could provide us with a "guest" centre-forward.

We were all ready to go on the field at three o'clock, still without a centre-forward, when Bobby Flavell, of Airdrie, dashed into the dressing-room, had a hurried word with Mr. Allison and then changed into our number nine shirt. Bobby, on leave from the Navy, was Mr. Peart's Xmas present to us. In the second half, the 5 foot 6 inch Scot beat three men and scored with a right-foot drive; thus enabling us to draw the game. Bobby played several games for us after that, and became a regular scorer

On Easter Saturday we were at home to Crystal Palace, and beat them 5-2. I had a good game at inside-left, and scored two of the goals, but I fully expected to be playing left-back again on the Easter Monday when we were to receive Brighton at White Hart Lane.

This was a match in which I was particularly anxious to do well, because Joan and her mother were coming along to watch. My mother-in-law had never seen a football match before. I met them both at Waterloo and watched them eat a good lunch while I had my usual tea and toast, after which we walked down Tottenham High Road from where Seven Sisters Road runs into the ground. That's quite a walk isn't it? I didn't realize it was so far, and we were rather late. I just had time to escort my wife and mother-in-law to their seats, and to tell mother-in-law that if she had any trouble in identifying me during the game she should look for the player with number three on his back. "That will be me!" I said.

I should explain, perhaps, that in those days I had quite a shock of hair, and was not so easy to pick out. Anyhow, mother-in-law got the idea. "Number three," she repeated. "All right, Walley, I'll keep my eyes glued on that number!"

But a shock awaited me in the dressing-room. There was all the playing kit laid out as usual, and I went straight to the seat

50

with the number three shirt, but somebody else's boots were underneath it. I looked right down the line of boots, but still couldn't find mine. I began to think I had been left out of the team; then I saw my boots. They were under the goalkeeper's jersey.

"Who's taking the Mickey?" I demanded to know.

"No one!" declared Billy Milne. "Everything is in order. George Marks phoned at midnight to say he couldn't make it. We couldn't get a replacement in time, so you're playing in goal this afternoon."

Well, there it was. So now I was a goalkeeper. I started to get dressed without further comment, and I took the field determined to make the best of a strange situation.

The match hadn't been in progress more than a few minutes when Tommy Hassell, the short, dapper winger who had partnered me at Southampton and was now playing right-wing for Brighton, waltzed inside the full-back and centre-half and prepared to pick his spot in the net. There was only one thing for me to do – advance to meet him. So that's what I did. Now I either had to dive on the ball like George Swindin, or tackle like full-back Walley Barnes. Undecided which to do, I neither dived nor tackled; I did what I must call a "dickle", or a cross between the two. My effort didn't even make Tommy lift an eye-brow. He avoided me with the greatest of ease, and left me sprawling while he pushed the ball home into an empty net.

Joan told me afterwards that I showed about as much gumption as a new girl playing netball!

Fortunately the next two shots I had to deal with were air balls and I saved them without trouble. Soon I got the hang of things, and the anticipation that I had developed as a full-back began to help me until, eventually, I became really confident. As soon as the ball left the foot of an opponent I could tell near enough whether I needed to do anything about it or not. If I saw that the ball was going to miss the goal I did nothing. Mr. Allison, sitting at an angle in the stands, didn't like these methods a bit. He told me afterwards that he thought every one of the shots I left alone was a certain scorer and that watching me had cost him ten years of his life.

But I don't think I did too badly, especially in the second half when I made quite a few spectacular saves. Raymond Glendenning, the famous BBC commentator, was good enough to tell me afterwards that he thought I had given a "brilliant performance" and he often reminds me of it when we meet today. Even the Arsenal lads were saying: "We needn't worry about George Marks any more. Barnes can take the goal-kicks almost as well."

Anyway, we won the match 3-1. The only snag was, of course, that nobody had thought to put my mother-in-law in the picture. Having watched "Number Three" throughout the game she was convinced that Walley Barnes had been the best player on the field!

Apart from a five-minute spell against Wolves in 1951-52 and a friendly against Ellesmere Port, the next time I played in goal was at Highbury at the start of the 1952-53 season, when we were due to give a demonstration of football tactics for television viewers. George Swindin was injured, and because of my cup final injury I was unable to take my place at full-back in the practise, so I volunteered to go between the sticks and show viewers "how to keep goal". Each member of the Arsenal team took a shot at the net – and my luck was in – I managed to save them all.

One Saturday in the 1943-44 season, after playing for Arsenal, I was returning by train to Gosport and found the Portsmouth team among my travelling companions. Knowing that Arsenal did not have an engagement during the Christmas holidays, I took the opportunity of asking Mr. Jack Tinn if Portsmouth had a vacancy in their team to play at Southampton. He didn't think there was much chance of it, but asked me to ring on Wednesday just in case. I did this, and he thanked me for phoning but said that Portsmouth had a full bill.

By now I was determined to get a game, however, so having failed with Portsmouth I thought I would try their opponents, Southampton. "No vacancies at the moment," the Saints director and acting manager, Mr. Sargantsan, told me. "But we'd be glad if you could be there. Bring your boots with you just in case...."

So on the Saturday, Joan, her father and myself went down to the Dell to watch. We were welcomed with open arms. "You're just the man," said Mr. Sargantsan. "We've had last-minute injuries and we'd be very glad if you could play for us at inside-left."

I couldn't help wondering what Jack Tinn was thinking as I ran on to the field in Southampton colours!

About ten minutes later we forced a corner and I had the satisfaction of heading the ball past Gilfillan for the first goal. A little later I scored number two, a deflection into the corner of the net. Then I completed a hat-trick with a first-timer from the edge of the penalty-box.

The experience was well worth the price of two phone calls!

Incidentally, newspaper reports credited me variously with one, two and three goals in this game, but I actually scored all three in the 3-0 win.

The author's first international appearance for Wales in 1944. Walley Barnes is third from the left in the top row.

The Welsh team that beat the rest of the United Kingdom 3-2 in the special 75th Anniversary Match at Cardiff on 5th December, 1951. The author has the ball at his feet.

Dai Rees gives the author a few tips to help him improve his golf swing.

The author during a boxing demonstration in the Aldershot gym.

55

Chapter Seven

"I've got news for you, Walley!" I was half-changed for a league match at the Queen's Park Rangers' ground on April 29th, 1944, when Mr. George Allison came into the dressing-room with a broad smile on his face, and made this announcement.

"The chances are that you will be playing at right-back for Wales against England at Cardiff next Saturday," Mr. Allison told me.

I could hardly believe it. After all, I had played less than a complete season as a full-back in top-class soccer, and although I was pretty confident that I had got the hang of the job, and there had been some nice things said about me by the Press and other experts, it honestly hadn't occurred to me that I was on the fringe of international rank. Naturally I was delighted with Mr. Allison's item of news and I celebrated it in the game which followed when, playing at inside-left, I intercepted a backward pass made by Dave Magnall, and scored an equalizing goal which saved Arsenal a point from a match we had looked like losing.

The following week I was on seven days' leave at my home in Gosport, when on the Wednesday, I received a letter from the Football Association of Wales confirming my selection for the international team, and instructing me to report, with properly studded boots, soap and towels to a Cardiff hotel on the evening of Friday, May 15th. I didn't want to give the selectors an opportunity to change their minds, so I immediately acknowledged receipt of this memorable communication. On the Friday morning I set off early for the journey to Cardiff, and my heart was thumping so loudly that I thought everyone else in the carriage could hear it and guess the cause.

I have since been told an interesting story about my selection for this, my first international match. I don't know how true it is, but as several people who should know have vouched for its accuracy I will report it here.

The story is that I had been on the short-list for the England team, the idea being that Laurie Scott and I should take over the Arsenal-England defensive partnership recently relinquished by Eddie Hapgood and George Male. The England selectors are supposed to have checked my birth qualifications at Somerset House and, discovering that I was born at Brecon, they passed this information on to the late Ted Robbins, secretary of the Welsh F.A. Mr. Robbins is reported to have said: "If he's good enough for your consideration, he's good enough for mine. In fact we'll give him a run against you at Ninian Park and see how he shapes."

It was Ted Robbins who greeted me first upon my arrival at the hotel, and he introduced me straight away to Don Dearson, Welsh captain for the match, and to Ronnie Burgess. That evening we all received a match fee of six pounds and travelling expenses in advance. This was quite a new experience to me, and I only hoped that I would be able to earn my pay by making a satisfactory debut in the game on the following day.

At ten o'clock in the evening Billy Lucas, Cyril Sidlow and I visited Ronnie Burgess's room for a chat. Before long someone produced a pack of cards and we started to play the famous Army game of Brag. I might easily have lost my shirt in such skilful company, but we were interrupted by the arrival of Ted Robbins's friend, a padre, who asked us to show him how to play. We explained the finer points to him, leaving out some of our sharper Army tricks, and he was quick to learn. So quick, that he won hand after hand. It was just as well that we were only playing for matches, because had the padre been a gambling man he would have emptied our pockets as readily as the Welsh F.A. had filled them!

Joan arrived just after lunch on Saturday morning, escorted by our friend, Captain Bill Harvey, but I only had time for a quick word of greeting before it was time for us to set off by coach for Ninian Park.

The bench in our dressing-room was littered with letters and telegrams for members of the team, and there were several good-luck messages among them for me from Mr. Allison and Arsenal players, relatives, Army pals and even members of the Gas Company team with whom I had played before the war.

"Taffy" O'Callaghan, the veteran international inside-forward who was still playing brilliantly for Fulham, was our twelfth man on this occasion, and he made a point of coming across to help put me at my ease while I changed.

I pulled the famous Red Dragon jersey over my shoulders and it was a jolly tight fit. As a wartime economy, the international jerseys had been worn and washed over and over again, until they were skin-tight on thickset chaps like Don Dearson and myself.

I often have a laugh at the photograph which we had taken before this game. Some of us look as if we were wearing strait-jackets.

Don Dearson led us out on to the field to the accompaniment of a great roar from 50,000 spectators, then the largest crowd I had ever seen at a football match, and a record attendance for Welsh wartime soccer I believe. Many of the spectators were in uniform, of course, and not only did they fill every available space on the ground but hundreds, at great personal risk, had perched themselves on top of the stands. In addition, the police had wisely allowed hundreds of youngsters to sit inside the concrete wall surrounding the pitch, thus easing the congestion.

You can imagine my feelings as I heard the roar of the great Welsh crowd for the first time. Funny things were happening inside me, and, I was glad that this time there were no formalities to go through before the game got under way.

Military priorities and injuries had made selection of our team difficult, and the centre-half and wing positions were only filled at the last moment. Fortunately, Idris Hopkins, of Brentford, had just returned to league football following a cartilage operation and was available to play at outside-right, and despite the unavoidable absence of key-men Tommy Jones and Billy Hughes, our team looked pretty capable. Here's how we lined up:

WALES: Sidlow (Army and Wolves); Barnes (Army and Arsenal); Lambert (R.A.F. and Liverpool); Dearson (Birmingham) capt.; Davies, R. (R.A.F. and Nottingham Forest), Burgess (R.A.F. and Spurs); Hopkins (Brentford); Davies, W. (Watford); Lowrie (Army and Coventry), Lucas (Army and Swindon) and Morris (Birmingham).

ENGLAND: Ditchburn (R.A.F. and Spurs); Scott (R.A.F. and Arsenal); Compton, L. (Army and Arsenal); Britton (Army and Everton); Cullis (Army and Wolves) capt.; Mercer (Army and Everton); Elliott (Army and West Bromwich Albion); Carter (R.A.F. and Sunderland); Lawton (Army and Everton); Rowley (Army and Manchester United) and Leslie Smith (R.A.F. and Brentford).

Although both England full-backs were Arsenal colleagues of mine, I hadn't met tall, handsome, Leslie Compton before. I was familiar with the brilliant English half-back line, of course, and had also played before against Tommy Lawton and Leslie Smith, the latter being the established international who I was required to mark on this occasion, and, incidentally, one of the best left-wingers I have ever played against.

I was soon in action as the play swept quickly from end to end; each team attacked in turn. Elliott gave Ray Lambert some trouble on the right-wing, and forced a corner, but Cyril Sidlow cleared easily enough and another Welsh attack was launched. From this, first Morris came close to scoring and then quicksilver Billy Lucas scraped the English cross-bar with a first-time shot.

It was thrilling football, and for the first quarter of an hour, encouraged greatly by the crowd, we were definitely on top.

Stan Cullis, the English captain, was a dominating figure in the middle of the field, but even he became ruffled when some bright sparks in the crowd began the throw leeks into the English goal whenever we attacked, and Stan complained about this to the referee, who was Mr. A. E. Davies of Aberystwyth.

"What can we do about these leeks?" Stan demanded to know.

"If I were you I'd collect 'em," Mr. Davies advised him confidentially. "They make splendid thickening for a stew!"

And soon Stan had more leeks to worry about, because George Lowrie and his fellow forwards started throwing in the shots one after another.

After half and hour's play, however, England returned to the attack, and Tommy Lawton opened the scoring for them with a typical effort. Gathering a loose pass he slipped past Davies and myself with a clever swerve and side-step and fired in a shot from twenty yards that gave Sidlow no chance.

All the same, I thought that England were a little lucky to be one-up at half-time. On paper they were much the stronger team, it was true, but my colleagues had impressed me by the way they rose to the occasion and gave as good as they received.

Ray Lambert and I were kept busy at the restart, but I thought I had got the measure of Leslie Smith, and I wasn't unduly worried. Then in a goalmouth scramble, I got an accidental blow in the stomach that laid me out. It was several minutes before I was able to get to my feet, and when I did I knew that I was booked to finish the game as a passenger. Skipper Dearson took over my position, and sent me out on to the right-wing to hobble along as best I could.

I was in no position to cause the England defence any trouble, as big Leslie Compton soon realized. When he tackled me he did so almost apologetically. Frequently he enquired how I was feeling, in that sympathetic way of his, until the stern Stan Cullis told him to "Stop fraternizing!" – quite rightly, of course. Although a club-mate of Leslie's, I was "the enemy" on this occasion; if I was given half a chance to put one over on the big fellow, injured though I was, I would have taken it without question.

Although enforced positional changes threw us rather out of gear, my team-mates continued to fight with spirit until a second goal for England, from the foot of Leslie Smith, more or less clinched matters in our opponents' favour. It hadn't been a very happy debut from my point of view, although Ted Robbins was very good enough to tell me that I had done very well up to the time of my injury, and that Wales would be wanting me again.

During the summer of 1944 I was posted to the School of Artillery at Larkhill, where I was to teach manhandling of guns to senior officers. I wasn't long at the job before I received a whole stack of invitations to join various football tours, starting with a British Army XI tour of the Highlands of Scotland at the beginning of August and continuing with other representative games right up to the end of September.

I went to see Major Williams, the Welsh hockey international who was my commanding officer, about it. When he saw the long list of matches for which my services were requested his eyes nearly popped out of his head.

"What am I to do, Sergeant?" he asked me. "There just isn't a leave-pass invented to cover the amount of time you want to be away!"

But Major Williams was not only a fellow Welshman, and a good sport, he was also a most resourceful commanding officer.

"Tell you what," he said, his eyes twinkling; "it's obviously no good giving you an ordinary leave pass. What I must do is to give you a pass that will get you back into the school when you're ready to return!"

And that's just what he did do, believe it or not, and I have the pass in my possession to this day. Surely no other soldier in history has ever dreamed up such a document!

On August 4th, I set off on my football travels, first taking the train for Dundee in the company of the following celebrated Army footballers:

Swift (Manchester City and England); Medhurst (Chelsea); Winter (Chelsea); Taylor (Wolves and England); Busby (Liverpool and Scotland); Macaulay (Rangers, West Ham and Scotland); Mercer (Everton and England); Fenton (Middlesbrough and England); Kurz (Crystal Palace); Heathcote (Queen's Park Rangers); Welsh (Charlton and England); Mullen (Wolves); Walker (Hearts and Scotland), and Tennant (Chelsea).

"Team attendant" was C.S.M.I. Rowe, now better known as the Spurs' boss, and another player, Jimmy Carabine (Third Lanark and Scotland), joined us at Dundee. The "first team", as we called the officials who accompanied us, included Colonel Hartley, a Rugby International and member of the Army Sport Control Board, and the late Major Sloan, Secretary of the Army F.A. They were later joined by Mr. (now Sir Stanley) Rous, the Secretary of the English F.A.

The purpose of the tour, Colonel Hartley told us, was to make friends, to give the troops and the civilian war workers a break, to stimulate interest in Association football and last, but not least, to raise money to augment such worthy causes as the Red Cross Prisoner of War Fund.

Well, the Army had certainly picked a wonderful side to do the job, and it was not only strong on paper. We started off with a 7-0 victory over a team selected from the best players stationed in the Dundee area, and Joe Mercer, Don Welsh and Andy Black, in particular, gave 15,000 enthusiastic spectators plenty to shout about.

Frank Taylor, now manager of Stoke City, was my full-back partner in this game.

The outstanding feature of our 7-0 victory was a wonderful goal scored by Don Welsh in the second half, with which he completed a hat-trick. Don shot from the corner of the penalty box with his left foot and the ball hit the top corner of the net before the goalkeeper saw it. It was one of the finest shots I have ever seen.

My Arsenal colleague, Alex Forbes, recalls that goal almost as vividly as I do. Alex was then one of the ball-boys on duty at the Dundee United ground.

On the Sunday we left Dundee for Aberdeen, where we were due to meet another all-star team the following day. Our spirits were high, but some of the smokers in the party were inclined to be bad tempered because they couldn't get hold of any cigarettes. Then, during the journey to Aberdeen, Frank Swift made a great discovery. The ever-thoughtful Archie Macaulay had more than five hundred "gaspers" packed away in his bag. For the rest of the tour Frank marked Archie more closely than a goalkeeper has ever marked a wing-half before!

"I don't know what Swiftie does with all the cigarettes I give him," sighed Archie, later in the week. "He must sell them back to the Naafi for a profit."

The game in Aberdeen, which we won by a much narrower margin, marked the first occasion I had played in front of big Frank Swift and, not being familiar with either his methods or his strong Northern accent, I made a mistake early on that might have cost us the game. Frank called out for me to take a ball, but I thought he was saying "Let it go!" and that's what I did. The ball ran across the goal and to the foot of an oncoming forward, but before the forward could size up the situation, Frank, recovering with amazing speed, dashed across and picked the ball from off his very toe. How the big fellow managed it is quite beyond me. He punted the ball up-field and then paused on his way back to goal to growl at me, "It's all right doing that once in a game, sonny, but don't do it too often – that's all." Believe me I took his warning to heart.

We were told to expect traditional hospitality at Inverness, the capital of the Highlands, and we were not disappointed. But first we were booked to spend a night, and play a game exclusively for the troops at bleak Fort George, one of the coldest, windiest and most unpleasant spots you can imagine. Perhaps you know it? If so, I'm sorry I reminded you about it.

Here, for the first time, somebody noticed that our party was made up of warrant officers, sergeants, junior N.C.O.s and even privates, and they wanted us split up accordingly. Joe Mercer insisted that we should all use the Sergeants' Mess, however, and when he and the other warrant officers were allotted private sleeping-quarters, they refused to use them, moving their blankets over to our hut in the dead of night. Tommy Walker went out to give them a hand with the moving, and was swallowed up by the darkness. He was missing for some time. Eventually a search-party found him up to his ears in a muddy slit trench, looking quite unlike the smart, gentlemanly figure we were used to seeing on the soccer field, and using unusually heated language!

When we played the match next day, the locals told us we were lucky to have such good weather conditions. I'd hate to be playing under conditions they called "poor", because I reckoned that the wind was blowing at nearly thirty miles an hour, and carrying stinging rain with it as well.

We won the match by 6-3, and Archie Macaulay scored a fine hat-trick. Centre-forward Anderson, of Hearts, was credited with one goal against us, and right-winger Newcombe two, but I think they would admit that it was the elements that had most to do with the beating of Harry Medhurst.

After that we sampled some of the grand Inverness hospitality. The Provost presided at a Rotary Club luncheon given in our honour at the Caledonian Hotel and we enjoyed a fine salmon lunch, as well as speeches by Sir Murdoch McDonald, M.P., once a well-known footballer himself, Mr. Stanley Rous and Colonel Hartley, while Matt Busby and Tommy Walker had a go on behalf of the players.

We were certainly well looked after, but Sir Murdoch told us that Highland hospitality was nothing compared with what it had been in days gone by. "At one time," he said, "they fed you well, they drank you well; and if anyone fell under the table they provided him with a boy to unfasten his collar."

Both the local Bowls Club and the Inverness Golf Club put their facilities at our disposal, and I tried both games for the first time without creating any sort of sensation. Finally a dance was thrown in our honour, at which Colonel Hartley taught us how to jitterbug!

There were about 7,000 people present at the Telford Street Park ground on the Saturday to see us put up one of our best performances, and beat a Services' Select XI easily.

This was one of the games in which Frank Taylor, my full-back partner, complained of the knee injury which was eventually to terminate his brilliant playing career.

This Army team was one of the best I have ever played with, and what's more they were a grand crowd of chaps. When Mr. Rous told us that we had helped to raise a sum of over £4,000 for the Red Cross we felt that, in addition to having a good time ourselves, we had done a worthwhile job.

Chapter Eight

The first time I opposed the great Stanley Matthews was when Wales met the R.A.F. at Wrexham on September 2nd, 1944, and press reports gave me a lot of credit afterwards for proving a thorn in his side.

I'd like to put that right. It was not I who deserved the credit for this fine performance but Ray Lambert. Although my name appeared as left-back on the programme, Ray and I actually tossed a coin to decide which of us should play in that position and, since Ray called correctly, I lined up at right-back to oppose Leslie Smith. Some of the Press must have failed to note our switch.

It has never really worried me to play on the right-flank, although my preference is for left-back because I like to have my stronger foot, the right, on the inside. Ray Lambert has the same preference, so we got into the habit of letting the toss of a coin decide which of us should enjoy this advantage.

Take a look at the teams playing that day, and you'll see that this match, arranged in aid of war charities, was England v Wales again in everything but name:

WALES: Sidlow (Wolves and Army); Barnes (Arsenal and Army); Lambert (Liverpool and Army); Dearson (Birmingham); Hughes (Birmingham and R.A.F.) capt.; Burgess (Tottenham and R.A.F); Leslie Jones (Arsenal and R.A.F.); Lucas (Swindon and Army); Lowrie (Coventry and Army); Alan Evans (West Bromwich and Army); Cummer (Arsenal and Navy).

R.A.F.: Marks (Arsenal); Scott (Arsenal); Hardwick (Middlesbrough) capt.; Shankly (Preston); Joy (Arsenal); Soo (Stoke); Matthews (Stoke); Carter (Sunderland); Drake (Arsenal); Mortensen (Blackpool); L. Smith (Brentford).

Alan Evans, a nineteen-year-old schoolboy international, was the "new boy" on this occasion. He showed a great deal of promise and have become a Welsh regular, but during the 1947-48 season his eyesight began to deteriorate, bringing his career to an untimely end.

The rain was pouring down a few minutes before kick-off time, but there was no question of the start being delayed. We were worried because Cyril Sidlow was missing and I was beginning to think that I should have to wear the goalkeepers' jersey when Cyril dashed into the dressing-room, cursing the curious behaviour of wartime trains, a constant source of irritation to us all.

Cyril certainly arrived in the nick of time, for the R.A.F. forwards kept him jumping about like a cat on hot bricks for the first twenty minutes, and he made some grand saves before Ted Drake put one past him.

We fought back well after this, but couldn't make much impression on the airmen's defence until early in the second-half, when Leslie Jones switched to centre-forward. Immediately he tested George Marks with a blazing shot, and led several subsequent raids on the goal, until after sixty-five minutes' play Billy Lucas pushed the ball coolly past Marks to score the equalizer.

The R.A.F. tried all they knew to regain the initiative, but we more than held our own and forced a draw, which surprised the experts, and pleased us, especially in view of the forthcoming international against England.

Although, as I have said, Ray Lambert was the hero of our defence, Mr. Ted Robbins gave me to understand that there was no reason why I shouldn't retain my international place for many seasons to come.

After the game I went home to Gosport for a few days. It wasn't worth reporting back to Larkhill, because on the Thursday I was due to accompany a Combined Services team to Northern Ireland, and in the meantime I still had my magic pass!

67

The Combines Services' party were due to leave Euston by the five o'clock sleeper on Thursday, so I set out to catch the two-twenty train for London which would have allowed me plenty of time. Foolishly, however, I failed to check whether the train was still running, and in fact it wasn't, so I was late and the team departed without me!

At once I telephoned the A.P.T.C. section at the War Office to confess my error and to ask what I should do. I was told to catch the Belfast train the following day.

Meantime I had to find somewhere to stay in London, so I went along to Highbury where trainer and Chief Warden Billy Milne kindly fixed me up with a bed and breakfast at Arsenal Stadium, or A.R.P. Headquarters as it was then. After breakfast I went out on to the ground and did my training with A.R.P. activities going on all around me. It was a strange experience, training at Highbury for the first time under these conditions.

That evening I really did catch the five o'clock boat train, and I was allotted a room with Bernard Joy, Raich Carter and Jimmy Mullen. When I started to explain my late arrival to Bernard Joy he cut me short. "You'll have to have that out with Major Sloan later," he said. "The important thing is that you're in the team to play Ireland this afternoon, so you'd better go straight to bed and get some rest."

I did manage to snatch forty winks, and was awakened at one o'clock for tea and toast, after which we were taken by coach to the Windsor Park ground where a record crowd – 50,000 strong – awaited us. For the last two seasons Ireland had beaten strong Combined Services' teams, and today they hoped to bring off the treble with nine of the team who had represented them the previous season.

This was the Irish team:

Breen (Linfield and Manchester United); McMillan (Belfast Celtic); Barr (Cliftonville); Walshe (Linfield); Vernon (Belfast Celtic); Jones (Blackpool); Cochrane (Linfield and

Leeds); Stevenson (Everton); McAlinden (Belfast Celtic and Portsmouth); Doherty (Manchester City), and Bonnar (Belfast Celtic).

We lined up like this:

Swift; Scott; Barnes; Macaulay; Joy (capt.); Busby; Matthews; Carter; Lawton; Mortensen and Mullen.

The game which followed created quite a sensation in football circles, and it thrilled the large crowd, but my own part in it is best forgotten because I played deplorably.

Playing at left-back alongside my Arsenal colleague Laurie Scott, it was my job to mark Ireland's live-wire right-winger, Davie Cochrane, and he led me a merry dance. Fortunately Frank Swift and Laurie Scott were both in great form and they covered up for me, otherwise we might have been several goals down in the first few minutes.

As it was, Horatio Carter scored for us after fifteen minutes. Nine minutes later, however, a penalty was given against us, and the Irish skipper, Peter Doherty, ran up to take it.

"You'll know where he's likely to put it at any rate," I said to Frank Swift, and Frank nodded confidently, for Peter was a colleague of his in the Manchester City team and he'd had plenty of opportunity to study his tricks.

But when Peter hit the ball it went one way, and Frank Swift went the other. Such was Peter Doherty's capability – he could even hood-wink a man who had played in the same team with him for years.

And Peter didn't stop there. I've never seen a man do so much work in my life; his energy appeared inexhaustible. A few seconds after stopping Stan Mortensen, almost on his own goal-line and clearing the ball up-field to Cochrane, he was back in position to take Cochrane's return pass and bang the ball home for a second goal.

Two minutes later, Carter again beat Breen, and so the score was 2-2 at half-time.

The second half was even more exciting, although I was still playing like a man with both his boots on the same foot. Mullen scored for us in the first five minutes, but Doherty equalized immediately. The thirteenth minute brought a goal for Mortensen and again Ireland equalized – this time through Cochrane.

Ten minutes from time, with the score four-all, Stan Matthews suddenly took control of the game, and led our forwards in a whirlwind *blitzkrieg* that brought four winning goals in as many minutes. Stan's dazzling footwork and bewildering body swerves had a hypnotic effect on the Irish defence, and every one of his runs finished with a perfect centre.

I remember our eighth and final goal very vividly. Stan Matthews picked up a pass ten yards inside the Irish half and started to weave his way through. When Lawton finally side-footed the ball into the net from Stan's pass there were four green-shirted players sitting on the ground wondering what it was that this will-o'-the-wisp had done to beat them. The last figure was goalkeeper Breen, perhaps the most puzzled of all.

Even then, Ireland did not give up. In fact they scored one of the finest goals I have ever seen, and were unlucky to have it ruled offside. Once again, I was the clinker that failed to put out the fire! Davie Cochrane cut inside me and sent a diagonal ball across between Scott and Joy. Paddy Bonnar, the Irish left-winger and "surprise choice", ran on to this pass and shot first-time with his right foot from the corner of the penalty-box, and although Swift must have seen the ball all the way, and dived full length to try and stop it, the ball was travelling so fast it beat him all ends up.

After the game I was sent for by Major Sloan, and I quite expected to be called over the coals for my inept performance, but, surprisingly, it was not mentioned. I was required to explain my late arrival, however, and after listening to my story the Major said, "Well, you were late on parade, Sergeant, and I suppose disciplinary action must be taken, but we'll forget it until after the next game, shall we?"

The next game was against the Irish League at Cliftonville on the Monday, and I was delighted to have a second chance when I fully expected to be dropped. As it turned out I had a fine match, and possibly because of that my breach of discipline was tactfully forgotten.

For the first half an hour our opponents were the better team. Their forwards moved sweetly together and swarmed all round our goal and, when our attack did get away, Scottish international centre-half Jimmy Dyke held Tommy Lawton in a grip of iron. On the two occasions that Tommy did manage to escape his policeman, in the thirty-fifth minute and one minute before half-time, he scored. Edelston and Mortensen added goals in the second half, and our defence resisted all attempts by the Irish League to retaliate, so we won 4-0.

If determination, not goals, decided the result, it might have been a different story. At one stage, for example, those fiery Irish forwards really piled on the pressure. They forced a corner on the left and, in trying to clear, Frank Swift was jostled about so much that he bit right into his tongue, causing a very painful quarter-inch cut. Frank was plucky enough to carry on after this, and made many brilliant saves, so few people realized how he was suffering.

The main feature of this game from my point of view was that this time I managed to keep Davie Cochrane under close control from start to finish. For once I don't think I put a foot wrong, and after the game Stanley Rous came into the dressing-room to congratulate me. I shan't easily forget his words.

"Well, Barnes," he said, "if I had known in 1920 what I know now, I would have personally conducted Mrs. Barnes over the border in the ambulance to make sure you were born in England."

71

That evening, team manager Arthur Rowe, several of the players and myself, were invited home by Jimmy Dyke. Jimmy had been working in the local brewery in Cliftonville, and he was anxious for us to taste the fruit of his labours. I'm sure I don't know what was in the glass he gave me, but I drank it, and when I got back to my hotel bedroom and removed by boots and socks my toe-nails dropped off too!

That's my story and I'm sticking to it.

The next day we boarded the homeward ferry, and while those poor sailors Laurie Scott and Tommy Lawton, fearing the worst, made for the sofas in the purser's office, Jimmy Mullen and I went on deck and swapped stories throughout the crossing.

Jimmy had been told that he would be required to replace the injured Leslie Smith in England's team to meet Wales two weeks later, so my parting words to him were, "Cheerio, Jimmy, see you at Liverpool."

Liverpool was something of a lucky ground for England, because on the three previous occasions that Wales had met them there the home country had won each time. We were determined to break the sequence.

The Welsh team selected was practically the same as that which did so well against the R.A.F., except that this time Leslie Jones moved to inside-right and Tim Rogers, of Swansea, took over the wing position.

Since Stanley Cullis was now on Army service in Italy, Joe Mercer became England captain for the first time, and our opponents lined up as follows:

Swift; Scott; Hardwick; Mercer; Flewin; Welsh; Matthews; Carter; Lawton; Mortensen and Mullen.

Reg Flewin, replacing Cullis, and Stan Mortensen, who had previously played, as substitute, for Wales *against* England, were the new caps.

"We won't bother to toss up for places this time," I told Ray Lambert. "You're playing on your own ground and the crowd want to see you tackle Stan Matthews so I'll play on the right."

Ray thanked me, for he was only too anxious to resume his duel against the great Stanley. I took on Jimmy Mullen, and as it happened he didn't have a very good game. In desperate efforts to score he continually shot into the side-netting, for which I scolded him playfully, but while doing so I made certain that he wasn't able to drop the ball into the middle, the last thing we wanted with Tommy Lawton around! Throughout, the match was played in drizzling rain.

English skipper Joe Mercer started as if he meant to win the match on his own, dribbling brilliantly past four men and going through with his forwards. But he did this too often, and tried too hard. Since Don Welsh also took an attacking role, Reg Flewin was very much over-worked. This caused gaps in England's defence that we exploited by using our inside-forwards as spearheads and our wing-halves close up behind in attack.

It made all the difference to have the midfield advantage and within fifteen minutes we had gained a two-goal lead. Dearson scored first from a corner after five minutes' play, and nine minutes later Billy Lucas hit the second, taking Leslie Jones's pass and placing the ball accurately past Swift.

I thought that Reg Flewin hardly deserved the blame that was put on his shoulders after the game. He was bound to be compared with his dominating predecessor, Stan Cullis, but the wandering of his wing-halves gave him no opportunity to show his own constructive ability.

It took England most of the first half to get on equal terms, and it was Tommy Lawton who led the recovery, first distracting Sidlow while Carter side-footed a goal, and then scoring himself with a header from Stan Matthews' centre.

Although we thought we had put Stanley Matthews in Ray Lambert's charge, Stanley had different ideas and began to wander a good deal in the centre of the field, causing Billy

Hughes and I a lot of trouble. On one occasion he nearly headed a goal, but I think Stanley, who has so rarely been seen to head the ball during his career, would be the first to admit it was an accident. In fact he had his back to the goal when the ball hit his head unexpectedly and flashed past Sidlow's clutching fingers inches wide of the post.

There was plenty of spirited play, but no score in the second half. Towards the end Tommy Lawton rounded Hughes at top speed, collided with me and got himself laid-out. I think Tommy still holds this against me, but I want to tell him here and now that the last thing I wanted to do was to come into collision with his mighty frame. The truth is I just couldn't get out of his way in time.

Seconds later we might have snatched a last-minute victory for Lowrie and Rogers both shot just wide.

Not a classic game by any means, but we were more than satisfied with a fighting draw against such powerful opponents, and as we came off the field, mud-stained and weary, Ted Robbins showed his pleasure with the result by shaking each of us by the hand and thanking us.

Chapter Nine

Towards the end of September 1944, with the Allies advancing farther every day into Hitler's stronghold, an F.A. Services XI made a flying visit to Europe to play matches in Paris and Brussels which would provide entertainment for battle-weary troops and civilians in those areas. I was proud to be selected for the trip in the distinguished company of: Swift; Hardwick; Hughes; Mercer; Joy; Busby; Soo; White; Matthews; Carter; Drake; Edelston and Mullen.

This team, which included the captains of England, Scotland and Wales, was valued and insured at £20,000 per player, so our pilot (who might easily have been mistaken for the original Flying-Officer Kite by his manner and appearance, but who actually was a D.F.C. and Bar, and a Flight Lieutenant) had the responsibility of carrying a quarter of a million pounds of football talent in his Dak transport.

In the "first team", which accompanied us, was Raymond Glendenning, the famous BBC sports commentator, who was to broadcast running commentaries of the games. While we were more than glad of Raymond's genial company it was sometimes a little confusing to see him sitting amongst us in one of the bucket seats that ranged either side of the plane. He and the pilot were as like as peas in a pod, such was the close resemblance between their moustaches, and the plane was hitting so many bumps that we thought that he would do better to concentrate on the job of flying the plane!

The real pilot frequently did pop back to ask after our comfort. I was finding my first flight a little hectic to say the least, but poor Stanley Matthews, who was also making his first flight, despite his many previous football tours in Europe, looked a picture of misery. Every few minutes he walked the gangway to the back of the plane to seek the only privacy our accommodation offered.

"Not feeling too good, eh?" barked our pilot heartily. "Better hold on to your seats then. I'm just going to land on a wizard bump that I can guarantee to have made myself on a previous trip. Look out, chaps!"

He went back to his cabin and a few minutes later we felt a bump that nearly threw us in a heap. My tummy sank dizzily to my boots and returned reluctantly as the cheerful countenance of the pilot appeared round the communicating door. "Ironed it out that time, what?" he chortled with satisfaction. No one answered him, we were busy with our own thoughts.

We found out later that this bump on the runway had a connection with our pilot's low-bombing exploits on the aerodrome, for which he had won the D.F.C.

You could sense the heartfelt relief of all our party now the plane had come to a halt at the end of this, the only runway still in commission at war-ravaged Le Bourget. The pilot was still chuckling as we thanked him politely for making the trip so interesting.

"Good show!" he said. "See you after the game tomorrow, chaps, and then we'll beat the record from Paris to Brussels."

"I can hardly wait," said poor Stan Matthews with feeling.

We were driven straight to a small hotel near the Madeleine where we soon got back to form with an excellent meal. Thanks to the generosity of the American troops who occupied Paris at the time, our rations were first class.

We received a visit from an N.C.O. of the Special Investigation Branch of the Military Police. He had been sent to warn us of the temptations to which we might be subjected in Gay Paree, and to tell us that dire penalties would be exacted if we allowed ourselves to become involved in any Black Market activities.

Having carried out his duty, the policeman became almost human. "I'm an Arsenal supporter," he admitted to me, and that put our conversation on friendly footing.

Stanley Matthews had been looking thoughtful. "Where are these places that you've been warning us against?" he asked. "How are we to know where we should go and where we shouldn't?"

"Well, that easy," said the police N.C.O. "If you're not doing anything special this evening I'd be glad to take you round."

So that evening Stanley, Frank Swift and I were taken on a personally conducted tour of the very places we had been forbidden to visit.

It was like being transported into film-land's underworld. Until I saw them with my own eyes I thought that only Hollywood could create sinister characters like those who leaned against cellar bars and talked monkey-business out of the corner of their mouths; the apache-dancer types, with striped jerseys, one with a black patch over his eye and a long knife in his belt; the oily spivs who engaged in muttered conversation and passed brown paper parcels under the table in exchange for wads of franc notes.

"If these are the men behind the Black Market we don't want any part of it!" said Stan Matthews. Frank Swift and I agreed wholeheartedly.

Even stranger things happened to us in Paris. For instance, the next morning we were enjoying coffee and doughnuts at one of the cafes on the boulevards when one member of our team, not noted for his generosity, produced a packet of twenty cigarettes and offered them round. This gesture surprised us, but it fascinated waiters and fellow customers, who began to crowd round in the hope that they might be included in the distribution. The embarrassed footballer quickly pocketed the cigarettes again, saying, "I only wanted to see if it was true that cigarettes are more valuable than money in Paris." Thus we all missed an unusual opportunity.

It was tragic to see the way Parisians coveted the everyday articles we produced as a matter of course.

One morning, as we strolled down the Champs Elysees I noticed Frankie Soo juggling abstractedly with a sixpenny bar of scented toilet soap and, as he did so, the eyes of passers-by were nearly popping out of their heads. Not only that, but motorists began to leave their cars, after parking them at the side of the road, to clamour round Frankie and plead to be allowed to buy the soap. Frankie couldn't have realized how long it had been since the eyes and nostrils of Parisians had been delighted by the luxury article he had so carelessly produced. Had he stopped to bargain he might have exchanged the Naafi soap for the Eiffel Tower itself.

I didn't play in the first match on the Saturday afternoon at the Parc de Princes Stadium, but I joined with the rest of the lads when they were presented to General Koenig and other high-ranking French officers; then sat on the side lines, with Major Sloan, to watch.

The French team was not at full strength, several of their players were away fighting with the Maquis, and the Services won 5-0, the main feature being a fine hat-trick by Horatio Carter. Ted Drake and Maurice Edelston scored the other goals.

The large French crowd, which contained a sprinkling of G.I.s, greatly appreciated the first soccer entertainment that had been able to enjoy since the occupation. From our point of view it was a most satisfactory result but there was one sour note. Jimmy Mullen was injured in the last few minutes, and it seemed unlikely that he would be able to play in our next engagement.

When we left Paris we had only one hour in which to make the flight to Brussels, because non-operational planes like ours were not allowed in the air after dark. Not that the bold Flying-Officer Kite had any fear of our being shot down. He had already vowed to break the record, and I've no doubt that he did so, for we arrived in Brussels with minutes to spare.

We remained at the Hotel Cecil that evening because the match against Belgium was to be played the following day. Our chief concern was to get Jimmy Mullen fit. Apart from that we were too close to the war zone to think about entertainment. The Germans were resisting very strongly along the lower Rhine with heavy fighting taking place barely thirty miles away.

The Darking Club Stadium, where our match was staged, had been in German hands less than a month previously, and we were told that soldiers were busy clearing land-mines from the terraces up to two hours before the kick-off. We were also provided with air cover while the match was in progress.

Air-Marshal Tedder was to have been presented to the teams before the kick-off, but so great were the crowds thronging the roads to the stadium that he arrived twenty minutes late and we missed the opportunity of meeting him. Our R.A.F. boys suggested that he ought to have been put on a charge, but the ground was packed and several thousands were unable to gain admission, so they let him off! Our audience consisted mostly of British Tommies.

One hour before kick-off it was decided that Jimmy Mullen would not be able to play, and I was detailed to take his place at outside-left. Thus our side read:

Swift; Hardwick; Hughes; White; Joy; Busby (capt.); Matthews; Carter; Drake; Soo and Barnes.

There was no way of informing the crowd of this change, however, and during the first few minutes, whenever I got the ball I heard the Tommie's shout "Come on, Jimmy! Up the Wolves!" I realized that under the circumstances I was the guardian of Jimmy Mullen's reputation, and I tried my best not to let him down.

I didn't have a brilliant match by any means, but I did have the good fortune to open the scoring after about thirty minutes' play with the type of shot that Jimmy Mullen might himself have made, a left-footed drive from just inside the box. If I did nothing else right, I did at least have the satisfaction of hearing the words, "Bravo, Jimmy!" from the crowd for that effort.

There was no further score in the first half, but a few minutes after the interval Smellincks, one of the Belgian backs, unluckily put through his own goal, and just before the finish Ted Drake made it 3-0. In a robust but thoroughly enjoyable game, it was Stan Matthews, as usual, who gave the Tommies their football treat during the last half an hour.

Incidentally, this marked the only occasion I ever had to toe the line before taking part in a match! The two teams were instructed to line up with the tips of their toes touching a taut string line in order to be presented to high-ranking Allied officers. Then two attendants staggered out of the dressing-room with a huge bouquet for skipper Matt Busby. As he accepted the offering poor Matt's face was as red as the flowers themselves.

That evening we were invited to the house of the Mayor of Brussels, and he threw a wonderful banquet in our honour. The wine flowed freely, and the Mayor told us that it was his best vintage, saved from the Germans through being concealed behind a false wall in the cellar.

After dinner we piled into cars which took us to a posh club, which featured everything from a first-class cabaret to indoor whippet racing. When we were introduced to the patrons we all got a splendid reception, but it was Ted Drake who got most applause because, I was told, he was remembered as a member of "the brilliant Arsenal team who had played in Brussels before the war".

The whippet racing was good fun, but Frank Swift provided the biggest laugh of the evening. He was persuaded to take part in the cabaret, and Big Frank surpassed himself in giving his well-known mime of a young lady taking a bath, followed by an imitation of a Wakes-Week holiday-maker at Blackpool eating fish and chips from a newspaper. Frank's act got more applause than any other in the cabaret.

To round-off the entertainment, Matt Busby, our skipper, was presented with a magnificent thoroughbred whippet by the club manager. Matt made a graceful little speech of thanks, but tactfully forgot to take the dog back to our hotel. The next afternoon, however, while we waited to board the plane for the homeward trip, a representative of the club arrived on the tarmac leading Matt's whippet and he insisted that Matt should take the dog back with him to England.

Our skipper had a terrible time trying to think up polite French words to refuse this generous gift. He was already red in the face when he turned to me and asked, "How the dickens do you explain quarantine in French?"

I couldn't help him, and anyway the rest of us had problems too. Between us we had collected enough presents to fill the plane, quite apart from its passengers. Sixteen cases of wine and grapes, presented to the members of the "first team", were already aboard, and there were more to come.

"We can't possibly take all this stuff!" said Major Roy White. "The plane will never take off under the weight."

But our "charabanc" driver, the intrepid Kite, was determined that we should not leave a single present behind. "You chaps have earned every one, and I'll jolly well see that you keep 'em," he said.

So we climbed aboard, arranging ourselves as best we could amongst the booty. Kite took the plane to the very edge of the runway, raced his engines and practically willed the machine into the air. Even so we brushed the top of a hedge as we left the ground, and Squadron Leader Tom Whittaker, who was at the airport on official business at the time, has since told me that no one on the ground thought we had a chance of making it. Make it we did, however, thanks to Flying-Officer Kite, who, for all his funny ways, was a brilliant pilot.

After returning from Europe I continued my duties at the School of Artillery, Larkhill, and played in various games for Southern Command, the Army and Arsenal.

I did not play in many matches for Arsenal during October and November because of service engagements, but when I was available my club still tended to regard me as a utility player, and

I had played in every position for the Club except centre-half and centre-forward. I never knew whether I should be appearing in defence or attack until the last moment. As a result of this, Frank Butler, the *News of the World* columnist who was then with the *Daily Express*, wrote something which started me thinking.

"It has been said that a good footballer can play in any position," he wrote, "but now Barnes has proved himself a full-back with a talent above average, I should have thought it advisable to keep him in defence."

On the whole I think I agree with Frank. Versatility is all very well. When you are learning it is a good idea to try as many positions as possible to get all-round experience, but once you show an aptitude for one particular place on the field it is better to specialize there in my opinion. Brilliant defenders like Bert Sproston, John Charles, John Aston and Leslie Compton were converted into successful forwards, it's true, and left-winger Jack Froggatt had made an outstanding centre-half, but that proves nothing, except that that these players were capable of doing whatever was asked of them. I made up my mind, after reading Frank's piece, that I would try to concentrate on the full-back position. As it happened, however, I was not able to put this decision to the test for some time.

In November 1944, I was posed to Aldershot – not to teach soccer, for Joe Mercer was the beginning and end of soccer coaching there – but to give boxing instruction. Dressed entirely in white, I demonstrated the correct moves, while an opponent, dressed in black, did everything wrong. We performed this drill for the troops' edification at sixty centres in Southern England, as well as at United States Army Headquarters where we emphasized the difference between the British and American code of rules. In addition, during school holidays, I was required to take Army cadets and members of junior training corps in a ten-day P.T. and leadership course at Aldershot.

It was while carrying out these duties that I met with an accident that threatened to end my playing days for good.

The author in Arsenal colours.

Walley Barnes scores a penalty against Stoke City in 1951-52.

Chapter Ten

On December 20th, 1944 while demonstrating high-horse vaulting to a squad of cadets at the Aldershot gymnasium, I cleared the vaulting horse but landed awkwardly, straining the ligaments in my left knee as a result.

I didn't worry much about this injury at the time, but since my knee appeared to be rather swollen the next morning I reported sick. The M.O. told me to rest in bed for a few days.

The swelling gradually subsided, so I resumed normal duties. After Christmas I travelled to Reading to play for Arsenal in a London Cup-tie, and I had quite a good game and no ill-effects from my knee until the last ten minutes. Then Wilf Chitty, the tall red-headed Reading winger, brought the ball up the touchline and suddenly made to cut inside. Turning sharply to check him my left boot stuck in the mud, my body rotated and my left knee went again as it had done in the gym. Billy Milne helped me off the field.

After that I did not play football for two or three weeks, and when Arsenal came to Aldershot to play the local team I was a spectator. I mention this game because in it Ted Drake scored a really remarkable goal. One often reads about goals being shot from thirty yards; in my experience many of these reports are grossly exaggerated; but Ted Drake really did do it this time. He got possession of the ball on the half-way line, took it forward on his own, and he was definitely no nearer than thirty yards from the goal when he shot with tremendous power. The goalkeeper saw the ball all the way, but so fast was it travelling that he could not stop it from entering the net.

I suppose that Ted Drake was past his best when I first saw him play, but he was still a very fine centre-forward and, next to Tommy Lawton and Trevor Ford, I rate him as the best of all.

My knee continued to trouble me, and I was put under the care of a medical officer who had dealt with so many knee injuries in the services that he had become a specialist. He was none other than that great Olympic miler, the late Jack Lovelock.

After giving my knee a careful examination , the famous New Zealander insisted that I should play no more football until he gave the word.

A whole month went by before Major Lovelock decided that the time had come for the test. Then, on his advice, I played at centre-half against the Canadian Army XI on the Aldershot Command ground. For seventy minutes my knee stood up to the task remarkably well.

Then I moved across field to try to cut out the Canadian left-winger, turned very sharply at speed and actually heard my knee give way with the sound of a dry twig snapping. "That's it!" I thought to myself. But since we were winning comfortably I stayed on the field and took things easily for the rest of the game.

Overnight my knee became very swollen. I stayed in bed for a few days receiving periodic visits from Major Lovelock. Gradually the swelling subsided and I was able to get about again. Now the Major put me on remedial work under instructor Armour Milne who, under the name of "Slip Saxon", had won the Powerball sprint. Armour later became well known as a sports writer. He certainly knew his anatomy and I benefited greatly from his treatment.

I was lucky to have such a skilful doctor as Major Lovelock, and an incident that occurred at Aldershot showed me, too, what a very great athlete he was. C.S.M. Dick Cordiner, a well-known Isle of Man runner, had reported sick with a knee injury two days before he was due to take his section on a two-mile forced march. Major Lovelock examined Dick's knee and told him to forget all about the exercise. "You're definitely not fit to take part," he said.

But Dick was insistent. "We're allowed sixteen minutes to complete the test, sir," he explained, "I can do that on my head."

"All right," said Major Lovelock. "If you think you know better than I do, you shall run. But just to prove that you're not fit,

I'll run too and guarantee that although I am much older than you, and out of training, I'll beat whatever time you put up."

Jack Lovelock was as good as his word. Dressed in full battle order, like the rest of the section, he covered the two miles in less than twelve minutes and such was his ability that he was back in the dressing-room and taking his shower before Cordiner finished. Yet Dick was a splendid runner who, despite his bad knee, had finished well within the sixteen-minute allowance. "Now perhaps you'll believe me," grinned the Major. "If you were fit you would have finished first." But I very much doubt if that was true.

In the spring of 1945 I carried on with fairly light duties in an executive capacity. By now I had been promoted to Sergeant-Major. Whenever I could I joined Joe Mercer and two other pals at ball practice. The others were George Bargh, of Preston North End and Bury, who had suffered a similar injury to my own, and Jimmy Morris, who played for Stockport and who was "guesting" for Aldershot. I am greatly indebted to these three fine fellows for the help and encouragement they gave me.

"You're going to be OK," Joe Mercer kept telling me, but I used to get fed up because of my inability to chase the ball. In the end Joe convinced me, and early the following season I persuaded Major Lovelock to let me play again. I hadn't heard anything from Arsenal all the time I'd been out of action, but I telephoned Mr. Allison and he invited me to come to Tottenham on the Saturday to play against Coventry.

I started this game at inside-right. After a quarter of an hour's play, however, as a result of an attempt to turn quickly in the penalty area, my knee rocked badly and Skipper George Male told me to go out on the wing. I continued in that position and the knee gave no further trouble.

Five minutes from the end, a goal down and pressing for the equaliser, we forced a corner on the left. As the ball came across I jumped and headed it straight into the net, but I was penalised for "climbing" so my equalizing goal did not count.

After the match I saw the Arsenal "powers-that-be", Tom Whittaker among them. It was the first time that they had seen me play since the Reading Cup-tie of the previous season and they expressed their disappointment that my knee had failed to stand up.

Actually there was no swelling or discomfort after the match, but when he saw my knee, Major Lovelock wasn't satisfied, and insisted on my visiting the Orthopaedic specialist at the Cambridge hospital. After an examination, this expert shook me by declaring, "I'm afraid your playing days are as good as over, Barnes!"

Just to make sure, however, he sent me to see a Brigadier-General, no less, at Byfleet, and the General put the tin hat on it!

"Well, Sergeant-Major, you're a big boy now, so I won't mince words," he said. "You'd better find some other way of making a living, because in our considered opinion you've played your last game of professional football."

You can imagine my feelings of dejection and acute frustration after hearing these words. At the age of twenty-five, through a simple accident on a vaulting horse, I appeared to have lost any chance of continuing the job of my choice.

Soon after this, too, the A.P.T.C. decided that they could no longer keep me at Aldershot as a semi-invalid, and I was posted for special duty. With the assistance of sixty men from the Pioneer Corps I was given the task of re-turfing the United Services' sports ground at Portsmouth.

It wasn't very exciting work, but it did have one redeeming feature – the type of work which I allotted myself enabled me to strengthen my knee. Gradually an idea formed in my mind that the specialists could possibly be wrong.

I elected to roll, cut and completely maintain one of the pitches by myself. For an hour and a half every day I walked behind the motor mower, which travelled at a fairly good rate and thus provided an ideal pacemaker.

With this exercise my knee began to improve. I was called upon to act as team manager for the Army team on two or three occasions and as I sat on the sidelines and watched the play, a fierce determination took possession of me. "The specialists can say what they like – I can beat this injury and play again," I told myself.

But my job at Portsmouth was soon brought to an undignified conclusion. One afternoon the G.S.O. of Physical Training decided to pop along to the United Services' ground to see how we were getting on with the turfing – and we weren't! The men had been working so hard I had declared a half-holiday while I gave a voluntary P.T. lesson to the men of a neighbouring tank regiment. I didn't have the chance to explain this to the staff officer, however. As colonels often do, he jumped to the conclusion that we had been slacking, and he had me posted to Salisbury to be "disciplined".

When I arrived at my new station it became apparent that I had a black mark against me. As far as the R.S.M. was concerned, my name was Mud. He and I didn't hit it off for the first week, and might never have done had not David Clelland, who was the Army quarter-mile and long-jump champion, mentioned something in the R.S.M.'s hearing about my experience in international football.

"What! Are you a professional footballer?" asked R.S.M. Harris, pricking up his ears. "Then you're just the bloke to fill in my football pools coupon!"....and that was the job he gave me. I am afraid I was no more successful at it than he had been himself, which seemed to make him a bit suspicious.

"If you're such a wonderful footballer, why don't you play for the regimental team?" he asked me. I explained about my injury. "Right!" he said. "We'll have to do something about this."

To the R.S.M. nothing was impossible; the difficult things could be done at once, miracles took a little longer. He certainly helped to accomplish a miracle with me. He devised an extensive programme of exercises which would strengthen my knee, and every evening after work the R.S.M., David Clelland and myself engaged in really tough physical jerks. How that helped to restore my confidence.

Before long I started to play soccer again, in inter-section matches. On occasions my knee rocked severely, but no fluid resulted so I kept on. My come-back had begun.

I also took up hockey again. Hockey was my first love in sport, and it is still my favourite. I firmly believe that it is possible to get to the top in more than one game at the same time, and I need only mention Denis Compton's name to substantiate this argument. But for a clash of fixtures I think I might have won honours on the hockey field. I was actually picked for an Army South v North hockey trial but since Arsenal wanted me for an important league game on the same day I had to ask permission to play football and lose my chance of selection for the Army hockey team.

Time marched on. The 1946-47 season had begun, and peace-time league football was in full swing. With such a strong incentive, in October I launched out on my major "come-back" campaign. Taking a month's leave which was owing to me, I came up to London and stayed in Southgate with my friends, Mr. and Mrs. Cottis. I want to pay a tribute to these grand folk right now. They were like a mother and father to me, and never wavered in the confidence that I would eventually play for Arsenal again, which was, of course, my main objective.

At once I saw Mr. Allison and asked him if I could train at Highbury Stadium, now in operation again despite the war damage. He gladly agreed. "We'd be only too glad to have you back again, Walley," he told me. "What's more, I'd like to wish you the luck that your courage deserves."

I didn't have any special treatment for my knee at Highbury. I just did solid routine training, morning and afternoon for three weeks. At the end of this period there was no sign of any rocking or swelling – the knee had stood up to all I had asked of it.

Meantime Arsenal had made a disastrous start in the league. After going down 6-1 to the Wolves away from home in the opening game, they continued to do so badly that by mid-November the experts were already beginning to accept relegation for once-mighty Arsenal as something more than a possibility.

The team that now floundered so badly bore little resemblance to the all-conquering pre-war combination. Stalwarts like Ted Drake, Jack Crayston and Alf Kirchen had hung up their boots for good, and a new set of players were trying desperately to mould themselves into the Arsenal pattern.

Tom Whittaker, who was now assistant manager and very much the "power behind the throne", had many problems to solve without my adding to them. At length, however, I plucked up my courage and asked him for a game. After watching me train he must have thought the gamble worth taking. "All right, Walley," he said thoughtfully, "we'll try you out against Cambridge University on Thursday."

So on Thursday, October 30th, 1946, at Cambridge I had my vital test. I played at left-back; the opposing winger was Trevor Bailey, the now famous English Test cricketer.

As fate would have it, the pitch was extremely wet and heavy and continual showers of rain were not improving the conditions. A stern test indeed.

How would my knee stand up? The game hadn't been in progress for more than ten minutes before I got the answer to that question. Trevor Bailey was running on to the ball and about to hit it very hard with his right foot, so I had to tackle him with my left leg fully extended. A split-second thought raced through my mind: "This is it: make or break!"

I came out of the tackle with the ball. Now – would the leg buckle?

It didn't. I made an effective clearance, and the game went on its way. I was called upon to make many further tackles. I made them without hesitation and without any painful effects.

91

As I walked up the pavilion steps after the game, the rain dripping down on my forehead, I felt a wonderful surge of exhilaration. Despite the verdict of the experts it began to look as if I would be able to continue my football career after all.

Tom Whittaker must have shared my thoughts because at once, in the Cambridge University dressing-room decorated so impressively with pictures of famous Varsity teams of the past, he asked me to sign a fresh form in order to establish my position as an Arsenal player. As I signed rainwater dripped steadily from my forehead, and the contract I handed back to Mr. Whittaker was just a smudge – but it represented the most important document in the world to me.

"How do you feel now?" Tom asked me.

"I feel great," I told him.

"That's good," said Tom, his eyes twinkling mischievously behind those thick horn-rimmed spectacles he now wore. He was nursing a bombshell with some relish. "That's very good," he continued, "because you'll probably be in the first team at Preston on Saturday week!"

And I was! Nine days after my come-back in a friendly match I took the field at Deepdale to play in my very first league game. And who should be opposing me but the great Tom Finney!

Although we lost 2-0, and Finney was at his brilliant best, I think I can say that I broke even with him and, what was even more important to me, my knee gave me no trouble. At the final whistle Tom Finney came across to congratulate me for my part in a keen tussle which, like the fine sportsman he is, he said he enjoyed. "Looks like you're back for good, Walley," were his parting words.

I went straight to hospital after the game – not because my knee had broken down under the strain, as many people assumed, but to have a minor operation. I turned out the following Saturday for my first match at Highbury, a London Combination fixture against Crystal Palace, and then regained my first-team place which I have kept, apart from absence through injury, ever since.

When we played Bolton Wanderers, at Highbury on November 30th, I welcomed a distinguished newcomer to Arsenal's ranks – Joe Mercer, the man with the "spiral staircase legs" who I already regarded as a good friend and who, to his own astonishment, was soon to add lavishly to the honours he had already won, and prove a tremendous inspiration to us all in seasons to come.

Up to December 14th Arsenal had collected only eleven points from eighteen league matches, and only Huddersfield were below us in the table by virtue of a slightly inferior goal average. That afternoon, however, we beat Charlton Athletic 1-0 and started an Arsenal come-back. From our next twenty-four matches we were to gain thirty points and finish Cock o'London in thirteenth position in the table.

The match that really set us on the road to recovery was played against Wolves, the league leaders and "team of the year", at Highbury on December 28th. From the word "go" we hit top form, and took the lead on our merits after twenty-five minutes when Ian Macpherson made an impertinent dribble for half the length of the field before passing to Ronnie Rooke. Rooke escaped Stan Cullis for once, and drove the ball into the net.

Four minutes later Wolves equalized, and set fire to an already exciting game in which there was no further score but plenty of thrills. Both George Swindin and Bert Williams were called upon to make spectacular saves, and right up to the last few minutes, when Bryn Jones made a brilliant forty yard pass to Rooke, only the see Ronnie miss a "sitter", the issue was in doubt.

So tense was the excitement that my wife, watching in the stand, bit the tops from the fingers of both her gloves, and I had to use my one pound bonus "lolley" to buy her a new pair!

It was some consolation, however, to read the Press comments the following morning. One critic went so far as to say that I reminded him of the great Eddie Hapgood, while Harry Ditton, of the *News of the World*, who was seeing me play for the first time, wrote "Barnes has come to stay!" Those words from such an experienced critic were a great encouragement to me.

In the third round of the F.A. Cup we met Chelsea at Stamford Bridge, and when Ian MacPherson gave us the lead with a "soft" goal just before half-time we thought we might be in for a good run. Then Scott, MacPherson, Bryn Jones and Logie were all injured, and Tommy Walker equalized late in the game to let us in for a marathon instead.

We were again first to score in the replay at Highbury and held the lead for seventy-five minutes. Then John Harris booted the ball up-field. I was ten yards outside the box when, instead of heading the ball first time as I should have done, I tried to kill it with my knee. The ball bounced to Walker who passed it on to Spence. Dicky Spence scooped the ball to Tommy Lawton and bang – there was the equalizer in the back of the net. George Swindin, who played brilliantly, was given no chance.

Even then we should have won the decider at Tottenham, but it was not our lucky day. In the first ten minutes our forwards hit the bar twice and the uprights three times and Reg Lewis missed a penalty. Then Tommy Lawton scored what I still think was a doubtful goal, since the linesman was flagging for hand-ball at the time. Seconds later, however, Lawton put the issue beyond doubt with another goal.

So we didn't get anywhere in the Cup that season. But we had begun to mould into a workmanlike team.

Laurie Scott and I had resumed our full-back partnership of war-time promise, and with reliable George Swindin behind us in goal and skipper Leslie Compton a tower of strength at centre-half, our defence had developed a confident look. Joe Mercer's superb general-ship brought the best out of such forwards as the temperamental Ian MacPherson, the then promising ball artist Jimmy Logie, veteran marksman Ronnie Rooke, who joined us from Fulham just as the tide began to turn and helped us considerably to sustain the effort, shrewd Reg Lewis, neat and clever Bryn Jones and big-hearted Alf Calverley, the outside-left who joined us from Mansfield Town and later moved on to Preston.

From my own point of view I had discovered the truth of the saying, "time is the best healer", and my knee now appeared to be perfectly sound. Naturally, I kept Major Lovelock posted with information and Press-cuttings right up to the time of his unfortunate death. I understand that he used to quote me as a miraculous example when giving medical lectures in America. I was particularly happy that my own come-back had coincided with Arsenal's revival and with the other players I looked forward to the future, confident that, with the ball running for us, we could achieve big things.

Chapter Eleven

I couldn't help laughing!

Everyone was perfectly happy about the soundness of my left knee except the medical officer who inspected it as a matter of Army routine one Monday morning during the 1946-47 season, and he was far from satisfied.

He pushed and he prodded. He moved my leg up and down, and he moved it from side to side. Then he pronounced judgement.

"You'll have to be very careful with this knee, Sergeant-Major," he advised. "Don't ever try to run fast or turn quickly. And never get off a vehicle while it's moving."

"Yes, sir!" I replied obediently, trying to keep a straight face, but hardly succeeding. Only two days previously I had played in a particularly robust league match for Arsenal and I had every intention of playing again the following Saturday.

I felt as fit as a fiddle, and needed to be fit to keep my place in the Arsenal team. But as far as the Army was concerned my tag remained: "Category B7, fit for light duties only".

One soldier who did follow the football news, however, was my commandant at Aldershot, Major-General Matthews. He sent for me one afternoon late in November 1946, and paid me the compliment of asking for my opinion. The advisability of introducing compulsory soccer training for cadets at the Royal Military Academy was being considered: did I have any ideas on the subject?

Yes, I did. I gave my opinion that since soccer was the number one game in the Army, I thought it essential that all officers should have a good basic knowledge of its rules, skills and organization.

"That's what we think, too," said the General, "and if the idea goes through we shall want an expect soccer coach to put the scheme into operation. Since you appear to hold strong views on the subject you may be just the man we shall need."

In due course, as a result of this interview I believe, I was appointed Association football coach to the R.M.A., Sandhurst, and for nearly three years, even after my discharge from the Army in March 1947, I continued to serve in this capacity. It was one of the happiest jobs imaginable, and I would like those officers who still write to me for advice regarding regimental soccer problems to know that they themselves taught me lessons of far greater value while they were at Sandhurst than I was ever able to teach them. They say that a teacher learns more than his pupils; the saying is certainly true in this case.

At Sandhurst I formed a lasting friendship with Q.M.S.I. Bert South who, through outstanding ability, has since become an organizer of Physical Training for the American Forces with the rank of Captain. Another crony of mine was George Brown, the Hants and England cricketer, whose expert coaching must have benefited the cadets enormously, while his dry sense of humour was a continual delight to me.

Among the cadets who figured in my soccer classes were those celebrated rugby international half-backs, Mike Hardy and D. Shuttleworth; and while their aptitude for the handling code was much the greater, their enthusiasm in chasing the round ball lent colour and excitement to our kick-abouts.

One rugby expert who might also have made a good soccer player was Captain T.G.H. (Graham) Jackson, a Sandhurst instructor, who often joined our classes. "Jacko" will be remembered as the fast, powerfully built Scottish international wing-three-quarter with a hand-off like the kick of a mule: but we converted him into a very creditable battalion centre-forward!

As I have already said, an athlete should be capable of reaching the top in more than one sport. But it is not often one finds a sportsman able to shine at both soccer and rugby football. The outstanding exception, of course, was my Arsenal colleague of the 1946-47 season, Dr. Kevin O'Flanagan, who played for

Ireland against France at rugby and then for Ireland against Scotland at soccer in successive weeks during 1946.

Although I was unable to join the rest of the Arsenal players in training at Highbury, I was very conscientious about my preparations, and used to train on the equestrian course at Sandhurst.

At the end of the first post-war season I had notice of an important change-over in the management of the Arsenal club. Mr. Allison, who had held the fort for thirteen years, had handed over the reins of office to Tom Whittaker.

Naturally, we were delighted at Tom's appointment. But I was not one of Mr. Allison's critics, and I did not hear that he was leaving us without a pang of regret. In some ways his rule was dictatorial; his football knowledge was not so great, and he lacked the flair for successful leadership possessed by Herbert Chapman. Despite this, however, the little man with the cello-toned voice had steered Arsenal through the difficult years, rebuilding, improvising and rebuilding again with a courage, skill and foresight that I, for one, greatly admired.

George Allison had been a good boss and a good friend to me; whatever faults others may have found in his methods I found nothing at which to complain. The results he achieved speak for themselves.

His health suffered through sustained effort, and when he no longer felt capable of giving the job the tremendous driving power he knew to be necessary, like the shrewd champion he was, he judged it time to retire and hand over to "Our Tom", the players' choice, and the man most capable of carrying on the Arsenal tradition.

Our new boss had already served the club for twenty-eight years as player, trainer and right-hand-man to the manager. Born at the turn of the century, Tom was discovered by Herbert Chapman while playing centre-forward for an Army team in 1919, and he was persuaded to join Arsenal instead of continuing a promising career as a naval engineer. Soon Tom became an outstanding half-back in the Gunners' team, excelling in the art of rugged defence.

In 1925, however, while playing for an F.A. team in Australia, Tom suffered a leg injury that brought his playing days to an untimely end. He became a trainer.

It was Sir Robert Jones, the great orthopaedic surgeon, who taught him his craft, and as a trainer Tom became famous throughout the country. Actors, Test cricketers, golfers, boxers, jockeys, speedway and ice hockey stars and celebrities from all walks of life paid tribute to his skill. In 1936 he took charge of the British lawn tennis team which retained the David Cup, and H. Roper Barrett, the non-playing captain, described him as, "The greatest masseur and trainer I have ever met."

During the war, still a qualified engineer, Tom was given the job of making battled-scarred planes airworthy again, and later he was awarded the M.B.E. for his secret work in connection with the water-proofing of vehicles for the D-Day landings.

Demobbed in 1945, Tom returned to Arsenal as assistant manager, in which capacity he had helped George Allison to rebuild an Arsenal team capable of maintaining the club's reputation.

There could be no doubt about Tom's qualifications for the job on paper; in fact, his appointment was even more appropriate for he had the affection and complete confidence of every member of the staff.

I always think of Tom as a first-class psychiatrist and philosopher rolled into one. He knows his job and his players inside out. No need for him to be a strict disciplinarian to achieve results. A hint or a suggestion from him is as good as a command to us, and we comply with it. Such is the strength of his personality. He is able to apply the Herbert Chapman principles in his own way and to get the very best out of each type of player without making himself the slightest bit unpopular in the process.

Towards the end of the 1946-47 season we had begun to settle down into a good side. Recognizing this our new boss did not rush into the transfer market, but like the good engineer he is he set about the task of making his existing staff "Arsenal-worthy". After giving a young player his first chance in the team I have heard Tom remark: "I could have bought an established player for a fantastic sum. Now I have got one for nothing and there is a new player in first-class football." That has always been his attitude.

He did make three astute signings, however. At the start of the season he obtained the services of two players well-known to me to strengthen the side. They were Archie Macaulay, who was now a P.T. instructor at the Acton Technical College and had been assisting Brentford, and Don Roper, who had developed into a robust, goal-scoring forward with Southampton and had begun to make a name for himself at cricket too, earning a trial for Hampshire during the close season.

It was Archie Macaulay who recommended the third newcomer, Alec Forbes, who, since first crossing my path as a ball-boy at Dundee, had gained a colourful reputation in sport. After showing early promise as a footballer he gave up the game to become an ice-hockey star, was persuaded back to soccer by Dundee North End, transferred to Sheffield United as a centre-forward in 1944, converted into a wing-half and capped for Scotland against England in that position in 1947.

When he joined us in 1948 Alec had to play second fiddle to his friend, sponsor, and fellow red-head, Archie Macaulay, for a time, but this did not stop him from developing into one of the game's most dynamic personalities and, of course, Alec eventually displaced Archie in the team.

We won our first five matches of the new season. Inspired by brilliant wing-halves, Joe Mercer and Archie Macaulay, the forward line of Roper, Logie, Rooke, Lewis and Macpherson, the latter successfully converted from outside-right to outside-left, struck a happy combination which scored seventeen goals, six of them against Charlton Athletic. In defence George Swindin, who had spent the summer coaching in Norway and had returned in better-than-ever form, Laurie Scott and myself, were helped by steady-as-a-rock Alf Fields, a centre-half who was to be robbed by ill-luck of the fame his brilliance deserved. But for Alf's injury, Les Compton would have had difficulty in regaining his place when cricket released him. We conceded only five goals to our opponents in this period.

Then we met Bolton Wanderers at Highbury. Early on Reg Lewis pulled a muscle and was moved to centre-forward. Crippled though he was, and only able to get to the ball on half a dozen occasions during the first half, still it was Reg, with splendid headwork, who made openings for his colleagues to score two goals. Then Alf Fields was injured and he had to leave the field altogether. Skipper Joe Mercer took over at centre-half and played the game of his life, inspiring us not only to keep Bolton at bay, but to launch attacks ourselves in an effort to increase the lead. Our 2-0 victory, won by nine men and a cripple, has always struck me as being an outstanding achievement in the club's history.

For the next game, at Preston, Leslie Compton came back to replace Alf Fields. Les, as previous captain, should have led us out, but in the dressing-room he handed the ball over to Joe Mercer, saying at the same time to Tom: "If you don't mind boss, I think Joe should have this. He's not done too badly with it so far."

So Joe continued as skipper, but Les gave such a wonderful display in our goalless draw at Preston that he retained the centre-half position for the rest of the season.

In this game, too, I renewed my duel with the tantalizing Tom Finney, and thanks to the way that the rest of the Arsenal players backed me up, on this occasion I was able to render Tom rather less effective than usual. It was a tremendous battle of wits, however, and I have no hesitation in naming this great artist as one of the trickiest wingers I have ever played against.

As a youngster, when running errands in the vicinity of Deepdale, Tom Finney always had a tennis ball at his toes. On

Saturdays he studied the craftsmanship of Alex James. At the time, he told me, his great ambition was to follow in the footsteps of this great inside-forward, who then played for Preston North End. Tom completed his football education as a member of the Preston club, who have always encouraged genuine ball players, and they persuaded him that his natural playing position was on the wing.

The Tom Finney that I know on the field of play is equally at home on either wing, and he is naturally two-footed, which means that a defender is constantly in two minds about which foot to watch. In addition, Tom has perfect balance and this is perhaps his greatest asset.

As Stanley Matthews does, Tom brings the ball right up close to you, shuffling it from one foot to the other while inviting you to tackle him. Unlike Stan, however, Tom's favourite trick is to sway towards the touchline and then move *inside* like lightening, taking the ball with his left foot (when playing at outside-right) which gives him two or three yards' start in the race for goal.

Tom's speed off the mark is terrific – it often carries him so far in advance of the other forwards that he is obliged to hold on to the ball until they are in position for a pass. Some spectators find this irritating, and others even blame him for "slowing up the play"! Speaking on behalf of his opponents, we would much prefer Tom to "get rid of it" at once, but he rightly waits until he can put over a really dangerous pass. This habit of his is certainly not a weakness, as I have heard it described.

How then should one play against a winger of Tom Finney's calibre?

The method of tackling a winger while he is in the act of receiving the ball, as every schoolboy knows, cannot be bettered. But one cannot always be Johnny-on-the-spot, so when playing Tom Finney the best idea is to try to force him outwards on to the touchline.

To do this I have found it best to take up position two yards away from him, lining up my left shoulder with his left shoulder, so that I am always in the inside position, and if he still wants to beat me by cutting-in he has to go very wide in order to do so.

When playing for Arsenal I know that if I can travel six yards or more with the winger, keeping him occupied without actually tackling him, my left-half, or the man who is playing in that position at the time, will get back and cover me, while the rest of the defence will so dispose itself that no matter which way the winger goes after that he will keep running into trouble.

The important thing to do is to delay the winger's progress, so that by the time he reaches your penalty area – at which point *you must tackle* – the rest of the defence are scientifically placed in the danger area, and whether your tackle succeeds or fails is no longer vitally important, because the way to goal is blocked by a human barrier.

This type of defensive play (shall we call it "fencing"?) is not likely to meet with the approval of all sections of the crowd. "Get into him!" they will cry. But to "get into" a man like Tom Finney, once he is in possession, and before your colleagues are in position is to invite disaster.

By mid-October we had played eleven games, won nine and drawn two, and we topped the league table with twenty-four points out of a possible twenty-six. While scoring twenty-five goals ourselves, we had conceded only six to opponents.

Yes, we had "come back" with a vengeance, and the anti-Arsenal fanatics were not slow to "come back" too, applying the "Lucky Arsenal" tag to all our efforts. They accused us of packing our defence, averting "goals against" by playing negative football, and of stealing points by snatching freak goals after our opponents had done most of the attacking.

They said that we beat Sunderland by "smash-and-grab" tactics, Sheffield United through their defensive lapses. The run of the ball favoured us against Manchester United and Preston. Stoke contributed largely to their own downfall, and had I not been "lucky" enough to head the ball off the goal-line with

Swindin beaten on two occasions against Burnley, and had we not snatched a soft breakaway goal on the rebound, we would have lost that one too. So they said.

Then as our run of success continued without any big scores in our favour, the critics changed their tune. Now it was not just luck but "deliberate strategy on our part", they declared. Whenever we took the field the boss reminded us that we already had a point in hand; if we failed to concede a goal then we could not lose it, so our instructions were simply "Stop the other chaps from scoring at all costs." This story persisted, and it is still believed by many people to this day.

Let me go on record as saying that never at any time while I have played for Arsenal, at home or away, have I known any such instruction to be given. Rather are Tom's last words to us: "You've got one point – *now go out and get another!*"

We have got a plan, and it's rather like that in which the Commandos are briefed: "Prepare carefully, attack boldly and retire swiftly."

Those who accuse Arsenal of playing negative football miss the finer points of our tactics, in my opinion. To my mind our tactics resemble those employed by a clever boxer who appears to be taking a lot of punishment, but is actually blocking, slipping and riding punches; ready to dart in and score points while his opponent is regaining breath for another onslaught.

When Arsenal defend the whole team defends. But they retire in formation, ready to switch to attack immediately the danger has been averted.

Each player, goalkeeper included, tries to use the ball constructively; to make each clearance a pass, preferably one that will enable the team to counter-attack in one rapid movement.

And in defence, we swivel to cover each other in such a manner that the goalkeeper is not necessarily the last line of defence. When I, or other members of the team, head the ball off the goal-line, our presence in that position is not always fortuitous

– more likely we have simply carried out the drill of covering the goalkeeper while he has advanced to narrow the angle of a shot.

The successful execution of these tactics depends on unselfish teamwork, which has always been Arsenal's greatest asset.

After each game Arsenal players take part in an inquest under Tom Whittaker's supervision. If a goal has been scored against us, its whole history is traced back to the individual fault which caused it. You see, the ability of our opponents apart, every goal is scored as the result of a mistake on someone's part, and that someone may be the goalkeeper, or even the centre-forward. No Arsenal player is immune from blame, and fortunately for the club, each one is prepared to admit to, and learn by, his mistake. At these weekly discussions we all have our say with the sole object of ironing out the flaws before the next game.

These methods, originated I believe by Herbert Chapman, are typical of Arsenal's approach to the game, and they remain in force to this day. Off the field you have eleven individuals who, being human, do not always agree. But on match-day it's different. Then we're a team with no differences, resolved to win as best we can *within the law*.

Our critics love to compare our pattern of play unfavourably with that of other clubs. Pointing to that brilliant attacking machine, the Spurs, they ask, "Why can't you play like that?"

My answer is, "We do; near enough," and that comment may surprise you, so let me explain.

Soon after the Spurs had regained their First Division status after the war by what the experts rightly described as "brilliant attacking football", I went to see them play against Hull City. Good Friday morning it was. On two occasions in the first quarter of an hour I saw Les Medley, the outside-left, dispossess an opposing forward inside his own box and, as the game proceeded, I noticed that he and the other Spurs' forwards spent as much time in their own box, looking for opportunities to start an attack, as they did at the other end.

This was typical of Arsenal team-work and, in fact, the only difference I observed in our respective styles of play was that whereas the Spurs progressed with short man-to-man passes, we favour long, sweeping attacking movements. Our system switches the play rapidly from one side of the field to the other, introducing a surprise element while relieving pressure on our own goal.

You must take my word for it that these long passes are deliberate tactics on our part, and not "run of the ball luck". Of course, any successful team needs a little luck, and we had our fair share in 1947-48. But it was more than a little disconcerting to have our every success attributed to this factor alone, and none of us felt happy about it at the time.

"No one can call us "Lucky Arsenal" after this," I remember Laurie Scott saying in the dressing-room after the classic Bolton game. But they could – and they did.

Yet we completed over a third of our league programme without defeat that year, and our defensive record was better than that of any other club under the present offside law as far as I know.

After we had played eleven games without defeat, conceding only six goals to opponents, I was feeling on top of the world, and to cap everything I was told that I had been selected to play for Wales against England at Ninian Park in my first full international.

Laurie Scott and Bryn Jones were also selected, and the only snag in this great honour as far as we were concerned was that we could not be in two places at once. Proud as we were to be wanted at Cardiff to assist our respective countries, we would also have liked to help our club at Wolverhampton where the boys faced their stiffest hurdle to date.

From Porthcawl post office, Laurie, Bryn and I wired good luck messages to the team, and I added a special word for my deputy, Joe Wade.

We needn't have worried. At Paddington, where we met the Arsenal team after the international, we learned that they had shared the points, that Joe Wade had played a blinder and that our unbeaten record was thus intact.

Chapter Twelve

In my first full international, on October 18th, 1947, I really did have the experience of marking Stanley Matthews.

Arriving in Cardiff on the Thursday evening, I found the whole of Wales had become "soccer crazy", or so it seemed. There is nothing Taffy likes better than a crack at the little country over the border, and the possibility of our upsetting one the most powerful England combinations of all time in this match had brought national spirit to the boiling point. The newspapers were full of conjecture, and one of the main topics appeared to be: "Could Ronnie Burgess" (skippering the Welsh team for the first time) "and I hold the Blackpool wonder-wing of Mortensen and Matthews?"

Stanley Matthews! That name began to haunt me. I tried to recall all that I had heard, and seen at first-hand, of the man who had been both my colleague and my opponent in services matches; the result was not very comforting!

To many people in all parts of the world Stanley Matthews was already "The greatest footballer in history." He was about to play in his fifty-second international for England, and such was his form that season that later he was almost automatically voted "Footballer of the Year".

Born in Hanley in the Potteries district in 1915, the Master had been groomed in Spartan manner by his father, Jack Matthews, once famous as a feather-weight boxer. Each morning, before breakfast, father and son performed Swedish drill in front of the open window. Physical fitness was their fetish.

As a youth, Stanley earned local fame as a sprinter. But football was his great interest: he had a natural ability for the game.

This ability he nurtured by constant and enthusiastic practice. A cheap rubber ball was his favourite toy – the garden wall his playmate. Kicking the ball against the wall for hours on end, and dribbling round the garden chairs were methods he employed to train the ball to obey him.

After earning schoolboy international honours, Stanley joined Stoke City, his local club, as a fifteen-year-old amateur player and professional office-boy. His father insisted Stan should walk the two miles back and forth to work, in all weathers, as part of his training.

At seventeen, Stanley became a professional footballer. Two years later he played his first game for England, and soon became his country's first choice for the outside-right position.

Stanley became the idol of millions of football followers all over the world through his unique ability and natural gift of showmanship. In Stoke he was far more than a football star, however. When he threatened to leave them for Blackpool in 1939, such was the public indignation in the city that, it was claimed, industrial output was disrupted.

Later, of course, he did make the move to Blackpool where he quickly enhanced his reputation as the darling of the crowds.

What was the reason for his fame? He was not a champion goal-scorer, although he once scored three goals for England against Czechoslovakia and I knew he had the knack. He *was* a champion goal-maker, winning matches and making reputations for others by allowing them the glory of converting his spade-work into hard goals.

Football had never seen, and would probably never see another player like him. Tall, shoulders drooped, hand resting casually on one hip, he paced the touch-line with a curious ungainly lope.

Then the ball would be flung in his direction: if despatched by a colleague then it would be aimed straight at him for choice. Stan would reach out a foot and bring it under control, and at once the ball appeared to become his personal property. He would not part with it until the opposition had been thoroughly undermined and confused, or until a colleague was in a position to receive a gift opportunity from which to score.

Stanley's habit was to take the ball right up under the nose of his opponent, inviting – or rather demanding – a tackle. Sometimes he would stop dead in his tracks to force a defender to take the initiative. Meantime his fellow forwards raced into unmarked positions.

Eventually the defender moved into the tackle, to one side or the other. Whichever way he chose, quick-witted Stan picked the right trick to hoodwink him. Once the defender moved a foot forward towards the ball Stan knew that his weight must be upon it and during that instant, while the defender was off-balance, he was ripe for the beating.

Often I had seen Stan sway his body to the left, encouraging a belief that he intended to cut-in towards goal, Tom Finney fashion. Unlike Tom in this respect, however, Stan would invariably check, flick the stationary ball towards the touch-line with the outside of his foot, and follow it like lightening down the wing.

Having made his escape, Stanley would select the colleague best able to convert his wizardry into a goal and then place the ball accurately to the very spot where the maximum opportunity existed.

It was with this problem-picture in my mind that I reached the hotel in Porthcawl where I had been instructed to report. I walked into the lounge and, believe it or not, the first person I set eyes upon was Stanley Matthews!

By a coincidence, the England team had chosen to stay at the same hotel as we had!

"Hallo there, Walley! Quite like old times seeing you again?" smiled Stan, in his usual friendly manner, and he and I spent five minutes of so together while Stan patiently signed a dozen autograph books on behalf of my friends. I didn't realize it at the time, but that was the nearest I was to get to Stan during our stay in South Wales!

The following day the Welsh team did some sprinting, and played head tennis on the common in Porthcawl, while the England team practiced under their coach, Walter Winterbottom, at Pencoed. That evening our team gathered together at the hotel to discuss a plan of campaign, but my particular role was obvious and it didn't need rubbing-in.

Here is how we lined up on that memorably Saturday afternoon, before a vast crowd of 55,000 enthusiastic spectators at Ninian Park.

WALES: Sidlow (Liverpool); Lambert (Liverpool); Barnes (Arsenal); I. Powell (Queen's Park Rangers); T. Jones (Everton); Burgess (Spurs) capt.; Thomas (Fulham); A. Powell (Leeds); Lowrie (Coventry); B. Jones (Arsenal) and Edwards (Birmingham).

ENGLAND: Swift (Manchester City); Scott (Arsenal); Hardwick (Middlesbrough) capt.; Taylor (Liverpool); Franklin (Stoke); Wright (Wolves); Matthews (Blackpool); Mortensen (Blackpool); Lawton (Chelsea); Mannion (Middlesbrough) and Finney (Preston North End).

This was virtually the England team that had beaten Belgium and pulverized Portugal, the latter by ten goals at Lisbon, and although Wales had won the only two full internationals played at Cardiff during the last thirteen years, the visitors were strongly expected to break the sequence on this occasion. And so they did! After twenty minutes' play it was all over bar the shouting.

In the ninth minute, after Mannion and Finney had exchanged pin-point passes at speed, Finney completed the move by half-volleying a brilliant goal from an oblique angle. Five minutes later, with the England attack still moving slickly at supersonic speed, Stan Matthews beat me and sent the ball across goal for the other Stan, Stan Mortensen, to tap it into the net. Then, to clinch the result in the twentieth minute, Tommy Lawton scored a third goal through Mannion, who deceived us all by racing across field to gather Taylor's throw-in at the corner flag.

By now I had "lost face" with a large section of the crowd. They considered that I was giving Stan Matthews too much rope. "Get into him!" was the familiar cry that rang in my ears. But I took no notice, retreating from Matthew's snaky runs like a cagey mongoose.

I refused to do the one thing that the crowd – and, I believe, Stanley Matthews – most wanted me to do: that was to "Tackle him!" Stan was dangerous enough as it was; if I allowed myself to be drawn I was sure that he would create havoc, and a Lisbon-like result would follow.

As I had found against Tom Finney, there appeared to be only one certain way to beat the master-winger and that was to stop him from getting the ball. Since I was rarely able to do that, I resigned myself to attempting to delay and hinder Stan from crossing the ball accurately. This I think I achieved fairly successfully.

But England gave a dazzling performance that day and well-deserved their win by three clear goals. Stan Matthews was their "master mind" and my master. But I got all the press! Taking their cue from the crowd, reporters criticized me for standing back in a "tackle-less trance", and allowing Matthews to mesmerize me.

All I can say in my own defence is that I played Stan the way I thought best, and if the game were to be played all over again I would not change my tactics. I believe the Welsh selectors appreciated this, too, for when our team was announced for the next international against Scotland, I retained my place and it was the unfortunate Ray Lambert who was dropped.

Two or three weeks after the Cardiff international, when Blackpool visited Highbury I again had the job of marking Stanley Matthews, I applied exactly the same methods to combat his wizardry as I attempted at Ninian Park, and this time I got a great deal of credit from the critics for "shutting him out of the game".

When Wales met Scotland at Hampden Park, only four members of our team and three of theirs had had previous international experience at this ground in Victory matches. An official Welsh team had last visited Glasgow in 1931; that was the occasion when the gallant "Welsh Unknowns" had forced their never-to-be-forgotten draw against the odds.

This is how the team lined up on Wednesday, November 12th, 1947.

SCOTLAND: Miller (Celtic); Govan (Hibernian); Stephen (Bradford); Macaulay (Arsenal); Woodburn (Rangers) capt.; Forbes (Sheffield United); Smith (Hibernian); Maclaren (Preston North End); Delaney (Manchester United); Steel (Derby County) and Liddell (Liverpool).

WALES: Sidlow (Liverpool); Sherwood (Cardiff City); Barnes (Arsenal); I. Powell (Queen's Park Rangers); T. Jones (Everton); Burgess (Spurs) capt.; Thomas (Fulham); A. Powell (Leeds United); Ford (Aston Villa); Lowrie (Coventry City) and Edwards (Birmingham City).

Although John Govan was the only brand-new cap, there was a great deal of dissatisfaction among Scottish fans about their team's composition. Chief complaint was that no less than seven Anglo-Scots had been selected in preference to home league performers.

Significant changes in our team were the introduction of Alfie Sherwood, of Cardiff City, as my partner at full-back and the recall of Victory-international Trevor Ford, then with Villa, at centre-forward. It was the first time I had played in the same team as these two great footballers, and I was greatly impressed by both of them.

A big worry before the game was the health of big George Lowrie, vital to our "double centre-forward" plan, who complained of a sore throat. Fortunately, Dr. Hughes, the welsh

113

F.A. Medical Officer, was on the spot as usual. He travels with us wherever we play, and "nurses" us right up to the moment we take the field. On this occasion Doc gave George an injection that made him "right as rain", so we entered the fray with all our big guns.

We had heard frightening stories about the Hampden Roar, and I found myself waiting for it, intent that, however frightening it might prove to be, it would not put me off my stroke. But it never came; and truth to tell, the Scots gave 68,000 spectators little to enthuse about in their performance. Right from the first whistle we were the guv'nors. We were given all the room in the world to move the ball about and made good use of it.

Actually, however, Scotland scored first. Gordon Smith, who was my particular "cup of tea", started as if he was going to take a leaf out of Matthew's book and gave me the run-around. It was from his centre that Andy Maclaren headed a goal after eleven minutes.

Then we bolted the door against those Scottish forwards. Tommy Jones, one of the best centre-halves I have ever played with, held Delaney in a grip of iron, and Burgess and Ivor Powell quickly stemmed any attempt by the opposing inside-forwards to set their line in motion. I think Gordon Smith might have given me a lot of trouble in normal circumstances. At first he was as full of tricks as a cageful of monkeys, and when running at speed with the ball he looked the perfect stylist. However, I was on top form, while Gordon must have had an off-day, because his bark proved worse than his bite.

After thirty-five minutes, Sid Thomas, who was able to do practically as he liked against Jimmy Stephen, took a centre on the right and "found" George Edwards with his centre. The Birmingham winger promptly back-heeled the ball to Trevor Ford who banged it into the net for the equalizer.

Just before the interval, George Lowrie scored the memorable goal of the match. Receiving the ball from Ivor Powell, twenty-five yards from goal, he tricked Alec Forbes and cracked the ball so hard that it entered the roof of the net with the velocity of a rifle bullet.

From then on it was all Wales, and only brilliant goalkeeping by Bill Miller, of Celtic, prevented us from adding to our lead.

One Scot who greatly impressed me in this game was Alec Forbes, who was shortly to join Arsenal from Sheffield United. He gave sterling service in the half-back line, although once he got in the way of a terrific free-kick by Tom Jones, that perfect kicker of a dead ball, and had to leave the field for attention by the trainer.

In the last few minutes of the game Bill Miller was injured, diving at the feet of Trevor Ford to prevent a certain goal. It was Alec Forbes who put on the goalkeeper's jersey and he proved just as much a thorn in our side in this unfamiliar position as he had done in the half-back line. On several occasions he saved the day for Scotland while our goal-hungry forwards peppered the net from all angles.

It was the first time that I had been on the winning side in an international, so perhaps I could be forgiven for the smug satisfaction I felt about my own performance. One national newspaper went so far as to use the headline: "Barnes and Wales beat Scotland" on their sports page the following day, and others were flattering enough to refer to me as "The man of the match".

I did not entirely escape Press criticism, however. A query was raised about my "risky cross-field clearances to the opposite wing". As I have already explained, we were using this move to good effect at Arsenal and I did not hesitate to use it at Hampden Park. While I would agree that can be dangerous, accurately employed at the appropriate moment it is a valuable means of taking the play away from the area where players are concentrated and of starting up a surprise attack on the other flank. For instance, imagine that you are playing at left-back, and the ball comes to you after play has taken place on your side of the field. If you are not hard-pressed you can trap the ball and take it forward for a few yards. A quick look round the field may reveal that players are still concentrated on the left and that your right-winger is isolated. The thing to do is to send a left-footed pass over the heads of the intervening players so that the ball falls just ahead of your right-winger, but not so far ahead that the opposing full-back can reach it first. Quite logical, isn't it, but of course it is a kick that needs a lot of practice.

Just prior to this international the Arsenal team had travelled to Paris and suffered their first defeat of the season at the hands of the Racing Club. Archie Macaulay and I rejoined the team for the next two league matches – at Blackburn and at home to Huddersfield – both of which we won, and then took part in the 1-0 defeat at Derby – our first league reverse in nineteen matches. This proved only a temporary set-back, however, and as Christmas approached we were still top of the league and in top gear.

Then, on December 20th, we made the long journey to Sunderland, where I was to meet with an injury to my "good" knee that put me out of action for nearly a month, and which might have crippled me. The injury was entirely my own fault.

During the first half the Sunderland forwards, led by that grand club man Dickie Davis (a great pal of Leslie Compton's, by the way), were very lively. We found Eddie Burbanks' corners, taken from the left wing, particularly troublesome, and it was from one of them that Davis opened the scoring with a back-header. Burbanks was sending the ball to the far corner of the box, to the spot from which goal-kicks are normally taken, and I didn't quite know what to do about it.

I now realize that, as left-back, I was the obvious player to intercept the ball and thus cut Davis out on these occasions, but through lack of experience with this particular manoeuvre I failed to do my job properly.

When Burbanks put over another of his special corners just before half-time, Leslie Compton succeeded in baulking Davis, and I, standing with my left shoulder up against the far

116

post, threw my right leg across to escort the ball safely over the goal-line. It was a stupid position in which to get myself. Davis and Duns both went after the ball and hit my braced right leg together.

I went down in agony, clasping my knee. Afterwards I learned that I had slightly torn the attachment of the internal lateral ligament of my right knee.

"How is it, Walley?" Tom asked me in the dressing-room at half-time.

"I can carry on all right," I told the boss, because the pain had begun to ease.

"All right," said Tom. "We'll try the same move that we used against Bolton. You take over at centre-forward, Walley!"

I readily agreed with Tom's decision. Providing a player is not too badly injured, and only the player himself can know the extent of his injury at this stage, he can make himself a nuisance at centre-forward, keeping three defenders occupied by simply standing up and walking about. For all the opposition know, even a semi-cripple might be capable of landing the one kick that makes all the difference to the result, so they've got to watch him. If the injured player goes on the wing, however, not only does he unbalance his own team's attack, but his opponents can afford to regard his hobbling efforts with some tolerance.

As it happened, although a complete passenger for most of the second half of this game, I was able to get a foot to the ball at a vital moment and send it to Bryn Jones to smash home a brilliant equalizer from eighteen yards.

One thing that my injured knee did do for me – it enabled me to have my Christmas dinner at home, a most unusual occurrence. But after Christmas I had the frustrating experience of sitting in the stand and watching ninety minutes' grim football in which "unfashionable" Bradford City came to Highbury and shocked the football world by licking all-conquering Arsenal in a Third Round Cup-tie.

After that reverse the danger was that we would lose confidence in the league battle, and crack at the vital moment, so it was with a grim resolve that we prepared for the encounter with our near-rivals in the table, Manchester United, at Old Trafford.

My knee had mended splendidly, and after a try-out on the Thursday I was declared thoroughly fit to resume my place in the team. I could not wish for a finer birthday present for, on the day before the big match, I reached the ripe old age of twenty-eight.

And what a match it was! There were 82,950 people at Old Trafford that afternoon, a record crowd for the English League, and those of them who managed to get a look at the game would no doubt confirm my own impression that it was a football classic.

After suffering a rather serious injury, as I had done, a player naturally hopes that he will not be called upon to do something early on in his first game after convalescence that will cause the injury to reassert itself. On this occasion, United set up a tremendous offensive from the start and after seven minutes play I was faced with the situation in which I either had to go into a difficult tackle or allow Johnny Morris a clear run at goal. Naturally, I took the former course, and Lady Luck smiled down on me because, although I had to extend my right leg to its full extent without much support, the leg stood up, saw me safely through the game and the rest of the season.

This wonderful game resulted in a 1-1 draw, restoring all the confidence that Bradford City might have knocked out of us. And but for a remarkable freak of fortune we would have gained both points. In the last few minutes we broke away, Reg Lewis slipped his "shadow" and placed the ball wide of the goalkeeper. Twenty-two players and 82,950 spectators watched the ball roll through the mud, hit the inside of the post and then – such was the spin on it – although hitting the *inside* of the post it somehow twisted from its path and rolled over the goal-line outside the same post.

Walley Barnes clears the ball from Jackie Robinson (Sunderland) in the Arsenal goalmouth at Highbury, 1948-49 season. Laurie Scott is covering the other corner of the goal.

"I must arrange to get hit on the head more often," says the author, describing a thrilling match at Highbury in 1948, in which Arsenal beat the Wolves. Despite a split forehead, Walley returned to the field after the interval with his head bandaged, and played one of his best-ever league games.

Chapter Thirteen

Monday, March 8th, 1948, is a date I shan't forget in a hurry. On that day I travelled to Wrexham to take over the captaincy of the Welsh international side for the first time. The scene was set for a keen encounter against Ireland, and by winning it we knew that we would go to the top of the international table.

I suppose that must have been the thought uppermost in my mind when I arrived at our hotel in Wrexham, because Tommy Jones, who was the first member of the team to greet me, told me that I looked as if I had all the cares of the world on my shoulders.

"Don't worry, skipper," he said confidently. "We're going to start you off with a good win on Wednesday."

But within a few minutes of my arrival I was involved in a spot of trouble, and it made me realize the wide extent of my new responsibilities.

"This hotel just isn't good enough, skipper," said one of the lads. "You'll have to do something about it."

"Look where we're expected to sleep," Cyril Sidlow chimed in, and he showed me the large upstairs room to which he had been directed. In it, a number of divan beds had been prepared *on the floor*.

"We had enough of that in the Army," said another member of the team. "It's hardly the way to treat the Welsh national side."

They were quite right. Our accommodation just wasn't good enough.

I didn't want anyone to think I was chucking my weight about at the first opportunity, but obviously something had to be done about this so, prompted and backed-up by well-established internationals like Tom Jones and Ivor Powell, I made my protest to Mr. Cookson, of Rhyl, the official representative of the Welsh

F.A. who accompanied us, and as a result we were allocated more reasonable rooms downstairs. They were available, you see.

On the Tuesday we did a spot of training at the Rhyl Football Club ground and I was introduced for the first time to our "new chum" Billy Baker, of Cardiff, who was to prove the best possible substitute for Ronnie Burgess at left-half. That evening all the players gathered together with Mr. Powell in the largest bedroom to discuss the tactics we should employ against Ireland the following afternoon.

The Welsh Amateur team had given England Amateurs a surprise beating at Shrewsbury on the previous Saturday, and we were naturally anxious to make it a good week all round for Welsh football.

I was asked for my opinion, and suggested one or two ideas, one of which was actually to pay a handsome dividend. As a result of my Arsenal training, I automatically looked for the suspected weakness in the opposing team, so that we could hammer away at it. In this case I estimated our chief hope to be that the veteran Billy Gorman, brilliant full-back though he still was, might be just that vital fraction slow on the turn and that we could beat him in flight. I said as much and it was decided that we should concentrate on the Arsenal plan of pushing long passes out to the wings, and especially to Sid Thomas on the right.

The lads' successful execution of this plan was undoubtedly the chief factor in our being able to establish an early superiority over the Irish defence. Right from the start, Aubrey Powell started lobbing accurate passes over Gorman's head, enabling Sid Thomas to run on to the ball and throw the other defenders into a panic with his crosses.

To take the plan a stage nearer to that adopted by Arsenal, I suggested to Alf Sherwood that he and I should swivel to cover each other, and not play square, as Alf is more used to doing with his Cardiff partner, and that Billy Baker and Ivor Powell should stay fairly consistently in position in order to check the dangerous prowling expected from Peter Doherty.

Mr. Powell and the rest of the players agreed to give these ideas a trial, and the fact that experienced players like Ivor Powell, Tommy Jones and Co. backed them up so splendidly gave my confidence a tremendous boost.

As we ran on to the field at Wrexham on the Wednesday afternoon my last words to the lads were the ones I nearly always use: "Play your natural game, fellows," I said. "That's what got you into the side, and that's what will help us most."

This is how we lined up:

WALES: Sidlow (Liverpool); Sherwood (Cardiff); Barnes (Arsenal) capt.; I. Powell (Queen's Park Rangers); T. Jones (Everton); W. Baker (Cardiff); S. Thomas (Fulham); A. Powell (Leeds); Ford (Aston Villa); Lowrie (Coventry) and Edwards (Birmingham).

IRELAND: Hinton (Fulham); Martin (Leeds); Gorman (Brentford); W. Walsh (Manchester City); Vernon (West Bromwich Albion); Farrell (Everton); Cochrane (Leeds); Smyth (Wolverhampton Wanderers); D. Walsh (West Bromwich Albion); Doherty (Huddersfield) capt. and Eglington (Everton).

Ireland had had an extremely good season, having beaten Scotland and drawn with England, and although steady and reliable Johnny Carey was missing from their defence on this occasion, they still looked a formidable combination with their tall, graceful centre-half, Jack Vernon, probably the outstanding player of the day in that position. Mind you, with two such powerful centre-forwards as George Lowrie and Trevor Ford opposing him, he needed to be good!

Although Ireland had beaten Wales in the only two internationals played since the war, it was a fact that they had been unsuccessful in their last seven visits to the Wrexham Racecourse ground, so there was little to choose between the teams on statistics.

It was a nice, sunny day, but the ground was hard and there was a stiff breeze, which meant that we all had difficulty in keeping the ball on the floor. At the outset, I remember, none of us liked the ball that had been provided so, by common consent, after a few minutes' play, someone gave it a hearty boot over the Racecourse stand. Another ball was provided immediately – but it was practically identical, and there appeared to be no future in losing this one as well. We settled down to play a quiet, methodical game, and it soon became apparent that Wales were top-dogs and that there was little Ireland could do about it.

The first goal came just before half-time. Edwards and Ford executed a brilliant change-of-position move, Trevor put over an accurate cross from the left wing, and Hinton barely diverted the ball from George Lowrie's header. Trevor Ford had a bang – his shot was blocked – and then Lowrie headed into the net. That's how I remember it.

Seven minutes after half-time George Edwards, the Birmingham schoolmaster, scored a weird and wonderful "number two" for us. While the Irish defenders were busy claiming a foul, George Edwards continued his run down the wing. In order to cut-out the cross he anticipated, Ted Hinton advanced towards Trevor Ford but, seeing this, George Edwards did not centre. Instead he cleverly angled the ball between Hinton and the goal-line and scored a "believe-it-or-not" goal. The odds against his hitting such a narrow target must have been pretty considerable.

There were no further goals, but we had already done enough to go to the top of the international table so that only England, by beating Scotland in the final match at Hampden, could take the championship from us. In fact England *did* beat Scotland in April, and we had to be content with second place above Ireland.

I was amused to read in the papers that "Arsenal tactics were obviously employed by the Welsh side which beat Ireland", and when Tom Whittaker kidded me about this, I could hardly deny that there was some truth in the assertion. "All the same," I pointed out, "imitation is the sincerest form of flattery," and Tom couldn't think of an answer to that one.

Arsenal were a good team to imitate, too. They were still top of the league and they kept on winning. After our memorable draw at Old Trafford, Aston Villa, Chelsea and Blackpool were the only teams to stop us.

On April 3rd we beat Blackburn Rovers 2-0 at Highbury, putting us seven points ahead of Manchester United with five matches to play.

I remember the Blackburn match for a particular incident. In the second half I was chasing Oakes, the speedy right-winger who had given me quite a lot of trouble. On this occasion I was quick enough off the mark to get to the ball a yard in front of him, and at this point, however, I got my feet tangled on the slippery ground and Oakes ran into me at speed, knocking me over the line so that I pitched on to my right shoulder in the mud.

Do you know, for three weeks afterwards I couldn't raise my right arm above shoulder height, and had to play with my thumb tucked into the button of my shirt! And further results were that, to this day, I cannot sleep on my right side – the pain wakes me up – and I'm not over-keen about robust charging with my right shoulder.

The following week we were travelling home after getting a point at Huddersfield, when Denis Compton made an important discovery. Studying the results and league table printed in the evening paper he had bought at Doncaster, he made a lightening calculation and announced: "We've done it! We can't be caught!"

It was true. Arsenal were league champions – for the sixth time in their history, and in Tom Whittaker's first year as manager – having topped the table from start to finish, as Leslie Compton was quick to point out.

What was more, our club had called on only eighteen players for league matches at this stage, and our defence had conceded fewer goals (30) than any other First Division club had done since the change of the offside law.

We felt pretty pleased with ourselves, I can tell you!

After that there were only two more games of note, and I didn't play in the second because of the first!

The first was our goalless draw at Portsmouth. At one stage I attempted a hefty clearance under the very nose of Duggie Reid, who for all his size is one of the cleanest players in the game, and Duggie blocked my kick in such a way that I was lucky not to break my ankle. As it was, the injury kept me out of the team for the last two games.

In the last game, on May 1st, I watched the boys speed Grimsby's passage into the Second Division with an 8-0 drubbing. Ronnie Rooke scored the first four, with all the lads helping him to top the individual scoring tables. On one occasion Alec Forbes beat big George Tweedy, turned on the goal-line and passed the ball back so that Ronnie could have the distinction of putting it into the net.

After scoring seven goals, Arsenal were awarded a penalty, and Joe invited Jimmy Logie, the only non-scorer, to take it. Jimmy put the ball one way, and George went the other, and although I could not hear George's comments from the stand, I can imagine that they would sum up the whole match, from his point of view, in the sort of language strong men use under an anaesthetic!

Immediately after the game I reported to the doctor, hoping against hope that he would pass me fit to fly to Portugal with the Arsenal team, who were to make their first post-war tour overseas.

I feared the worst, because not only did I have a shaky ankle and a pad on my right shoulder, but the plaster bandages I had been wearing on both knees had given rise to a form of dermatitis, and I had a painful boil behind the joint of my right knee as a result.

126

The Doc must have realized how keen I was to make the trip. To my great delight he gave me his OK.

Trainer Billy Milne was not so lucky. Poor Billy – he had played more than his share in our success that season, and no one deserved a holiday trip more – but the Doc's final check-up revealed that he had contracted a contagious skin disease.

From an administrative point of view this did not cause a last-minute crisis because, according to Arsenal custom, deputies had packed and were prepared to substitute for anyone forced to drop out at the last moment. Jack Crayston had said "cheerio" to his wife in case he had to take the boss's place, twenty reserve players were standing-by in case they were needed, and Bert Owen, Billy's able assistant, was equally ready to step in as trainer.

As it happened all the first team players were available except Leslie and Denis Compton, whose services were required by the Middlesex County Cricket Club.

Before leaving for London Airport we had a send-off party in the restaurant under the West Stand, with players' wives and friends present, and what with our league championship success, the big win over Grimsby, and the prospects of a happy holiday trip to sunny Portugal, the party was a success from the word "Go" and we were in the best of spirits when we left the ground by coach at about ten o'clock.

In the early hours of Sunday morning, the wheels of our extremely reliable but noisy York aircraft touched down at Lisbon. In just about five hours we had travelled a thousand miles from the scene of our party at Arsenal Stadium and everyone, except Alec Forbes, who was a temporary casualty because he doesn't take kindly to air travel, felt ready to make the most of the ten days' "holiday" that lay ahead.

Chapter Fourteen

"If I were a romantic novelist, this is where I would get my inspiration," said Joe Mercer, his eyes scanning the starry scene from our bedroom window. We were quartered in the luxurious Palace Hotel on the sea-front at Estoril, the millionaire's playground, sixteen miles from the Portuguese capital of Lisbon. Borne on a light breeze, through the open window, came the mellow tones of a dance orchestra from the nearby Casino, clear, but not loud enough to drown the gentle lapping of the waves on the beach below.

"It certainly is beautiful," I agreed, "but personally, I'm going to wallow in the bath and then get some shut-eye."

"I'll bet you won't find water coming out of those taps – it'll be asses' milk," grinned Joe, and such was the luxury that surrounded us it would not have surprised me if he had proved right.

We woke late on Sunday morning, and our first task was to select breakfast courses from a menu as large and as packed with detail as a half-time scoreboard. Fortunately, our waiter had heard of "bacon and eggs". He spoke impeccable English, as did most of the friendly Portuguese, though Ian Macpherson preferred to imagine that they understood his French better.

After breakfast Laurie Scott, the only member of the Arsenal party who had visited Estoril before, as one of the never-to-be-forgotten England team which had shattered Portugal a year previously, offered to show us round.

He took us first to the hotel next door, and showed us the magnificent indoor swimming-pool that the England team had used. Then we took a stroll along the front and watched the millionaires at play on the golden beach.

Joe Mercer and I were particularly interested in the colossal goldfish pond in the ornamental gardens in front of our hotel. It was 150 yards long, and it contained the biggest goldfish I've ever seen; some of them were at least two feet in length!

"I must tell Jimmy Morris about these fish!" declared Joe Mercer. His remarks required and led to an explanation.

Apparently, after playing in a wartime league match in London, Joe Mercer and Jimmy Morris had been invited to stay the night at the London District P.T. School. They spent a convivial evening together, as was the habit of even warrant officers on short leave, and were returning through the grounds of Hendon Police College, where the P.T. School was situated at the time, when Joe lost sight of his companion.

Joe found Jimmy Morris eventually. He was on his knees beside a large goldfish pond, watching the fish swim placidly round and round.

"Did you ever see such beautiful fish?" asked Jimmy. "I'd like to have one of those to keep in my bunk at Aldershot."

Joe looked at Jimmy, and then at the goldfish. "If you want a goldfish, old chap, you shall have one!" he declared, and so saying he rolled up his battledress trousers and waded into the pond up to his knees. After a few minutes he held one bare hand triumphantly aloft, and in it was a plump, slippery goldfish.

Carrying their prize with great care, the bold fishermen retired to the "guest" bedroom. "It'll be all right here," said Joe. He placed the goldfish lovingly in the wash-bowl, put in the plug and turned on the tap. "Now you can swim about all night if you like, my beauty," said Joe, and he and Jimmy hit the hay.

Unfortunately, however, Joe forgot to turn off the tap and the next morning, when he and Jimmy awoke, not only was there no sign of the goldfish, the bedroom was flooded and the water had flowed down the passage and was steadily trickling under the door of the R.S.M.'s bunk opposite.

Joe and Jimmy decided not to waken the R.S.M. and put him in the picture. Instead, with great presence of mind, they hastily mopped the water from their own floor, exchanged their sodden doormat for a dry one from a neighbouring bunk, packed their bags, and stole away to the railway station, leaving the R.S.M. with a mystery to solve that would have taxed the best brains ever housed in Hendon's celebrated Police College.

After hearing Joe's story I took another look at the mammoth goldfish in the Palace Hotel pond and promptly suggested that it was time for us to join the rest of the party at lunch.

On Sunday afternoon, Tom Whittaker, who had been reading Ernest Hemingway's celebrated book *Death in the Afternoon*, suggested that we should follow local custom and attend the bullfight held weekly at Lisbon. "I understand that it's not such a cruel business in this country," Tom told us. "They go through all the motions, but don't actually kill the bull. After a fight the animal is put to pasture."

Although bullfighting was foreign to British ideas of sport, Tom thought it might teach us something new about footwork and agility. Of course, we were all keen to go, and told him so.

Without going into the right and wrongs of "blood sports" I must say I was greatly impressed by what I saw that afternoon.

The bullring turned out to be a circular building of dark red brick surrounded by impressive colonnades. Tiers of seats overlooked the sand arena and the whole scene was reminiscent of pictures I had seen of the Roman Colosseum. Plastering the walls of the ornate entrance hall were glossy, still and action photographs of famous matadors and we soon caught the excited and expectant attitude of the fans who had come to watch these heroes of their national sport. As the time approached for what was called the First Performance, excitement rose to fever pitch, and a veritable "Hampden Roar" greeted the appearance of the picturesquely dressed peones, banderillos, matadors and picadors, the latter mounted on magnificent horses.

The entertainment was to consist of three different forms of combat between men and bulls, each contest being repeated with fresh participants, and each lasting about twenty minutes.

130

The first bull was brought through the giant double doors and into the arena. It was a magnificent specimen, obviously bred for strength and savagery, but for the first event its horns had been padded. The picadors, mounted on horseback, made their entrance carrying barbed darts of varying length. The bull was incited to charge them, and as he did so, the picadors tried to receive this charge on the point of their darts, first irritating the bull with the long barbs and finally administering a sharp thrust with the shortest dart. We particularly admired the horses, one black and one bay, who appeared to know as much about the art of bullfighting as did their riders. An early thrill occurred in the first contest when, with the bull charging blindly at full tilt, the bay horse slipped, and might have been gored but for the skill of the elderly picador on its back. Although handicapped by the dart he carried, with the aid of one arm and his knees he lifted his horse and pulled it away at the vital moment. It was superb horsemanship.

When this bull was exhausted, another was brought in to face the "second team". The new bull was obviously not up to standard: indeed he sat down on his haunches and surveyed the scene with the placid indifference of "Ferdinand". Angry peones took him away, and when they brought him back five minutes later he was in more belligerent mood.

For the next act, seven men wearing "pixie" hats filed into the arena, the tallest man in the front and shortest in the rear. This spectacle was too much for Arsenal! Here were the "Seven Dwarfs" come to life!

These dwarfs were supposed to taunt the bull, evade its reckless charges, and finally reduce it to a state of physical exhaustion. On this occasion, however, the bull was released too soon, even as the little men were preening themselves and turning to wave at members of the audience. As they crossed the arena, the bull made its charge. Just in time, the leader saw it coming and stopped dead in his tracks; his followers, however, unable to see the danger, were still busy making their bows and they folded up on top of the leader like a pack of cards.

Once the dwarfs had recovered their equilibrium, however, they gave a very courageous performance. At one stage the leader stopped three of four yards from the bull and called tauntingly "Bull, bull, bull!" until the incensed animal charged with its head down and its tail up. Undismayed, the leader stood his ground. His fists were clenched on his hips while he allowed the bulls head to pound against his padded cummerbund; then his arms encircled the bull's neck in full lock.

While the leader held the bull's head in chancery, the smallest dwarf sped from his position at the rear of the file and grabbed the bull by its tail! Between them, in this fashion, the daring little men forced the bull to its knees.

Next came the star attraction: the matador, who performed classical passes with the muleta (a red cape) and attempted to plant six darts in the bulls neck before administering the *coup de grace*. Portuguese matadors use a wooden sword for this purpose, and do not actually turn their adversary into corned beef!

The crowd's favourite matador was a tall, slim, handsome figure with slicked-down black hair, and an assurance of manner which reminded us vividly of a famous footballer. In fact the resemblance was so close that we could not refrain from hailing him. "Tommy Lawton!" we exclaimed, laughing away the black looks of our neighbours.

With impertinent passes of the muleta "Tommy" encouraged the bull to attack him, only stepping out of danger at the last conceivable moment, at the same time pricking the neck of the frustrated animal with a short dart. The bull wheeled in fury and attacked again, and this time the matador drew it past him on the wrong side with another impudent side-step.

"If only I could sell a dummy as well as that I'd be the best football in the business," sighed Joe Mercer, with deep appreciation of the matador's skill.

But on one occasion "Tom" left his side-step too late, and he was thrown. The bull towered angrily over his tormentor, his needle-sharp horns poised to gore.

"Good for you, bull!" shouted a member of the Arsenal party. "Now you've got him on the floor *get the clog in*!" It was easy to tell which of the contestants he supported!

Not only did the matador recover, however, eventually he got the bull into such a state of exhaustion that he was able to move up close and actually pat the bull playfully on the top of its head!

Then Tommy asked the President for permission to "make the kill". Permission was granted, whereupon the matador went through the traditional motions with his wooden sword.

We rose to go, thinking this was the end of the entertainment, but it was merely the end of the "first performance" and we found that we were expected to sit through a repeat of the whole business from beginning to end.

Discussion continued amongst us for a long time as to whether bullfighting could be fairly called a "sport", but none of us would have missed it for anything.

We didn't see much of Lisbon on this trip, but the following morning most of us decided to visit the capital on a shopping expedition, dividing naturally into our usual groups. Jimmy Logie teamed up with his pals Bryn Jones, Alec Forbes and Ted Platt, our tame humorist, while Reg Lewis, Laurie Scott and Don Roper had George Swindin, an authority on all foreign cities, as their trusty guide. Tom Whittaker joined Commander Bone, the Arsenal director in charge of our party, and "Willie" Webb, the well-known Scottish international referee who was to officiate at both of our matches in Portugal. As usual, Joe Mercer and I were together; Archie Macaulay went quietly off on his own.

Built on seven hills overlooking the River Tagus, Lisbon is a city of vivid contrasts. On the one hand are the clean, white thoroughfares, elegant buildings and delightful public gardens of the residential quarter; close upon them are the steep cobbled streets and pitiful dwellings of the slum areas. On the outskirts I remember seeing a block of ultra-modern luxury flats cheek-to-cheek with squalid huts made from corrugated iron, strips of wood and hessian sacking, built on an extension of the modern building's earth mound foundation. Thus do dozens of poor Portuguese slum families live side by side with their rich, luxuriously-housed neighbours.

On our shopping expedition I was pleased to be able to buy a splendid leather bag for Joan, which she treasures to this day. Two of our lads claimed an even better bargain, however. Intent on buying flimsy undergarments for their wives they made the intriguing discovery that it was the custom in one shop to "model" such articles for husbands with a poor memory for sizes! The players concerned were loth to reveal the address of this establishment, however, and I cannot deny that they may have been pulling our legs.

One curious local custom I can vouch for concerns the behaviour of Portuguese courting couples. Since even engaged parties are not allowed out without a chaperone it is not unusual to find them consorting in "Romeo and Juliet" fashion, the girl leaning out of a window two stories up, while the boyfriend stands on the pavement below and whispers sweet nothings into her ear. This, despite the competition he gets from the traffic's roar!

I can't think that engaged couples continue their romance in this manner after marriage, because the Portuguese birth-rate is already impressive and continues to rise!

After a sumptuous lunch, Mr. Whittaker took us to see the famous National Stadium where we were to play our first match of the tour against Benfica, the Portuguese champions. The grandeur of this £750,000 super-Wembley quite took our breath away; without doubt there is no stadium in the world to match it.

It is shaped like a bowl, with one-third of the bowl cut away to form a main entrance which gives access to all parts. The long approach, quite fifty feet wide, is fashioned of mosaic paving, and growing flowers, banked on either side, reach well into the stadium itself to provide a brilliant splash of colour.

Inside the stadium, which is built of solid white marble, you get an immediate impression of height looking up at the marble terraces that will seat 65,000 spectators and provide a perfect view for all.

The National Stadium is equipped for all athletic events, and there is even a "horse gallop" which runs round the top of the horseshoe bowl. This is in use whether a football match is being played or not, and I believe it is not unusual for a bored soccer spectator to leave his seat, hire a horse and gallop his blues away on this handy circuit.

But the greatest joy of all is the pitch itself which, incidentally, can be hired by any club for an important game. This rich green carpet of closely knit Cumberland turf is the finest playing-pitch I have ever walked upon, and George Swindin voiced the thoughts of all of us when he remarked, "It seems sacrilege to run about on this turf in ordinary shoes, let alone in football boots."

When we marvelled at the greenness of the turf, which contrasted violently with the parched countryside we had seen all around us, it was explained that a regular water supply had been made available by pipeline from Lisbon, five miles away, at a cost of £2,000 a year, and that the absence of frost, unknown in sunny Portugal, was another factor that helped to keep the turf fresh and healthy.

Almost equally luxurious was the marble-paved dressing-room accommodation. There were dozens of showers, and wooden clogs were provided for a player's use while crossing the wooded duckboards.

I was bitterly disappointed to be left out of the Arsenal team for this match, but Tom did not think it advisable that I should play since my knees were still infected. George Male partnered Laurie Scott at full-back, and I became a spectator, sitting on the trainer's bench with Bert Owen.

The chief wish of the large, enthusiastic crowd which attended this match was to see their favourites slay the British giants, but in this they were to be disappointed because our lads romped home comfortably by 5-0. Although the smallish, brunette-complexioned Benfica players were all good ball-players in midfield, they broke down in front of our goal and became panic stricken in front of their own.

And after Arsenal had scored four goals the Portuguese crowd broke down too! They showed their own team exactly what they thought of them by hurling cushions on to the field. These cushions are similar to those available for hire at our country cricket grounds. They were particularly popular at the Portuguese National Stadium, partly because they made the hard marble seats more comfortable, but also because they made excellent ammunition with which to express public opinion.

At the superb banquet which followed this game, Benfica representatives complimented Arsenal on their "classic exhibition of teamwork" and, contrary to what we had been led to expect, all our opponents turned up and took their defeat in a sporting manner.

The next day we were due to fly to Oporto to play our second match. George Swindin informed us that Oporto was the second largest city, situated three miles from the sea in the Douro Valley, centre of the port wine trade. I think that George must sit up half the night swotting up such facts in case anyone asks him for information! But whatever his secret may be, he is never at a loss and we have learned to rely on him as a guide in a country he hasn't visited before.

The last article I packed in my bag was a full bottle of liquid paraffin necessary for the removal of the paste with which I treated my affected knees, and I placed this carefully in an upright position on top of a new shirt. But when my bag was unloaded from the luggage lorry at the airport it was thrown on to the tarmac top-end first. The bottle broke, soaking all my clothes in liquid paraffin. It wasn't so funny!

136

That night, Bert Owen and I mooched around Oporto market trying to buy another bottle of this stuff that I needed for my infection. For three-quarters of an hour we had no luck. Then Bert spotted the very article on the shelf of a chemist's shop. We went inside and tried to explain what we wanted by addressing the young lady in sign-language.

The girl regarded our gestures with a tolerant amusement. Then, addressing us in perfect English, she asked: "I gather that you want a bottle of liquid paraffin. Do you want a one- or a two-pint bottle?"

We had twenty-five escudos worth and left the shop blushing furiously.

The next day we were taken to the Stadio Lima to see the pitch on which we were to play. This time we had an unpleasant shock. While conditions at Estoril had been more than perfect, these were too rugged by far. The main part of the pitch, which was marked by sawdust lines, was completely bald. Where grass did grow, in each corner, the wiry tufts were at least six inches high. With some difficulty we managed to persuade local officials to have this grass cut to a reasonable length, and men armed with billhooks did have a somewhat half-hearted attempt at the job.

This time the boss decided that the condition of my knees was sufficiently improved to allow me to play. Frankly we did not expect much opposition, for Oporto had just suffered severe defeat at the hands of Benfica, who in turn had been our easy victims.

It was in a very hot, lethargic atmosphere that we strolled on to the field. An early goal by Oporto's international centre-forward and captain failed to upset our easy confidence. Plenty of time to get that back with interest, we thought. But when their centre-forward added two further goals in the next twenty minutes, we began to sit up and take notice!

We faced an irate Tom Whittaker during the interval. He told us that we must pull our socks up, because not only were we endangering the club's reputation but that of the country as well.

So then we got cracking. Bryn Jones scored just after the interval, and Ronnie Rooke added a second, but although we attacked continuously and hit the Portuguese with everything bar our own goalposts, we couldn't notch the equalizer.

Ronnie Rooke's goal was scored from a penalty, awarded to us by referee Willie Webb who may or may not have been aware that local referees risked lynching for less. Not that he would worry. After all, he had often handled Rangers v Celtic battles, and what was the anger of 12,000 Portuguese compared with that of 100,000 Glaswegians?

I think Willie only got away with it this time because the crowd were too surprised to act. Many of them had never seen a penalty before. Their own referees had learned to turn a blind eye towards controversial issues which rated this punishment.

Willie could turn the "blind eye" too when the occasion demanded and, when giving a factory lecture, I often quote his action, or rather lack of action, at one stage of the game as the "acme of diplomacy". Ronnie Rooke and Don Roper were busily engaged in an all-in wrestling match with two defenders, and since it was a case of six of one and half a dozen of the other, Willie chose to turn his back on the distressing scene in order to fuss over a manufactured throw-in dispute with Joe Mercer. A little tact goes a long way on such occasions.

As the game proceeded, a regular "bullfight" developed between the Oporto goalkeeper and our forwards. So successful were the Arsenal "matadors" in goading this particular bull that, suddenly, to my utter amazement I saw the goalkeeper grab the ball, tuck it under one arm and disappear with it down the tunnel to the dressing-room where he sat and sulked, refusing to return either himself or the ball to the field.

A substitute goalkeeper and another ball were provided, and for the last fifteen minutes of the game we bombarded the Oporto goal, and a new custodian, from all angles. But although we traced a dusty pattern all round the framework, we just couldn't get the ball between the posts, and when the final whistle

138

sounded, a tremendous roar from the crowd celebrated our shattering defeat.

Our opponents were good, but no better than an average Third Division side, and we should have wacked them hollow. But we didn't and I blame our apathy and dangerous over-confidence for the failure. Tom warned us that our defeat would be regarded as a National victory, but I admit I had not realized the full significance of his warning. I do now.

At the inevitable banquet which followed, after Joe Mercer had made a speech to congratulate our hosts, the Oporto "trainer" (who corresponds to our manager, their trainer being known as "masseur") rose to say a few well-chosen words. The gist of his speech was that everybody knew that Arsenal were English champions, and since English football was the best in the world, Arsenal must be regarded as *world* champions. But now Oporto had beaten Arsenal and that meant that they had succeeded to the title of "world champions".

A chorus of "Hear, hear's" greeted this simple logic, and the outcome of it was that a public subscription was raised to provide a six-feet-tall trophy, on a marble base, to commemorate Oporto's victory. This monument, unveiled by civil and military dignitaries, was erected in the main square of the city. It stands there to this day, a permanent reminder of Arsenal's most memorable defeat.

We did not let this humiliation spoil the enjoyment of our remaining days in Portugal, however. And as a matter of fact the game not only taught me a valuable lesson, it provided ideal medicine for my dermatitis!

The fierce sun beating down on my knees, which I had treated with liquid paraffin before taking the field, literally fried the affected skin, which came off in strips under a hot shower and cured the unpleasant business for good.

All the same, I wasn't taking any chances so I didn't join the rest of the lads when they went swimming at Estoril. What I did do, however, was roll up my grey flannels and paddle in the sea up to my calves, in good old English "tripper" fashion. And didn't I shock some of the more haughty beach lizards!

On our single visit to the swank Estoril Casino, we risked a few chips of low denomination on the "wheel". Reacting to a flash of inspiration, while the wheel was spinning, Ronnie Rooke changed his bet from one to another. He obviously hadn't heard that it is unwise to change horses in midstream − luckily, for the alternative he chose turned out to be the winning number! − and although his action was against the rules, the croupier paid up with a smile.

We had promised ourselves a visit to the attractive Egyptian leather and sandalwood shop opposite the Palace Hotel, and when we did go, several of us picked out attractive gifts we wished to purchase. But the shopkeeper would not allow us to have them. "No, messieurs, a thousand regrets," he apologized. "All these articles − they are reserved for the Ginger One. He is to buy them for his mansion in Scotland."

The Ginger One was, of course, Archie Macaulay, who possessed the flair characteristic of his race for finding a good bargain. He had certainly been having the shopkeeper on a piece of string!

All too soon it was time for us to return to England, but there was a pleasure in store for me, since my wife and I had managed to obtain a home of our own at last − a flat near Farnborough Experimental Air Station.

That summer I managed to see quite a few events in the Olympic Games at Wembley, and I enjoyed a great personal thrill in playing for an Army hockey team against the superb Olympic Hockey team from Pakistan. This match was played at Sandhurst, where I was still engaged as soccer coach.

An incident occurred only the other day which enables me to add an "amazing but true" tailpiece to the Portuguese story. I was busy in my sports shop opposite Harringay Arena one Saturday morning, when a chap came in to buy a pair of my special football boots. He appeared to be in a terrific hurry and I heard him mumble something about wanting to use the boots in Oporto that very weekend.

I pricked up my ears, because Oporto was still a sore point with me, and I thought he was trying to be funny! But it was true: he was a native of Oporto, and was determined not to miss the London-Portugal plane leaving that afternoon.

"Why the hurry?" I asked.

"You should know!" he said. "Monday is the day of our great fiesta – the annual celebration of Arsenal's defeat in 1948!"

Won't we ever live that down?

Chapter Fifteen

Spectacular leaps and daring dives are the tricks of the acrobatic goalkeeper, Soccer's Number One Showman. He's grand to watch, but when you're playing in front of him – that's a different matter! It's a wonder to me that Continental full-backs do not all develop ulcers.

No, if a chap's a really good team goalkeeper, then you hardly realize that he's there. By correct positioning he is always on the spot to make his job look easy. By safe handling he makes strong shots look weak; and such is his anticipation that he rarely needs to resort to the dramatic last-second leap.

Such a goalkeeper is my Arsenal colleague, George Swindin.

There's nothing easy about keeping goal, as I have discovered for myself on a few occasions when I've gone between the posts. You need a quick-thinking brain and a quick-seeing eye: you must be really fit and full of confidence, and always keep cool under pressure. It is no good just being destructive, you must think constructively, too, and maintain a close understanding with your fellow defenders.

I've had the advantage of playing in front of some outstanding goalkeepers in my time, among them George Tweedy, George Marks, Cyril Sidlow and Billy Shortt, but if you were to ask me to choose the goalkeeper I would most like to have playing behind me, then I should choose George Swindin. Not only does he possess all the qualities I have named, but he and I have learned to think as one on the field of play, and very rarely does a misunderstanding occur between us in an emergency.

George, a Yorkshireman, joined Arsenal from Bradford City in April 1936, and gave the club continuous service of a high standard for ten seasons, earning a Cup-winners' medal and two League Championship medals in that time, before a fractured wrist caused him to lose his first team place, temporarily, to Jack Kelsey.

George has never gained an international cap, and although he may shrug this bad luck away with typical Yorkshire independence, I know he feels the disappointment deeply. And no wonder, for surely no better player ever went uncapped.

He was particularly unlucky, because he represented the Football League on several occasions, and played in many trials: he was twelfth man for England's junior team as a schoolboy, and also twelfth man for the seniors, but he never actually took the field in an international.

I think George has had a raw deal from the selectors. Of course, luck plays a big part in the life of any goalkeeper. Perhaps that is why they're so superstitious.

Most players have got pet fads and fancies, and I'll readily admit that I'm no exception. When I'm not leading the team out on to the field, I like to be last man out of the dressing-room. There's no reason for it – just put it down to silly superstition.

But goalkeepers are the giddy limit! They must touch the left post before the right, approach the goal area without stepping on any lines, or handle the ball once with bare hands before putting on their gloves.

They have their lucky caps, their lucky gloves – like Jack Fairbrother's white policeman's gloves – and their lucky jersey.

Like the rest, George Swindin was provided with a new jersey for the 1952 Cup Final, but he would not wear it until it had been laundered. That wasn't just a superstition, however, Arsenal had lost a previous final, in 1925, when Dan Lewis covered a Cardiff shot comfortably, only to have the ball slide on the sheen of his new, unlaundered, sweater. It slipped out of his arms and over the line for the goal that decided the result.

George was something of a lucky prophet too. In 1949-50, he stated right from the start that Arsenal would be drawn at home four times and then win the Cup. He was right! And in the later stages he even named our opponents for the Final correctly – Liverpool!

In our first Saturday home match of the 1948-49 season Arsenal, reigning League champions entertained Manchester United, the Cup-holders, at Highbury. The first half saw a grim, unrelenting struggle, with no goals given away by either side. Then, after the interval, we faced the sun, so George Swindin donned the white, wide-peaked skiing cap that he had brought home from a coaching trip to Norway. Almost immediately, Delaney put the ball across our goal and Mitten headed it in to score what proved to be the match-winner.

George took off his new white cap and threw it into the back of the net in disgust. He never wore it again.

In 1948, George Swindin kept goal just as brilliantly as he had done throughout the previous season when he played in every league match. Early in December, however, he was injured, giving a chance at last to the ever-faithful Ted Platt who had been kept out of the first team by George's brilliance ever since 1939, when Ted joined the Gunners from Colchester.

Now see how the luck works out. We were playing at Charlton, and the first ball that was hit in the direction of our goal, a shot from the wing by Chris Duffy, suddenly dipped in flight and deceived Ted, who thought he had it well covered. Two minutes later, Phipps took a free-kick from forty-five yards that also swerved in flight to beat the unlucky Platt. And was Ted's face red when Charlton added a third goal through O'Linn in the fifteenth minute of the game!

"Never mind, Ted," I said sympathetically, "not even George could have saved those shots." But Ted was terribly upset; and for once he had no funny remarks to make.

It certainly was a cruel debut for the faithful reserve who had waited nearly ten years for this chance. But later in the season, Ted had chances to redeem himself, and so he did, particularly in the game at Wolverhampton, in February, when he made a heroic save from McLean's rasping shot in the closing seconds and helped us to gain our first away points for nearly three months.

In 1948-49 we failed to keep a grip on the championship we had won the previous season. Far from repeating our feat of playing the first seventeen matches without a loss, we made an indifferent start; but we hit our best form in autumn and played thirteen games for only one defeat. We tailed off again at Christmas and eventually finished fifth, nine points behind Portsmouth, the worthy champions. And although we reached the fourth round of the Cup, after beating the Spurs at Highbury, we went out in the next round at Derby.

Injuries played a large part in our less-distinguished record – particularly the cartilage injury suffered by Laurie Scott in the international match against Wales in November, which put my partner out of action for most of the season.

Poor Laurie! While coaching Storm F.C. in Norway during the summer he lost his appendix. While he was away, too, burglars broke into his house at Southgate and stole, among other things, all his medals and international caps, the priceless possessions of any footballer skilled enough to have won them. To cap everything, the season was not four months old before, through serious injury, Laurie lost his cartilage, and his place in the England and Arsenal teams. I'm glad to say that these set-backs were only temporary, however, for Scottie returned to play for us in the Cup Final, and for the England team too.

Like George Swindin, Laurie was a Yorkshireman who came to Arsenal from Bradford City. A serious, studious type of chap, he nevertheless had a strong sense of humour. He was always trying to improve his game, even when at his peak – as he was in 1948. Speed was his greatest asset; particularly speed off the mark. He was superb on the turn, always calm under pressure, and able to use pretty well every ball to advantage. Obviously he could have filled the bill equally well as a wing half, or even as a winger when he started his playing career.

I missed Laurie as much as the club did during the 1948-49 season, for we had built up a wonderful understanding on the field, and I owed a great deal to his experience and helpful guidance.

Fortunately, however, in Lionel Smith, Arsenal had yet another splendid Yorkshire defender ready to fill the gap. Lionel was to follow in the footsteps of Eddie Hapgood, George Male, Laurie Scott and myself and gain international honours.

Our long, gangling, "Gary Cooper of the football field" had always been a centre-half (he stood-in for Leslie Compton on the Portugal tour), but such was Lionel's all-round football ability that he quickly settled down to the left-back position, while I moved across to take over Laurie Scott's usual berth.

Another reason why Lionel was able to fit into the league team so readily is that Arsenal's basic tactics are the same throughout the club and our "new chum" was obviously familiar with our defensive system. He had been drilled in it by Jack Crayston, the Combination team boss.

A quiet chap, whose off-the-field hobbies are carpentry, gardening and cricket, Lionel rarely gets flustered, and he and I soon got used to each other.

Let me pick out the highlights of the season. The first game that stands out in my memory, for personal reasons, was played against the Wolves at Highbury at the end of September.

Inspired by Billy Wright, who I was to oppose as rival skipper in the England v Wales international later in the year, the Wolves set a cracking pace from the first whistle. Joe Mercer, Les Compton and I had our work cut out to deal with Hancocks and Dunn on the left, and with wing-halves Forbes and Wright throwing themselves into the fray as well we had virtually a seven-man attack with which to deal.

Nevertheless, it was Arsenal who scored first after twelve minutes, through Denis Compton, who was playing his last home game for Arsenal before leaving for South Africa with the M.C.C.

team. Denis bobbed up in the centre-forward position at the right moment to drive the ball well out of Williams's reach.

Wolves retaliated, trying all they knew to pierce our defence by short passing and frequent interchanging of position. Then, during one hectic goalmouth scramble, I received a nasty cut in the forehead and had to leave the field for treatment. For Arsenal to face that inspired Wolves' attack successfully with only ten men was asking a great deal, and it was no surprise when, just before half-time, Smyth headed in an equalizer for the visitors. But Alex Forbes stood in brilliantly for me at right-back, and Jimmy Logie performed the combined jobs of right-half and inside-right to such good effect that he nearly made a second goal for Arsenal.

Meantime, Dr. Pepper, the Arsenal medical officer, was examining my cut in the treatment room. It was two inches long, bone deep in line with my nose – just like an orange with the skin split. The doctor swabbed, cleaned the cut, and put in three stitches.

I pleaded impatiently, "I've got to get back on the field."

The job was completed in time for me to resume my place after the interval with a bandage round my head.

"His skin's so tough we had to use the biggest needle in the place to pierce it!" Billy Milne told the rest of the lads at half time.

In the second half we staged a remarkable recovery. Although scores were level, Wolves were definitely on top throughout the first half, but now, inspired by Joe Mercer and Archie Macaulay, our forwards took command, and Reg Lewis was able to score two brilliant winning goals.

As for me, I think I must arrange to get hit on the head more often, because I had one of my best-ever league games despite the dangerous raiding of Jimmy Mullen.

On October 6th, 1948, Arsenal gained a great 4-3 victory over Manchester United to win the F.A. Charity Shield, after one of the finest games I've ever played in.

As early as 1908 it had been decided that the two leading F.A. clubs should play an annual match for a trophy and gold medals, so that charity should benefit by receiving the gross receipts. Manchester United were actually the first-ever winners of the trophy. Since 1930, the teams selected to contest this annual fixture have been the League Champions and the Cup – holders. Except for 1932 and 1937, Arsenal had been concerned in every one of these games, and they had won the shield five times. The brilliant match against United on this occasion marked Arsenal's sixth victory. I shall always treasure my gold medal.

My wife, Joan, attends all Arsenal's home games, but like thousands of others this time, she missed the biggest thrill. So that United could catch an early train, the kick-off was brought forward five minutes. Before Joan could find her seat Arsenal were three up! Reg Lewis scored twice, and Bryn Jones once in an inspired four-minute burst. What my wife did see, in the fifth minute, was a terrific shot from Ronnie Rooke which might easily have meant number four, had the ball not rebounded from the cross-bar with Crompton well beaten.

Then skipper John Carey rallied his team to such purpose that, despite Arsenal's sensational opening burst, United fought back and actually threatened to make a draw of it until Ronnie Rooke clinched matters by scoring another good one for us. It was top-notch soccer from beginning to end.

Ten days later, after gaining a hard-won point at Deepdale, the Arsenal team flew to Dublin to play Bohemians, the famous Irish amateur team. We arrived in time for dinner at our posh hotel in O'Connell Street, in the heart of Dublin, and thanks to the tireless efforts of the management committee, and of the honorary secretary, Mr. Vincent Rochford, we received a wonderful welcome, and the best of everything in this fair city.

At the beginning of the season the Arsenal players had combined in a business enterprise and had produced a really lavish Championship Souvenir book which we sold at 2s 6d a copy. Although having the blessing of the Club, this was financed

148

entirely by the players and it wasn't going too well so, at Joe Mercer's suggestion, we took about 2,000 copies with us to Dublin and went on the terraces of the famous Dalymount Park ground before the Bohemians' match to peddle them to the crowd. I think you'll agree that this was a very "Bohemian" idea indeed, and it probably wouldn't have worked anywhere but in Eire, where the spectators were very friendly indeed and didn't seem to think our little idea at all unusual.

A fine sporting match followed, and although we won comfortably by six goals, the Bohemians, who have won every honour in their country at one time or another, lived up to their famous Three Golden Rules: Never Say Die; Keep the Ball on the Floor and The Best Defence is Attack.

After the game we had a slap-up dinner followed by a "hooley", at which George Swindin, Archie Macaulay and secretary Mr. Bob Wall made contributions to the musical entertainment.

In November we played our annual match in Paris against the celebrated Racing Club. Through a quick-fire goal in the closing minutes, Racing gained a well-merited draw in an exciting match and thus maintained their proud boast that Arsenal had not beaten them since the war.

After a good autumn run in the League we were beaten at home by newly-promoted Newcastle United, and then provided Portsmouth with the opportunity of celebrating their Golden Jubilee in no uncertain manner – conceding as many as four goals for the first time for two seasons.

So keen were Pompey to show a distinguished audience what they could do on this auspicious occasion, that it would have taken an Arsenal team playing at its best to have held them while, in fact, the Gunners all seemed to be playing with two left feet.

Before the game both teams were presented to the Portsmouth President, Field-Marshal Viscount Montgomery of Alamein. When "Monty" reached me in the line, Joe Mercer said,

"This is Walley Barnes, another former A.P.T.C. instructor and the present Sandhurst football coach."

"Monty" gave me a soldierly handshake while I stood stiffly at attention. "You might have been playing in blue instead of in a red and white shirt today, young man," he said.

And of course the great soldier was right! Obviously there was little he didn't know about the world of football.

Early in the new year we were all broken-hearted to hear of the death of our popular Chairman, Major Sir Samuel Hill-Wood, Bt., D.L., J.P., who we were used to welcoming in our dressing-room after a game – whether we had won, lost or drawn. He was always ready with a friendly smile and a kind word for the players, and his death was a sad loss not only to the Arsenal but to the game as a whole.

Arsenal were fortunate enough to have Sir Bracewell Smith, Bt., K.C.V.O., Ll.D., B.Sc., to take Sir Samuel's place as Chairman, and so the efficient administration of the club's affairs was in no way interrupted. Sir Bracewell Smith was elected Lord Mayor of London in 1946, and I shall never forget that he and the Lady Mayoress were kind enough to invite the whole Arsenal playing staff to a banquet at the Mansion House after we'd played our thirteenth match without defeat, an honour most of us could not have foreseen in our wildest dreams.

What of the Cup? In the third round we were drawn at home to the Spurs, and it was the first F.A. Cup meeting between these two great London clubs although they had been together in the competition for fifty-four years. The Press built this match up as the "Tie of the Century", and made much of the great rivalry and so called enmity between the teams. So much publicity was it given that on the day of the match thousands of spectators, fearing a dangerously large attendance, stayed away, and the outcome was a meagre crowd some 40,000 strong and the biggest financial flop in Cup history!

Even a bigger anticlimax, perhaps, was our easy victory by 3-0.

In the next round we were knocked out of the Cup by what I am sure Billy Steel, the scorer, would admit was a "fluke" goal. The expensive Scottish inside-forward received the ball from a throw-in near the penalty box and, as Archie Macaulay went to tackle him, Billy hit the ball with his left foot quicker than he intended, and not where he intended, with the result that it dropped over George Swindin's head, just under the bar in the left-hand top corner of the net.

At the beginning of this chapter I wrote about goalkeepers, and I want to close by referring to the greatest goalkeeper I ever played against – Frank Swift, who made his farewell appearance for Manchester City against Arsenal on April 27th, 1949.

I'll never forget the roar of cheering, the flashing of cameras, the brass band playing and the crowd singing "For He's a Jolly Good Fellow", as Frank led the City team out for his last game before the home crowd. It was a unique occasion, and undoubtedly Frank deserved every cheer he got.

It was certainly not his fault that Arsenal won this game by 3-0. His goalkeeping was as brilliant as it always had been and, in a way, we felt a bit ashamed at taking the points, well though the Arsenal team played. Two of our goals came from the more-than-useful head of Duggie Lishman, the strong, forceful opportunist, who had joined us from Walsall at the beginning of the season.

After the game Frank's City team-mates chaired him off the field, while Arsenal players made a tunnel of honour for him to pass through. Frank was obviously very touched as the crowd sand "Auld Lang Syne" and thousands of youngsters ran on to the pitch to pay homage to their idol.

I made a point of asking Swifty to sign Joan's autograph book, which she kept at the time, and I was very proud to recall that I had played both with and against this giant among goalkeepers.

Frank was a giant in more senses than one. Half an inch over six-feet tall, he had an exceptionally long reach and huge hands. For all his size he was as agile as a cat, and his cool judgement and accurate kicking and throwing were unrivalled in the game.

In 1933, when only nineteen years of age, Frank played his first league game to become the youngest goalkeeper in first-class football at that time, and the following season he won a Cup-winners' medal at Wembley, fainting on the field as soon as the final whistle sounded, such was the ordeal he had faced.

First gaining international recognition against Scotland in 1941, he went on to play thirty-three times for England. He was the only goalkeeper ever to captain an England side – against Italy in 1948.

Not only was he a great goalkeeper and a great personality, but hundreds of players, like myself, must have benefited by his advice.

"There goes a great player and a great gentleman," said Joe Mercer as we watched Frank Swift leave the field.

And I thought, "There's not much wrong with a profession that gives one the chance to win glory like this."

Tommy Jones and the author make a sandwich of Tom Finney in the Wales v England international at Villa Park on 10th November, 1948. This was the match in which Walley Barnes became established as captain of Wales. Also seen in the picture are Burgess, Milburn and Shackleton.

The author makes a desperate leap, but fails to stop Morris from scoring a fine goal for Manchester United in a league match at Highbury in 1948-49.

Chapter Sixteen

An unfamiliar Scottish international team, containing seven new caps, faced Wales at Ninian Park on October 23rd, 1948. From the first whistle they made obvious determination to gain revenge for the defeat we had administered at Hampden in 1947.

How well they succeeded! It's only fair to confess that we were outplayed in this match, and Scotland's 3-1 victory started a great revival in their fortune, for they went on to beat both Ireland and England and to win the 1948-49 international championship.

The new caps were Hugh Howie, a wartime discovery who had been converted to right-back from centre-half, and his partner Davie Shaw, brother of Rangers' "Tiger" Shaw, a small but stocky ex-miner; Bobby Evans, who replaced Archie Macaulay, and Willie Redpath, a clever ball-player who had partnered Tom Finney for Army teams in the Middle East during the war; centre-forward Lawrie Reilly, the very fast, two-footed, now famous Scottish leader, who was then only nineteen years old; tricky inside-right, Jimmy Mason, and Johnny Kelly, the latter partnering his former Morton colleague, Billy Steel.

Ronnie Burgess resumed the captaincy of our side which I had taken over temporarily in his absence. Injury kept Tommy Jones out, and his place at centre-half was taken by young Freddie Stansfield, of Cardiff (later player-manager of Newport County), while Ernie Jones, a former Swansea amateur who had been showing great speed and goal-scoring ability for the Spurs' left-wing, replaced George Edwards.

It was a mistake by Cyril Sidlow that gave Scotland their first goal after seventeen minutes play. Howie took a free-kick from the touchline and, with half an eye for Lawrie Reilly, Cyril misjudged the flight of the ball. Although he half caught the ball he dropped it again and actually pushed it over the line. "That was Sidlow – own goal!" admitted the unhappy Cyril as he booted the ball up-field for the restart. "Sorry, lads." The goal was credited to Howie.

I've already mentioned that Cyril is one of the best goalkeepers I've had the pleasure of playing with, but he didn't always have the best of luck, and occasionally he made such costly mistakes as the one I have just described.

Seven minutes later, however, Bryn Jones equalized with a terrific volley shot on the run that deserved, and received, the biggest ovation of the afternoon.

Alas, we were not on level terms for long. Within two minutes, Willie Waddell nodded the ball into the net from Kelly's free-kick to put Scotland ahead.

Waddell was credited with a third goal in the thirty-ninth minute, although I feel justified in claiming that this shot, knocked down by Sidlow, actually failed to cross the line. Indeed, not one, but dozens of photographs taken of the incident, proved to my satisfaction, at least, that the ball was eighteen inches from the line when Sidlow recovered it.

Caught by the high speed of the play, the referee, Mr. D. Maxwell (Belfast), was on the half-way line at the time. The linesman flagged to attract his attention, but the ref decided at once that it was a goal. An international pitch is not the place to argue with the ref's decision so we left it at that. But the decision was a minor tragedy and enough to take the fight out of us, temporarily, when we were already up against it.

In this game I was very impressed with the play of Bobby Evans, who kept thumping the ball through to Jimmy Mason, and also with the way little Jimmy, a will-o'-the-wisp with a style similar to that of Jimmy Logie, used it. Johnny Kelly, too, was a real danger on the left-wing.

But I didn't have much time to stand about in admiration of the Scottish stars – in fact, I probably had the toughest opponent of all to mark in Willie Waddell.

I've already told you of my experiences in playing against Stanley Mathews and Tom Finney. Well, at his best, Willie

Waddell was a combination of both, and of the fast, strong and direct Billy Liddell as well – a fairly useful combination, you'll agree!

Strong, forceful and dangerous whenever he got near the ball, Willie was extremely tricky for a well-built player, and he was always ready to cut inside and have a powerful shot at goal.

In order to mark him, I could only apply the basic principle of trying to be with him when he got the ball, and then bar his progress without tackling for as long as possible, while my colleagues got back into position.

On this occasion I may have allowed Willie that little extra bit of room a winger covets, because I was also concerned with covering the centre-half position, where Freddie Stansfield, new to international football, had a full-time job trying to hold Lawrie Reilly in check. Ronnie Burgess, too, had an off-day and in the long-run, the combination of Evans, Mason and Waddell proved a bit too much for us.

But don't let me fail to give Scotland credit for a fine performance in this game. Their so-called "experimental" team turned up trumps in every way.

In or next international, against England at Villa Park on November 10th, 1948, I again took over the captaincy of the Welsh team.

Mr. Herbert Powell told me the Welsh F.A. had decided that Ronnie Burgess should be relieved of the burden of captaincy so that he could concentrate all his energies on watching the Mortensen and Matthews wing. For some reason, Ronnie's own form suffered when he had the added responsibility of leading the international side.

And presumably because I had not had too good a game against Stan Matthews on our last international encounter, I was chosen to play at *right*-back and was given the responsibility for marking Tom Finney instead. Talk about "out of the frying-pan and into the fire!"

No need to emphasize the great honour that the captaincy meant to me. I was determined to grab the chance with both hands: in fact, I was to have a good game and remain Welsh skipper from that match onwards.

On the Wednesday before the match, in company with the Arsenal team, I took part in a golf match at the South Herts Club. The Arsenal golfers were led, on this occasion, by the famous British Ryder Cup golfer, Dai Rees, and when Dai was introduced to us he said:

"It will be my pleasure to play with the Welsh football captain."

"He means *you*, Walley," grinned Joe Mercer, giving me a friendly nudge.

So that's the way it was, and such was the prowess of my famous Welsh partner, that our best score for 18 holes was 62, and Dai inspired me so much that we actually picked up on 4 holes.

Playing golf with Dai was a great education. He's bright and breezy, and very unserious, even about golf.

He's also a great soccer fan. The day before Wales met England, at Wembley for the first time, in 1952, Dai met Walter Winterbottom, the English team manager, on the links.

"I do hope all your players are fit and well," he asked solicitously.

Mr. Winterbottom was surprised. "Why, yes, thank you, Dai. Not a complaint among 'em."

"That's good," nodded the Welshman, well satisfied. "I just don't want any alibis afterwards, that's all!"

I must spoil that story with a reluctant reminder that it was Wales who had to look for the alibis afterwards. In 1952 England gave us a hiding.

This is how the team lined-up at Villa Park on November 10th, 1948:

ENGLAND: Swift (Manchester City); Scott (Arsenal); Aston (Manchester United); Ward (Derby County); Franklin (Stoke City); Wright (Wolves) capt.; Matthews (Blackpool); Mortensen (Blackpool); Milburn (Newcastle United); Shackleton (Sunderland) and Finney (Preston North End).

WALES: Hughes (Blackburn Rovers); Barnes (Arsenal) capt.; Sherwood (Cardiff City); Paul (Swansea Town); T. Jones (Everton); Burgess (Spurs); E. Jones (Spurs); A. Powell (Everton); Ford (Aston Villa); Rees (Cardiff City) and Clarke (Manchester City).

Billy Wright, who had become English skipper at the age of twenty-four, was the chap I shook hands with at the centre-circle. Billy had captained every team he had ever played for, whereas Wales was the first team I had ever led!

England had begun the 1948-49 tournament with a 6-2 win at Belfast, and you've only got to glance at their team to see what a task we were up against. As it turned out, however, we gave them a tremendous battle, and they were somewhat lucky to win by a single goal.

This was the match in which my pal Laurie Scott suffered his unfortunate injury, and it came about in a similar way to my own experience in the 1952 Cup Final.

In the twenty-third minute Laurie went to tackle Roy Clarke, the Manchester City winger, who was playing in his first international for Wales, and caught the studs of his right boot in the holding turf, putting his weight on the ligaments of his right knee which gave under the strain.

After Laurie had been carried off the field, Tim Ward moved to right-back and Stan Mortensen to right-half. Prior to this incident we had been having the better of the play, Trevor Ford having two unfortunate lapses when more than favourably placed with the ball in front of goal; but now, strangely enough, the England team started to press. Mortensen actually got the ball into our net, but was rightly ruled off-side.

The game developed into a grim, tight struggle, with our opponents playing doubly hard to make up for the absence of their right-back. Stan Mortensen and Tim Ward, in particular, played a noble part in defence, making numerous last-second interventions to prevent us from scoring. Ward, I think, was most unfortunate not to retain his place for England's next international.

The only goal came in the first half, when Jackie Milburn, stopped by Tom Jones, quickly flicked the ball to Tom Finney, and Tom scored with a left-foot shot.

While I was naturally disappointed by the result, the fighting spirit of the England team undoubtedly deserved the reward of victory.

"Never mind, Walley," said Bill Dodman sympathetically, as we chatted outside the dressing-room after the game, "we've got the makings of a good side, and I'm sure you'll have the chance of leading them to victory in the next game against Ireland."

I must explain at this point that the gentleman I refer to somewhat presumptuously as "Bill", is actually Alderman Dodman of Wrexham, who has been mayor of the town several times, and has done so much for Welsh sport. We players had come to regard him as our lucky talisman, as well as our guide, philosopher and friend, and he attends all our international matches, home or away.

It wasn't until just before the Villa Park international, chin-wagging with Alderman Dodman at our Leamington Spa hotel, that I realized he was the Bill Dodman who had trained and had so much to do with the success of the famous Welsh boxer Johnny Basham. On hearing this, I remarked on the fact that my father had boxed exhibitions with Basham, and Alderman said immediately that he remembered "Sergeant Teddy Barnes" well, and had thought him "a very useful customer in the ring".

160

From this moment the Alderman and I struck up what I would call, and hope will remain, a firm friendship. What's more, I'm pleased to record that he was right about our next international at Belfast on March 9th, 1949. I did lead the Welsh team to a comfortable 2-0 victory.

It was by no means a brilliant game, and it was played throughout in snow and bitter wind, but I shall always remember it for two other reasons. First for the magnificent play of Trevor Ford, who made the first goal for Billy Lucas and scored the second himself, and secondly for an incident that occurred that has since given me much food for thought.

Should a player own up to the referee that he handled the ball with the intention of stopping a goal from being scored? That was the problem provoked by an incident in this game, and I was the player concerned.

It happened like this.

After Lucas scored our opening goal in the twenty-fifth minute, the Irish team put on the pressure and penned us in our own half for five or six minutes, which represents a long time in a game of football. They forced numerous corners, and one of them, taken by O'Driscoll on the left, was a high cross aimed at the far post and practically on to the head of Davie Walsh, the Irish centre-forward. I went up to head clear, realized that I couldn't get to the ball, and in last, despairing effort to get an extra inch of height, threw up my right arm to divert the ball from Walsh's head.

In all fairness, I realized that but for my intervention Walsh, who was very accurate with his head, would have scored. The referee, Mr. Leafe (of England), had been on my blind side, and could not have seen what happened, and as we all know, referees do not give decisions on impressions, but only on something they, or the linesman, have actually seen.

In this case neither linesman gave him a signal, so Mr. Leafe waved play on.

161

Immediately there was an appeal from the Irish forwards. What did I do? Let me be honest. I held my breath and hoped that I'd got away with it.

Why didn't a linesman raise a flag? The one in our half had been standing on the goal-line on the side from which the corner was taken, while the other was on the half-way line, to cope with a possible breakaway from the corner. Thus both were out of the picture.

"You know darn well you handled the ball, Walley," grumbled Davie Walsh, reasonably enough, as the play continued.

"Yes," I admitted, "but what do you expect me to do?"

Davie shrugged his shoulders and said sportingly, "I suppose I'd do the same as you're doing – keep quiet about it."

But did I do the right thing? My argument is, that while it may not have been very sporting to keep quiet, football is a TEAM game, and one makes split-second decision like this not on one's own behalf, but with the team's interest at heart.

And suppose I had owned up? It is extremely doubtful if the referee would have altered his decision once it had been made.

Chapter Seventeen

As the 1948-49 season drew to a close, with Arsenal out of the Cup but respectfully placed in fifth position in the league table, thoughts at Highbury began to turn towards South America.

All season we had been hearing rumours of a "Grand Tour of Brazil". Now rumours began to blossom into facts. "Are we still going?" and "Is the tour still on?" became leading questions in our everyday conversation, until the knot was finally tied that was to take us 6,000 miles across the world to the glamorous city of Rio de Janeiro.

This was the first of two tours Arsenal have made to South America. A further visit was made in 1951. I was fortunate enough to be a member of both parties, and to play in each of the thirteen games against Brazilian clubs, only three of which the Gunners managed to win. Statistics, however, cannot tell the full story, so I'll do my best to fill in the gaps.

Some of our adventures and experiences were so fantastic that now, as I write, were it not for the supporting evidence of colleagues who shared them, I would find it difficult to believe they really did happen.

"They happened all right!" Tom Vallance (Stan Matthews's brother-in-law) is saying over my shoulder as I write these notes. "In fact the experiences started a little too early in the trip for my liking, remember..."

All right, Tom, I'm coming to that!

No doubt because of the Turin air disaster, in which the whole of Italy's international football team were tragically killed, Arsenal officials and players divided into two parties for "Operation Rio", a precaution now taken by most clubs. The parties for our 1949 tour were made up as follows:

Party No.1: Messer. Whittaker, Milne, Daniel, Lewis, Lishman, McPherson, Rooke, Roper, L. Smith, Scott, Swindin and Vallance.

Party No.2: Commander Bone, Messrs. Wall, Fields, Forbes, Grimshaw, Goring, Jones, Logie, Macaulay, Platt, Wade and myself.

Our party went to see Mr. Whittaker and Co. fly away from London Airport on the journey we ourselves would start the following day.

"I hope you don't have too bad a trip," I said to Laurie Scott. Despite his R.A.F. service, I knew that Laurie was subject to airsickness.

Laurie told me that he'd taken a liberal quantity of special tablets. "They should see me through all right," he said.

"You'll need plenty of tablets to cope with this trip," Ronnie Rooke said grimly. He turned to the others. "These York aircraft are death-traps," he told them. "I hope you chaps know what to do when the engines pack up!"

But the rest of the lads were not to be scared so easily. They were only too well aware of Ronnie's leg-pulling ways.

No sooner was the plane airborne, however, than one of the York's engines did pack up! No one in the plane was more surprised than Ronnie Rooke, the man who cried "Wolf" once too often. Or very nearly. Actually, after circling Sandown racecourse, the pilot returned to the airport for a check-up, much to the relief of his passengers. We were still in the waiting room.

"We didn't even see the first race at Sandown, let alone Rio," said Ray Daniel.

"Were you sick?" I asked Laurie.

"No," he said seriously, "it's the first flight I've made without being airsick. Those pills are pretty good."

164

There was a great deal more backchat before it was announced that the plane's engines were now OK, and this time the party got away safely.

The next day we took off without incident, although I must admit that I wasn't altogether happy in York aircraft – I found it both noisy and uncomfortable.

First stop Lisbon! – where old friends and officials of the Benfica Club met us, entertained us to lunch, and wished us a successful trip. Then on to Dakar, where we landed at midnight. Here we were "fumigated" by spray-guns before being allowed to leave the place for a meal.

At this stage, according to normal practice, a new air-crew took over all the jobs – except one. When our pretty air hostess heard that her relief was ill, she cheerfully agreed to carry on for the rest of the journey, although it meant being on continuous duty, alone, for thirty-two hours.

"I always thought that air hostesses had a soft job," admitted Bryn Jones. Me too! But it's not all glamour, as I can now testify for, remembering my training as a married man, I helped our air-hostess do the washing-up for the remainder of the flight.

Incidentally, the young lady we are discussing was selected as air hostess to the Queen, then Princess Elizabeth, and the Duke of Edinburgh, when they flew to South Africa in 1952.

Our plane flew on through the starry night and then, in the early hours of the morning we saw barren, red soil stretching below us and soon our wheels touched down at Natal Airport. We were in Brazil, but still 1,500 miles from our ultimate destination. Once again they wheeled in a chemical tank up to the plane and "fumigated" us with a spray-gun as we sat there, just in case we had picked up any disease since leaving Dakar. We were also given a quick once-over by Customs officials to make sure that we were not engaged in any smuggling activities.

On the last stage of our flight, down the Brazilian coast, we passed over dense forests and mountain ranges. There were no

165

lakes, as far as I could see, and the reddish-coloured soil predominated. It was May, and therefore winter on this continent, yet we began to feel quite warm in the aircraft and most of us took off coat and tie. Bob Wall spotted the hull of the *Magdelina*, the British ship that had recently broken up in a storm on her maiden voyage, and we observed this tragic sight in sober silence.

Then we saw Rio – a natural and architectural wonderland, with mountains, sea and skyscrapers mingling to form a breathtaking panorama in the morning sunlight. Our excitement mounted as each of us visualized the "Hollywood-style" romances that awaited us at this magic location.

We were soon to discover, however, that Rio's glamour is confined to technicolour films, and to the first glimpse one gets from the air. In other respects, dear old Portsmouth and Southsea are equally glamorous, and a great deal more healthy in my opinion!

Dr. Carlos Martins da Rocha (who, at his own suggestion, we learned to call "Uncle Charlie"), the President of the Botafogo Club, and his friend, the late Dr. Amando Barcellos, were at the airport to meet us. These gentlemen, the sponsors of Arsenal's tour, were both millionaires, and they were wonderfully helpful and hospitable throughout the trip.

Dr. Barcellos spoke quite good English and interpreted for his colleague. "Uncle Charlie" was every bit as big, if not bigger than Leslie Compton, and had been an outstanding athlete in his day.

These gentlemen placed every facility at our command, and we learned to regard Botafogo Stadium as a second Highbury, as far as training was concerned. Later, because of his firm friendship with "Uncle Charlie", Mr. Whittaker was able to arrange similar training facilities for the England World Cup team when they found themselves without a ground.

We were driven along the winding main thoroughfare leading from the Trans-Continental Airport, through Rio to the Hotel Luxor, overlooking the famous Copacabana Beach. The

Arsenal players of the first flight were already established here, and they lost no time putting us in the picture.

I joined George Swindin on the balcony, and let my eyes wander over the mosaic promenade to the silver sands of Copacabana where playboys sunned themselves, and bathing belles reclined under gay umbrellas.

"This looks a bit of all right!" I exclaimed.

"Yes, it *looks* all right," agreed George, who was our skipper for this tour; "but get a little nearer and you'll find it somewhat dingy to say the least."

"See that stagnant pool over there. That's water that has run straight on to the beach from the street gutter, and it'll stay there for days. The tide never washes these sands."

"The sea looks most inviting, anyway," I said.

"So it does," said George, "but look at those tough customers at the water's edge. They're lifeguards, and they have a full-time job by all accounts, so strong is the undercurrent. You'll notice that none of the swimmers venture outside those white markers – if they were to do so they'd get caught in the undertow and disappear. As a matter of fact the beach is out of bounds, because it's easy to pull a muscle on those loose sands."

George went on to tell me about the delights of our luxury hotel. "The food isn't too bad, and the kitchens on the top floor are regularly visited by sanitary inspectors," he said. "I wish the inspectors would pay more attention to the bedrooms, though. None of us got any sleep last night. Our beds were invaded by an army of cockroaches!"

Already the romantic picture I had conjured up in my mind had begun to fade. I decided to change the subject.

"Have you seen any football yet, George?" I asked.

"We saw Brazil play Uruguay under floodlights last night," said George.

"Believe me, these Brazilians are going to give us some shocks. They're wonderful ball-players, and crack shots too! Why, they scored eight wonderful goals last night!"

167

"Never mind, George," I said heartily, "they won't score eight against us."

"Maybe not," agreed George, "but if they don't the crowd are going to get annoyed. You remember what Bill Dodgin told us about the crowds out here? It was no exaggeration. If they feel like making a demonstration, neither the moat nor the eight-feet high fence surrounding the pitch will stop them. Not only do they throw oranges, fireworks, bottles and so on, they don't stop short of murder if they really take a dislike to a referee or a player!"

"Well, thanks for marking my card, George," I said with heavy sarcasm.

But I soon found that George had not been pulling my leg! He was right in every detail, except for the cockroaches. My room-mate, Peter Goring, and I were luckier than the rest – we didn't have any to cope with.

Our first game at the Vasco da Gama Stadium, in Rio, turned out all right. Heavy rainfall beforehand made conditions favourable for us, and we were able to give one of our best exhibitions before a large and enthusiastic, but reasonably well-behaved crowd, who watched us beat Fluminense by 5-1.

Despite the wire fence surrounding the pitch, the circular Vasco Stadium is so designed that every spectator has an uninterrupted view of the game. The pitch, like the others we came across in Brazil, was on the bitty side.

A strange feature was the ball, smaller than our size five, while opponents, we found, wore light-weight slipper-boots, and none of them used shin-guards.

As advised, we took the field twenty minutes before kick-off time, and it was just as well we did, because we were expected to pose for hundreds of pictures, and to give radio interviews to half a dozen different commentators on the field itself.

It took us a little while to get used to the unfamiliar conditions, but Don Roper fired home the first goal just before the interval, and in the second half Doug Lishman became Brazil's Number One Pin-up Boy by scoring four times. "Leeshman!"

roared the appreciative crowd – they dearly love a man who can score goals.

As I have said, the crowd weren't too bad on this occasion, except towards the end, when they wanted the lights turned on and, because they couldn't have their way, cleared spaces on the terracing and lit bonfires to set up their own floodlighting system. I didn't worry too much about the fireworks that banged and crackled all round us – after all, they are not unknown on English grounds round about the fifth of November – but I did find those bonfires a little disconcerting.

Next we played two hectic games in the industrial city and provincial capital of Sao Paulo, drawing the first game against Palmeiras, and then beating Corinthians 2-0.

Sao Paulo is about 300 miles from Rio, so we travelled by air, leaving from the City Airport which claims to be the busiest in the world, coping as it does with one plane landing, and one taking-off every two minutes of the day. With officials and fellow-passengers rushing hither and thither, shouting and chattering, pushing and shoving; with unintelligible voices competing against each other, and the roar of aircraft, over rival loudspeaker systems, the whole place has the atmosphere and appearance of a madhouse. But it is actually a most efficient organization, relying on split-second timing, and achieving it.

It seems incredible that under these conditions planes are able to land and take-off in quick succession with scarcely any trouble at all. I say "scarcely" because actually we did witness a spot of trouble when flying back to Rio from Sao Paulo in 1951.

As we approached the City Airport our twin-engined Douglas ran into bad weather. Flying ceiling was practically zero, but we came in at the correct height and in the lane that had been allotted us by Flying Control. The plane due to land ahead of us went down through the cloud-banks and we waited to follow it two minutes later, but time passed and we continued to circle. For thirty-five minutes we stayed up there in the clouds, while our

169

pilot waited for the "all clear". Then we were given permission to land and did so quite safely.

Afterwards we learned the reason for the delay. The plane ahead of us had missed the landing-strip and crashed on to a mountain road just outside Rio. Nine times out of ten a plane touching down there would have barely skimmed the road before tumbling 3,000 feet over the mountainside, but on this occasion, by a miracle, the machine pancaked to a halt on the edge of the precipice and all the passengers were saved.

The 1949 match against Palmeiras was our players' first experience of a match under floodlight conditions. The sixteen lamps at each corner were extremely effective, but didn't always allow the goalkeepers a perfect view of the ball. The strangeness of the artificial lighting, the white ball and the continual firing of the photographers' flash-bulbs during the game were not all we had to cope with, however. In addition the Palmeiras players, mostly of Italian extraction, were both livelier and tougher than our previous opponents. What with one thing and another, we were more than content to get away with a draw.

While in Sao Paulo our head waiter, anxious to please, asked if there was anything special that we fancied to eat. I told him we would appreciate some English food for a change – steak, egg and chips, for instance? Of course! Our slightest wish was his command. We got our steak, egg and chips, and very good it was too. But after we'd had the same thing for lunch, dinner and breakfast two days running, I began to wish I hadn't spoken. After all, there's such a thing as having too much of a good thing.

Corinthians, our other Sao Paulo opponents, were also a fine attacking side, but they hadn't met a defence like ours before, and with George Swindin in brilliant form they were unable to convert clever approach work into goals. In fact it was Doug Lishman and Tom Vallance who did the scoring, to give us a 2-0 victory.

Back in Rio excitement was mounting in anticipation of our floodlight encounter with Vasco, the Brazilian champions, which was to take place on Wednesday, May 25th, with the kick-off at nine o'clock in the evening. So far Arsenal were undefeated, and already the Press were referring to us as the "Kings of Soccer", and by other similarly extravagant terms. Girl athletes of the Botafogo club had even composed a song in our honour, and it was sung to a traditional chorus that sounded just like "Two Lovely Black Eyes!"

> "O Arsenal! O Arsenal! Quen te conbece
> Nao esquece jamais. O Arsenal!"

Just try that little number in your bath-tub! Apparently it simply means: "The Arsenal. You, who we have met we shall never forget."

All this was very flattering, but we had no illusions about the real cause of Rio's excitement. It was not so much an exhibition of British football at its best that they were keen to see, as Arsenal's downfall at the hands of their own crack club. What could be more natural?

The crowd for this game exceeded 70,000, and £20,000 was paid, a record for any match other than an international and then only bettered in the World Cup series.

Let me say at once that this was one of the best games of football in which it had been my good fortune to take part. From the start it was obvious that Vasco, who provided more than half of Brazil's national team, were our equals in every department of the game, and that if either team managed to score a goal, it would probably be the winner. So it proved, and it was Vasco who, during an inspired burst in the last ten minutes, got the ball into *our* net.

The crowd went crazy with delight, and the closing minutes of play took place to the accompaniment of a continuous "Hampden Roar" (Brazilian version, with plenty of fireworks to pep it up!). We bombarded our opponents goal with every shot in

171

the locker but, taking a leaf from our own book, they set up an impregnable defensive barricade.

Yes, we tried everything within the law to beat Vasco – but we failed. The exciting news went ringing round Rio: "Vasco had beaten the British Soccer Kings! The Lion had got its tail down."

But it hadn't, you know. We'd been beaten, yes....fairly and squarely in a great game....but in no sense were we downhearted. Who could be after such an enjoyable tussle? When we left the stadium in our coach for the ten-mile trip across Rio, we were in the best of spirits, joking, laughing and singing at the top of our voices. Whenever we stopped at the traffic lights, Brazilians stopped to stare. They couldn't believe the evidence of their own eyes and ears. And the next morning, although the newspapers featured Arsenal's defeat in banner headlines across the front pages, they also carried a centre-page spread declaring: "The English people are mad. Although they lose, they still sing!"

I've been lucky enough to take part in some great victories in my time, but none of them have made me prouder than this defeat – and my club's attitude towards it. It's an attitude that foreigners find difficult to understand, although it's taught to every British schoolboy.

Teach me to win when I may, and if I may not win,
then, above all, I pray, make me a good loser.

The lads at Dunkirk were "good losers" – and they were good enough to come again and *win*. We tried to take a lesson from them and I believe we succeeded. When we left Brazil the Press were to write:

The Arsenal season is now over and we are left with a feeling of regret because we shall miss their fairness, the beauty of their game and the sportsmanship shown at all times. Arsenal leaves behind a reputation which no other foreign team has yet

172

achieved, as well as a very useful lesson in football which we hope to profit by, although we have excellent players of our own. They may also be assured that as a result of their visit here there will be a great number of admirers of British spirit, its fairness and composure.

While *A Gazete*, the Brazilian sports newspaper, said:

As to discipline, gentlemanliness and sincerity which they always show we simply cannot speak too highly. We have not seen a single dirty trick or anything like it. Grabbing the opponent or deliberately handling the ball in order to keep the game away from their opponents simply does not exist for them. There is not the slightest doubt that the eleven have a lot of football in their feet, much discipline in their bodies, and not a little grey matter in their brains. The Arsenal may lose games in our country, but there is one thing of which we can be certain – they will always play good football, characterized by science, originality, heart and particularly, extreme discipline. That is why, once again, we must state that the football played by this famous team, which England has sent us in its first exhibition in our country delighted the eye and warmed the heart.

I hope you will forgive me for having those reports reprinted here. I do so in order that the reader may understand the great pride I felt – to be a British sportsman and a member of a team that was able to show the rest of the world what that means.

Chapter Eighteen

The only thoroughly unpleasant incident in Arsenal's 1949 tour of Brazil occurred during the second half of the match against Flamengo and, looking back now, even that had its funny side.

It arose out of the well-known tendency of foreign crowds, officials and players, to champion the goalkeeper; and from their lack of understanding of the rules when Bryn Jones, known throughout Britain as one of the cleanest players in the game, attempted to dispossess the Flamengo goalkeeper.

Actually, I didn't feel too happy about this game from the word "go". Sprinkled among the large crowd were Brazilian "Red Caps" – looking not unlike our own military policemen. We were already familiar with their methods when trouble threatened. Advancing among the ringleaders in a body ten strong, they drew their three-foot truncheons and flattened out everyone within reach. Not until all spectators in the area, innocent or guilty, had been sorted out did the Red Caps start asking questions.

Civilian police were also present in large numbers and, contrary to regulations, half a dozen positioned themselves inside the wire barrier surrounding the pitch, on the pretext that they were on "special duty".

Even the referee – a Brazilian named Snr. Mario Viana – was a major in the Special Police. This gave him the authority to pack a six-shooter in a holster under his shirt, which he wore throughout the game.

When Peter Goring received the ball from a typical Logie dribble, and scored for us in the opening minute of the play, such was the crowd's reaction that I thought the referee might have to use the revolver in his own defense before the game was much older.

Instead, he took the safe course of awarding free-kicks to the Brazilians whenever an Arsenal player was fouled. From one of these, the Flamengo inside-left scored the equalizer ten minutes later.

Bryn Jones came on to the field just before the interval as a substitute for Archie Macaulay, who had pulled a muscle.

The second half had not been in progress for more than nine minutes when a mix-up took place around the Flamengo goal. The goalkeeper went down on all fours and the ball was on the ground between his arms and thighs. According to the local custom, he expected to be left severely alone. But Bryn didn't know anything about local custom. He did what any other British forward would do in similar circumstances – rushed in and challenged the goalkeeper for possession of the ball.

Immediately the crowd howled protests. Brazilian players and officials crowded round Bryn, convinced that he was about to kick their goalkeeper. One of the Flamengo full-backs jumped on Bryn's back from behind and attempted to strangle him. Policemen rushed on to the field to preserve law and order and, in the general fracas, Bryn was struck in the Adam's apple by a truncheon. Delivered with more force, this blow would have resulted in serious injury. As it was, the little Welsh forward was in considerable pain for several days afterwards.

Whatever would Brazilian goalkeepers make of a rumbustious forward like Trevor Ford?

After this incident we refrained from tackling any opposing player during the time that remained, and this silent protest appeared to win the sympathy of the crowd. The next day's papers made full apologies to Arsenal in respect of the incident, and praised us for not losing our heads. We were also told that the policeman who had struck Bryn had been suspended from duty and thrown into jail for a short time.

Perhaps I should add that we lost this game by 3-1. We also lost by a single goal to Sao Paulo in the final game of the tour, and before that drew 2-2 in a floodlight match against our hosts, Botafogo.

175

The latter was a very friendly game, with hardly a foul in it. So friendly was it, in fact, that the crowd decided there was "Marmalade" involved.

"Marmalade", we discovered, is the Brazilian expression to describe "an arranged result between two crooked sides". But although the Botafogo players and ourselves were good friends, I can assure you that no such arrangement was made!

Incidentally, I became particularly friendly with the Botafogo goalkeeper, Brasileino Osvaldo. We often trained together, and before Arsenal set off for home he presented me with a package of Cigarros, autographed "*Ao Grande Barnes, Uma Recordacao do seu grande amigo*", which I took as a great compliment.

While, like the majority of the rank-and-file Brazilian footballers, Osvaldo lived in "Nissen hut" accommodation at his club's grounds, the real top-notchers lived like film stars, with house, car and servants all provided.

This was made clear to Mr. Whittaker when certain officials approached him on behalf of a prominent Brazilian club. They wanted to "buy" Jimmy Logie, George Swindin and myself.

The boss fingered his chin thoughtfully. "How much do you think your stadium is worth?" he asked the Brazilians.

"One hundred thousand pounds!" they decided.

"Well, sell your stadium as the first securing part of the transaction, and then I'll consider your offers," said Mr. Whittaker, tongue in cheek.

The Brazilians didn't smile. They thought the boss meant what he said, and at once started making plans among themselves as to how his demand could be met.

In the end the boss had to explain that he had been joking; that he would not part with any of his players at any price and there was, therefore, no need for the Brazilians to part with their stadium.

From a romantic aspect I was disappointed with Brazil, and from a playing point of view we all found the tour strenuous.

But it had been a wonderful experience, and a financial success because the club made around £20,000 as the result of seven games.

Obviously the standard of football on this side of the world was high, and although our opponents' defensive system was less reliable than our own, and they were inclined to be shot-shy when attacking, there were lessons in the art of ball-play that they could teach us.

In the Autumn of 1950, Dr. Amando Barcellos invited Arsenal to tour Brazil again, at the end of the 1950-51 season. This invitation was accepted, but before arrangements were completed we were grieved to hear of the doctor's death. We were to miss him in more ways than one.

Still, tour arrangements went ahead and details were completed when the Argentine F.A. invited us to extend our tour and play two matches in Buenos Aires. The Arsenal directors delayed their decision regarding this invitation until the team's reaction to a heavy tour of six matches in Brazil was observed, and since it did prove a hard tour, whilst we were in Sao Paulo, Arsenal informed a representative of the Argentine F.A. that their invitation must be declined. These were the facts behind the rumours that flew about at the time, suggesting that Argentine F.A. had withdrawn their invitation because of Arsenal's poor form.

It is true that Arsenal were not the attraction they had been in Brazil two years previously, but this was not entirely due to our play, although we lost every game but one.

For one thing a decided apathy towards football was apparent on the part of the Brazilians, who had been shocked by their country's defeat at the hands of Uruguay in the 1950 World Cup competition: for another, television had become the craze in Brazil, and all our matches, except the one against Botafogo, were televised.

Generally speaking, the smaller clubs were glad to have their matches televised in order to cash-in on the commercial fee, but clubs like Vasco and Botafogo were far from happy about it because if undoubtedly reduced their attendances. The winter temperature; of sixty degrees, was enough to cause Brazilian ladies to wear fur coats in the cinema, and their men-folk to stay home, or sit in cozy cafes to watch their favourite team on the television screen instead of in the flesh.

In the absence of Tom Whittaker, whose health did not allow him to make this trip, our party was under the capable direction of Jack Crayston, Arsenal's assistant manager, and Bob Wall, the assistant secretary. Laurie Scott was skipper, and a fine job he made of it too.

We again trained at the Botafogo ground, and stayed at the Hotel Luxor where, oddly enough, I occupied the same room as before – the one without cockroaches! This time my room-mate was Albert Gudmundsson, the Icelandic amateur, who played many games for Arsenal before becoming a professional with the Racing Club de France. Tall, slender, fair-haired Albert was a quiet, likeable companion, and a keen soccer student. An excellent linguist, he was able to act as our interpreter on a number of occasions in Brazil.

From a footballing point of view, our poor results on this tour were not due to a deterioration in our standard of play, but rather to a spectacular improvement in the play of our opponents.

We soon found that the Brazilians had completed a successful change of tactics, modelling their new style on that of the Arsenal team which had impressed them so greatly in 1949.

Not only had they copied our system of defense in every detail, except for our "retreat and delay" plan, but in attack, too, they favoured the Herbert Chapman principles, with a wandering inside-forward to link defense and attack in the Alex James manner.

We met Brazil's "Alex James", a black inside-left named Didi, in our first match and he completely dominated the play. Instead of repeating our 5-1 victory of the previous tour, Fluminense beat us by 2-0 and I was the culprit as far as the goals were concerned. The first was the result of a poor back pass to George, and the second I deflected into my own net.

But the Brazilians were not only good imitators, they added ideas of their own which made them superior to any sides we had ever met previously.

Their marking was grim, they moved at great speed, blending sparkling individual artistry with good teamwork and crack sharp-shooting.

Each member of every team we played was a ball artist, and among our opponents there were at least half a dozen players whose skill was equal to that of Stanley Matthews!

Another thing that impressed me was the way our opponents moved and made their own openings without waiting for the defender to move and create an opening for them. This created havoc in our ranks, and but for Arsenal's fighting spirit, the scores against us would have been very much greater.

As it is, several of us, and Ray Daniel, Laurie Scott and myself in particular, reckoned that we were playing as well as we had ever done; yet we were not good enough to hold the opposition.

Of the six teams we met, America, a team of dark-skinned Brazilians and not the America of the World Cup series (!), were outstanding. Their speed of movement and the precision of their passing was breathtaking, and although Gudmundsson scored a fine goal for us, America's eight-man attack twice forced the ball past George Swindin in reply.

Nothing would satisfy me more than to see the America side, or Vasco, who beat us 4-0 under floodlight, come to Britain and play on some of our first-class pitches. This would enable the British public to appreciate how far other countries have advanced in such a short space of time.

We players know; but do British supporters really appreciate that tours abroad are no longer "bright lights and sweet music"? British teams are made to fight to the last breath to preserve the shreds of their reputation.

Defeated by Fluminense 2-0, Botafogo 2-0 and America 2-1, we gained our only victory by floodlight, in the fourth match against Sao Paulo. Steady rain before the start made the clay subsoil very slippery, and under these conditions the standard of football was surprisingly good. No goals were scored until, in the closing stages, Don Roper replaced Reuben Marden in the forward line and scored with one of his cannon-ball drives from fifteen yards out.

Again under floodlight, and in drizzling rain, we lost our next match to Palmeiras who, although Champions of Brazil at the time, did not seem as strong as the other teams we had played. This is a game we should have won, and in fact we opened the scoring through Logie in the twentieth minute, but the game was thrown away in the last fifteen minutes when Palmeiras were allowed to score three quick goals.

To conclude the tour we suffered our heaviest defeat, by 4-0, to Vasco, partly because of an unfortunate injury to Dave Bowen, and partly due to our failure to snap up scoring chances.

In our off-duty moments we got to know Rio pretty well, but one thing we could not get used to was the Brazilians' attitude to road accidents. If a pedestrian was knocked down by a car, the driver stepped on the accelerator and drove away from the scene as quickly as possible: and no one else would go to the assistance of the unfortunate pedestrian for fear of being called as a witness to the accident.

The reason for this attitude was that all witnesses in Rio are liable to be taken into custody by the police, and kept under lock and key until the case comes up before the courts. This might involve detention for several months.

Knowing this, Reg Lewis risked a "long sentence" by going to the assistance of an elderly woman knocked down by a car on the main road opposite our hotel, and only the fact that he was recognized as an Arsenal player enabled him to get away with it!

Incidentally, they do send out ambulances when road accidents occur – cream ones for the injured, cream and blue for the dead!

When we arrived home from this tour Arsenal were invited to a tea-table reception given by the Anglo-Brazilian Society at the Hyde Park Hotel, and since Jack Crayston was unable to attend I was sent along as spokesman.

I made a little speech in which I said: "British football must pull up its socks. Arsenal were outplayed and no excuses. The Brazil teams soon learned how to tackle our defense – which is something few teams in the last few years have been able to do."

I pointed out that although a normal player in Brazil was paid about £140 a week, and a star player as much as £400 against our weekly £14, in my opinion that didn't make any difference, because we all played our best, and extra money wouldn't make us any better.

"We should improve our tactics and learn how to counter opponents' play by a study of their style," was my summing up.

I was thanked very graciously for my speech, and then, as I was putting on my hat and coat in the cloakroom a waiter presented me with a bill for the drinks that I and my Arsenal colleagues had consumed at the reception!

Since I made that speech, subsequent events have somewhat modified my concern with regard to Britain's international football.

Having gleaned tremendous knowledge from the Southampton tour of 1948, Arsenal's two trips, the English World Cup visit and the Portsmouth tour which followed ours in 1951, Brazil have not encouraged further visits by British clubs. Can it be that they feel they have nothing more to learn from us, and will continue to play blithely along the lines that proved successful in 1951?

If that is so, they are making a big mistake!

There's nothing new in soccer, nor anything else. Arrange the letters of the alphabet in the right order and you can write a best-seller: with 1, 2 and x in the right order you can win a fortune on the Pools. Hit on the right combination of everyday soccer moves and you can develop a wonder team.

But there's more than one winning combination in all these fields, and it's always possible to produce a tactical combination even better than the wonder team of the moment.

Varied opposition creates new ideas, and it is teams that keep pace with each new development that thrive. If the Brazilians are content to assume that they have reached the peak of perfection, I would remind them that the peak of any structure is a very small space, from which it is easy to slip.

British sport has now settled down again after the war, and young blood is coming back. I am confident, too, that the powers-that-be are constantly seeking new ideas for the improvement of our football generally, and there is not so much danger of our becoming set in our ways so that we are liable to be beaten by the unorthodox.

But there's nothing new about one thing that the British player possesses; that is, in my opinion, his greatest asset, and I hope he will never lose it. It is "that little something extra" that he is able to call upon when all seems lost – a good old-fashioned quality known as Guts!

Was it hands? With the goalie beaten, Walley Barnes fists the ball out of the goal to prevent Carlisle United from scoring in the Third Round Cup replay of 1950-51 at Carlisle.

The Great Moment! Arsenal win the Cup at Wembley in 1950 and chair their skipper, Joe Mercer, the Footballer of the Year.

Chapter Nineteen

While I have experienced most of my memorable moments in the red jersey of my club or country, it was in Arsenal's "lucky change" of old gold, that I gained my coveted Cup-winners' medal at Wembley on April 29th, 1950.

"Lucky Arsenal!" they were soon calling us again, because we won the Cup without playing a single tie outside London!

I won't deny that we had luck: a team needs it to win the Cup. But give us credit for using it to advantage, and for helping to serve up what Sir Stanley Rous called, "The best footballing final I've seen at Wembley."

We didn't start the 1949-50 season too brilliantly. In fact, after the opening games, we found ourselves sharing bottom place in the league table. "Too lengthy a tour" was the cry of the fans and the Press, but it was really just one of those things which make football so unpredictable. And, suddenly, we hit winning form. By Christmas we were challenging the league leaders.

And strangely enough it was Liverpool, our Wembley opponents, who gave Arsenal's league title aspirations a jolt at this stage, ending our good run by administering a 2-0 defeat just before the Third Round Cup-ties.

There was a general optimism about at Highbury that this might be our year in the Cup. Indeed, as I mentioned in an earlier chapter, George Swindin went so far as to prophesy that we would be drawn at home four times in succession, and would then win the Cup.

How right he proved; and how fortunate we were to have all those home draws! But don't get it out of proportion. Speaking personally, it never worries me whether we are playing at home or away – one piece of grass is like another as far as I'm concerned. And don't tell me we had an easy path to the Final, with such doughty fighters as Sheffield Wednesday, Swansea Town, Burnley, Leeds and Chelsea to overcome.

Our Third Round tie against Sheffield Wednesday was only thirty minutes old when their young full-back, Vincent Kenny, collided in mid-air with Ian McPherson and was carried off with a dislocated shoulder. Mac had actually netted the ball, but was ruled offside.

After that, Wednesday's ten men fought gallantly and the Gunners' shooting was very much off-target. I counted half-a-dozen gilt-edged scoring opportunities missed by our forwards, and things were beginning to look sticky until two minutes from the end, when Reg Lewis did manage to find the net and score the winner.

Those great triers, Swansea Town, didn't allow us an easy win in the next round either. On this occasion I managed to score the decisive goal in our 2-1 victory from a penalty.

It happened just after half-time. When Reg Lewis beat goalkeeper Parry with a header, Keane, the Swansea left-back, fisted the ball over the bar in desperation.

"Don't forget the Welsh selectors are with Swansea," Roy Paul warned me jokingly as I ran up to take the penalty.

"There's only one place for the ball after a penalty," I told Roy. "That's the back of the net!"

And that's where I put it, hitting the ball hard so that even if Parry had been able to get to it he could hardly have stopped it.

Earlier in the season, on the train journey to West Bromwich, the boss asked me to take over Arsenal's spot-kicks in future. Strangely enough we were awarded a penalty in that very game, and also in the return league fixture against West Bromwich Albion the following week, and I scored both of them. During the season I converted six spot-kicks altogether. Bert Williams was the only keeper to save one from me.

When given the job I decided that the method I would use would be to hit the ball really hard, aiming at the iron support on the left-hand side of the goalkeeper. Many kickers, I know, favour

186

a push with the inside of the foot to a spot just inside the upright, but with such a slow-travelling ball a keeper whose anticipation is good can get across and stop it. So I've stuck to the theory of hitting it hard and in the same place every time. In practice this has paid good dividends. Against Fulham on Guy Fawkes' day, for example, goalkeeper Kelly got a hand to my forceful penalty-shot, but without a hope of stopping the ball in its flight.

After placing the ball on the spot I go back to the edge of the semi-circle, which allows me to get in six approach strides before hitting the ball on the seventh. The main thing, I've found, is to keep your eye on the ball the whole time – don't worry whether the goalkeeper is trying to beat the kick or not the ref or the linesman will ensure that he stands still.

Those readers who have seen me take penalty kicks at Highbury may think that I adopt a policy of "hit hard and hope for the best", but I can assure them that I have put a lot of hard practice to enable me to place the ball where I want it in actual play.

After I had scored my second penalty-goal against West Bromwich I heard one of the Throstles' defenders remark: "Our goalie should have saved that, Barnes put it in exactly the same place as he did last week."

It was a pity that we had to beat Swansea by a penalty, although after the game Keane readily admitted that the ball would have entered the net from Reg's header had he not fisted it out. Swansea had put up a fine show, and Mr. Tom Whittaker visited their dressing-room afterwards in order to congratulate them.

For the next game against Burnley the boss made what many critics described as a "bold gamble" by restoring Denis Compton to the outside-left position in Arsenal's Cup team. Denis had put on weight, and was said to be troubled by his knee injury. In addition, cricket duty allowed him to play little more than twenty league games for Arsenal since the war, and it was suggested that he was past his best as a footballer.

With great satisfaction we observed that the critics were wrong again. Not only was Denis out match-winner on this particular occasion but his dash and enthusiasm proved a vital factor right through to the final whistle at Wembley. This was his last season in first-class football, and he finished in an appropriate blaze of glory.

How good a winger was Denis Compton at his best? There have been very few better, I would say.

His very first kick in Cup-tie football gave goalkeeper Strong a nasty moment. He helped Reg Lewis to score our first goal against Burnley, and went on to score the second himself with a crafty "cannon" that went into the net off both posts!

Our next victims at Highbury were Leeds United, who played pretty football but met an Arsenal team now resolved to "reach Wembley or bust!" Opposing us at centre-half was eighteen-year-old John Charles, who was to be my international colleague against Ireland three days later. I was impressed by his surprisingly mature ability. He only made one mistake, but learnt that to make a slip in the penalty area with Reg Lewis anywhere in the vicinity was asking for trouble. John's minor slip enabled Reg to score the only goal of the match.

One more hurdle to Wembley – Chelsea, but what a hurdle! The Blues always seem to pull something special out of the bag when they play against us. At Tottenham it was two smash-and-grab goals in the first half by Roy Bentley, and they nearly shattered our Cup ambitions for good.

Then, with the whistle just about to sound for half-time, Freddie Cox, who had joined Arsenal from the Spurs earlier in the season, took a weird and wonderful corner. The ball spun from his boot and hovered tantalizingly in the air before taking a last-second twist into the roof of the net. It was a right-footed slice-kick that Freddie had practiced during training, though undoubtedly it was helped by a lucky gust of wind on this occasion. Lucky or not, however, it gave us just the tonic we needed to recover and then save the game.

"Don't panic lads," was Mr. Whittaker's advice at half-time. We tried to pretend that this was just another game, and failed. The tension was terrific.

"Tension!" exclaimed Arthur Milton just the other day. "I was watching from the stand, and I've never known a game so packed with thrills." My wife agrees with Arthur. Indeed the nervous strain proved too much for her and made her ill for several days afterwards. After watching Arsenal's vital game against Burnley, in which they clinched the league title by goal average, in 1953, I know how they must have felt. Arthur and I sat together in the stand on the latter occasion, and we agreed that this was the worst form of torture a footballer can suffer – to see his team fighting desperately for honours and he unable to play any part to help them. After the match – with its happy ending for Arsenal – Arthur and I were exhausted as if we'd made every kick in it ourselves.

Many readers will recall our memorable equalizing goal in the 1950 Cup semi-final, scored by the Compton's "double-act" fourteen minutes from time. Denis, about to take a corner on the left, signalled his brother Les to come up. At Joe Mercer's shouted counter-order to "Stay back!" Les hesitated. Then he deliberately disobeyed, trotted up-field and arrived in front of goal at precisely the right moment to meet and to head home Denis's accurate centre between the startled Danny Winter and Harry Medhurst.

In the act of scoring, Leslie lost his balance and fell. Joe was the first to help him to his feet and to congratulate him.

The replay took place at Tottenham on the following Wednesday. The night before the match, Eileen Cox, Freddie's wife, dreamed that Arsenal won 1-0 and that her Freddie scored the winning goal. Without wanting to steal George Swindin's thunder as a prophet, I must record this as an equally accurate forecast: that's exactly what did happen. Seconds before the half-way stage in extra time, Freddie received the ball from Peter Goring, skirted Chelsea's defensive barrier and let go a beauty with his left foot. As the ball entered the net, hundreds of Arsenal supporters rushed on to the pitch to mob him, and to form singing, cheering and dancing circles round us until chased off by the police.

But hard luck, Chelsea! You tried all you knew, and failed gallantly. "Pity we couldn't have stayed apart until the Final," I remarked to Harry Medhurst, my former Army chum, as we left the field together.

"It's all in the luck of the game," said Harry. "Don't forget my tickets for the Final!"

Arsenal and Chelsea players had agreed that whichever team got to the Final the winners would make sure that Final tickets were made available to the losers.

I kept my part of the bargain and strangely enough, as I write – four years after the event – I met Harry Medhurst and he paid me for those Cup Final tickets. Since Harry joined Brighton, we just haven't run into each other at all. It was his first chance to "get it off his conscience", as he put it.

As the day of the Final approached so the excitement mounted, and there was plenty of confidence at Highbury despite rumours that Liverpool had already organized, and started selling tickets for a Grand Victory Ball! Our confidence did not go as far as that, but when George, our tame prophet, looked into his crystal ball he saw an Arsenal victory quite clearly, and that was a good omen.

We made no special preparations – took no "atomic cocktails" or "pep pills", made no seaside visits, no secret plans – it was just normal training beforehand, and an early lunch together at Highbury on the morning of the big game, an arrangement we had followed in every Cup-tie.

The only sign or nerves was shown by the coach-driver, who got the Arsenal team to Wembley a quarter of an hour ahead of schedule. We stopped along the road leading to the stadium, much to the delight of the Cup Final crowds, many of whom stopped to wish us luck.

Entering the No.1 dressing-room (the *lucky* one!) three-quarters of an hour before kick-off time, we sorted through hundreds of letters and telegrams that awaited us. Mr. R. V. Jones, representing our Supporters Club, visited the dressing-room to present Mr. Whittaker with a magnificent floral gun, made entirely of red and white carnations, and we appreciated this good-luck gift enormously.

With time to spare, I walked down the tunnel as far as the entrance to the famous pitch itself. I was hoping to absorb "Wembley atmosphere" before taking the field there for the first time, and luck was with me when I bumped into Captains Jaeger and Statham, directors of music for the Welsh and Irish Guards respectively, both of whom I had known at the R.M.A, Sandhurst. I was able to spend a good twenty minutes at the entrance, scanning the huge crowd, getting my bearings and soaking-in atmosphere while chatting to my friends. This helped me considerably.

Then it was time to change, and to play my part in ensuring that Denis Compton got ready in time! But we didn't have to worry about Denis – he set up a personal record for punctuality!

All at once, time, which had so far hung heavily on our hands, made a spurt, and before we quite realized it, zero hour was upon us.

"Go out and play football. Play your normal game. Good luck!" were the boss's last words as we started on the long walk to the pitch. Knowing Leslie Compton's wish to be last out, and not wanting to interfere with our luck in any way, I left the tunnel just in front of him. It was raining as we lined up opposite the Liverpool team, ready to be introduced to His Majesty the King, and the water trickled down our backs, inside our jerseys, until our excitement became a little dampened by discomfort. This had the effect of steadying my nerves.

I remember calling across "All the best" to Cyril Sidlow, and Cyril grinned back in response.

191

As we lined up for the kick-off it gave me a great feeling of confidence to know that behind, alongside and in front of me I had such talented colleagues. George Swindin, behind me, had played nearly two hundred great games for Arsenal. Laurie Scott, my full-back partner, had made a splendid come-back after a second operation for cartilage trouble during the season. In front of me was big Leslie Compton, one of Arsenal's "Old Reliables", who had served the club for eighteen years and had been a great hero in earlier rounds of the Cup. Flanking him on the right was robust, red-headed, red-blooded Scottish terrier Alec Forbes, and on the left skipper Joe Mercer, who on the evening of the Final, and in his twentieth season as a footballer, had been presented with his trophy as "Footballer of the Year".

On the wings we had Freddie Cox, outside-right, making a sensational debut that season in Arsenal colours, and Denis Compton, outside-left, on the crest of an equally spectacular "come-back". The inside men were that thrustful, ice-cool opportunist Reg Lewis, and ball conjuror Jimmy Logie, while twenty-two-year-old, ex-butchers' boy Harry (Pete) Goring, a Ted Drake-type leader with a shot in either foot, was creating something of a record by appearing at Wembley during his first season in first-class football.

What of our opponents? Cyril Sidlow had won international honours as a junior, an amateur and as a professional for Wales, and I knew his capabilities only too well. Equally, I respected my two-footed, reliable Welsh colleague Ray Lambert who, incidentally, first signed for Liverpool at the age of thirteen and a half! His partner, Eddie Spicer, the Liverpool-born ex-Royal Marine Commando, I knew as a hard tackler, quick in recovery.

The Liverpool half-backs, consisting of English international Phil Taylor, utility defender and hard tackler Bill Jones and wiry and industrious Bob Paisley, looked equally powerful.

I have previously made mention of international duels against Billy Liddell, the opposing outside-left, and now we had good reason to mark him as "Dangerous if unattended", while my particular "cup of tea", Jimmy Payne, sleight-of-foot specialist, was well known for his "goal-creating" activities. Willie Fagan, the experienced Scottish schemer, and diminutive Kevin Baron would take some watching, while big, red-headed Albert Stubbins I knew as an extremely fine centre-forward, and personally I feared him most of all.

Remembering Tom Whittaker's advice, Arsenal soon settled down to their normal game, and actually I thought we were much better together than in recent league matches. After sixteen minutes play, Cyril Sidlow cleared the ball down the middle. Les Compton intercepted and headed out to me. I pushed the ball along the carpet to Jimmy Logie, who swiveled with it in his possession, drew the defense and then slipped it through to Reg Lewis who was in the inside-right position. Reg flicked the ball past Sidlow as coolly as if in a casual kick-about game during training, and Arsenal were one-up!

Immediately after this, Billy Liddell got away down the left-wing and put across a wonderful centre that found our defense wide open. If Albert Stubbins's head had made contact with the ball it would certainly have been a goal and so sure was I that Albert would get it that momentarily I relaxed. Well, the ball shot past the Liverpool centre-forward, past me and, fortunately, wide of Payne, allowing me the necessary time to recover, to turn and to block the right-winger's shot at goal. The ball rebounded from me – Payne shot again, and this time the ball struck my left instep and went over the line for a corner, which came to nothing.

This was a vital incident, as I saw it, and the game might have gone differently if Stubbins had scored. As we came off the pitch at half-time I asked Albert how he came to miss.

"I wasn't getting it from the moment Billy Liddell hit the ball," declared Albert Stubbins.

This may sound strange to many readers, but timing and anticipation are acute with crossed balls like this and I realized at once what Albert meant. As soon as Billy shaped to make his centre, Albert's instinct and experience told him that even though he could cover six yards in a second, he still would not be able to get the ball kicked hard from a distance of thirty yards; a ball which would probably travel at sixty miles an hour. Who could blame him? Yet to me, and to many on the terraces, it had looked a fairly easy chance.

There was no great jubilation among Arsenal players at half-time, just a keenness to get out on the pitch again and finish off the job well begun. The boss asked for another goal from us as soon as possible, and twenty minutes after the interval Reg Lewis obliged with a smashing right-foot shot from Freddie Cox's pass. Number two from Reg and another beauty!

As the game went on, we seemed to get more and more on top, and every member of the team seemed to be playing on peak form. Laurie Scott and Alec Forbes were doing a great job in holding Billy Liddell. I was sorry to see Alec accused in some Press reports of fouling Billy Liddell maliciously in one incident. Despite Alec's tigerish tackling, it was, and always is, perfectly fair, and on the particular occasion referred to, Alec's knee barely came into contact with Liddell, and at no time was it above thigh height. If Alec had really been guilty of a malicious foul, the outside-left would have been flat out on a stretcher, and not flying down the wing again seconds later.

Towards the end, inspired by their skipper Phil Taylor, Liverpool staged a fighting rally, and there were a number of goalmouth scrambles, but our defense managed to hold out until there seemed little doubt in my mind that we were home!

Three minutes from time there was a stoppage while Phil Taylor received attention from his trainer. Joe Mercer, Les Compton and I were together in the middle of the field, and I said to Les, "What's it feel like to know you've got a winners' medal coming to you, Big Fella?"

194

"Enough of that, Walley," snapped Joe. "There's still three minutes to play, and the game's not won yet!"

That was typical of Joe, and a typically *correct* attitude for him to tale, too, as I quickly realized. A lot can happen in three minutes in a game of football. What a part our skipper played in our ultimate victory! Thinking back, I don't recall a better display from Joe, or any other wing-half-back, and no one could have carried the title "Footballer of the Year" more deservedly.

I find it difficult to write without prejudice about Arsenal's skipper, because he is a very close personal friend of mine, but putting friendship aside – I must state that in my humble opinion Joe Mercer is the complete wing-half-back and captain.

Jokingly before the game I had promised friends who were to watch the game on television that I would smile at the cameras especially for them as I went up to collect my winners' medal, but the occasion proved too much for me, and I forgot to do so.

Joe Mercer was even more overcome by the situation. After receiving the Cup, and thereby realizing a lifelong ambition, he accepted a medal from Her Majesty the Queen without noticing that it was a *losers'* medal he had been given! Fortunately, however, His Majesty the King noticed the mistake, and smilingly drew the Queen's attention to it, so that Joe got his just reward in the end.

Lucky Arsenal? "Yes – call us lucky Arsenal," said our Chairman, Sir Bracewell Smith, after the match. "We're proud of the title. It is our talisman. We are lucky to have such wonderful team spirit."

And just to prove his words and to provide some consolation for those Arsenal supporters who were unable to see us at Wembley, we concluded the League season with our two best displays of the year, beating League champions Portsmouth, 2-0 at Highbury, and Stoke City 5-2, at Stoke.

Soccer fans still talk about Arsenal's performances in these two matches, rating them with the semi-final match and replay against Chelsea, and of course the classic Cup Final, as the highlights of the season.

We finished sixth in the League and but for a bad start, that elusive Cup and League double might have been achieved in 1949-50.

Chapter Twenty

"Beat England today and you'll be well on the road to Rio, with a chance to win the championship of the world!"

With these inspiring words from Mr. Milwyn Jenkins, who succeeded the late Mr. B. Watts-Jones as Chairman of the Welsh F.A., we took the field against England at Ninian Park, Cardiff, on October 15th, 1949.

This was our first match of the season in the British International Tournament, and also the first World Cup preliminary match ever to be held in Britain. We knew that if we finished tournament champions, or runners-up, we should be eligible for the World Cup Final at Rio.

So with our team, which contained seven 2nd Division players we faced a star-studded England side who were equally anxious to stake a claim to a Rio passage. This was the line-up:

WALES: Sidlow (Liverpool); Barnes (Arsenal) capt.; Sherwood (Cardiff City); Paul (Swansea Town); T. Jones (Everton); Burgess (Spurs); Griffiths (Leicester City); Lucas (Swansea Town); Ford (Aston Villa); Scrine (Swansea Town) and Edwards (Cardiff City).

ENGLAND: Williams (Wolves); Mozley (Derby County); Aston (Manchester United); Wright (Wolves) capt.; Franklin (Stoke City); Dickinson (Portsmouth); Finney (Preston North End); Mortensen (Blackpool); Milburn (Newcastle); Shackleton (Sunderland) and Hancocks (Wolves).

Frankie Scrine, a young utility forward discovered by Swansea Town when playing in local football, was making his international debut. Mal Griffiths, at outside-right, had done well on the Welsh overseas winter tour which I had missed through accompanying Arsenal to Brazil. Mal had been on Arsenal's books for a time, before joining Leicester City in 1938.

Derby County full-back, Bert Mozley, was making his international debut for England, and our opponents recalled Mortensen, Milburn, Shackleton and Hancocks to their forward-line following defeat by Eire in September.

Len Shackleton and Stan Mortensen, both in brilliant form, were the schemers we feared, and at a pre-match conference it was decided that wing-halves Ronnie Burgess and Roy Paul would have to stick closely to them, and not indulge in their favourite, and often effective, liberty of going through with the ball.

We also planned a surprise move to give Frankie Scrine a goal-scoring opportunity straight from the kick-off, and this worked well. In the opening seconds Frankie found himself in possession right in front of goal, just as we had hoped. But through over-eagerness, natural enough in his first international, he hit the ball much too soon and missed a golden opportunity. Had he been as accurately "on the target" as the team of four archery experts who gave an impressive exhibition of their sport to the 60,000 crowd before kick-off, the whole course of the match might have been different.

It was England who scored first, through Stan Mortensen in the twentieth minute. Five minutes later, Milburn added a second, and then a third with a low hard drive before half-time.

Curtains? Not yet! In the second half we fought back with all the fervour appropriate to the occasion, and Ronnie Burgess was unlucky to have a crashing drive tipped over the bar by Bert Williams. Soon afterwards, Jackie Milburn virtually put the match in the bag for England by completing his hat-trick with a header, although Mal Griffiths reduced the deficit two minutes later with an angled shot.

It wasn't such an easy passage as it sounds for England, however. The score of 4-1 flattered them because their forward-line did not hit it off too well together, in my opinion, and three of their goals were decidedly "edgey".

Len Shackleton, in particular, had an indifferent game, and his poor form in England colours was to be emphasized when he played in a later international in front of his home crowd. Why, I wonder?

Potentially, Len Shackleton is a really great inside-forward. His uncanny gift of ball control excels that of any other player today. He has a variety of freak tricks, and shots at goal that can penetrate the best organized defence. But, possibly through a peculiarity of temperament, this Yorkshire-born near-genius has failed, in internationals, to reach the heights of which his natural skill make him capable.

A schoolboy international, Len first joined Bradford when still thirteen years of age. He might have been an Arsenal player instead, but he slipped away from the Gunners during the war when he was called up for service in the pits.

Soon after the war, Newcastle United paid £13,000 for his transfer. He played his first game for the famous Northern club a few days later and scored six goals on his debut, sharing in an amazing 13-0 rout of the Welsh team, Newport County. In the same season, 1946, he gained his first international cap as a senior player.

In February 1948, he was involved in another move – this time to nearby Sunderland, who paid over £20,000 for his services. At times he has been the inspiration of his side, dreaming up defence-splitting moves that have made his fellow forwards look like world beaters. There have been times, too, when the ball would not run for him, and at such times he has been condemned as "too unorthodox".

He's a curious figure on the field, with hunched-up shoulders and flopping arms – one minute lost in the tactics of the game, the next musing to himself with his typical wide-toothed grin as if gleefully working out some new, devilish manoeuvre.

Once he is in possession, however (and few can match the dexterity with which he brings a ball under control), the ball becomes his slave. All the skills of inside-forward play, such as dribbling, feinting, correct positioning and accurate passing, are his to command. He was the inspiration of the Sunderland attack which gave Arsenal a 7-1 hammering in September, 1953.

Len's poor form in internationals has got me puzzled, I don't mind admitting. But, whatever he does, he is always the artist, and time may yet prove him something more.

That defeat by England gave our World Cup hopes a bitter blow, and worse was to follow. We lost 2-0 to Scotland at Hampden in November, and figured in a goalless draw with Ireland at Wrexham in March. At season's end, far from earning a trip to Rio, we found ourselves in a sorry plight. We were wooden-spoonists in the International Tournament.

What can I say about these disappointing results? We had plenty of talent, as we frequently showed. And heaven knows, we tried! I've yet to play for a Welsh side that didn't do its darndest to win from the first to the last whistle. I suppose it was just one of those seasons when the ball didn't run for us.

Wales played one other international during the season, on November 23rd, 1949, against Belgium, and this marked the first visit of a Continental side to the Principality. During the winter, Belgium had beaten the Welsh touring team 3-0 at Liége, and we Red Dragons were intent on revenge against the Red Devils.

These were the teams:

WALES: Shortt; Barnes; Sherwood; I. Powell; T. Jones; Burgess; Griffiths; Paul; Ford; A. Powell and Clarke.

BELGIUM: Meert; Aernaudts; Gillard; Auwera; Carre; Mess; Lemberechts; Govard; Mermans; Chaves and de Hert.

While the Belgians lined up as they had done at Liége, only Ivor Powell, Tommy Jones, Ron Burgess, Mal Griffiths and Trevor Ford remained of the Welsh team on that occasion.

It was the first time I had played against the Belgian national side since my appearance against them at outside-left for Combines Services during the war. They played good football, but so did we. Wales were better than in any other match of the season and strolled home victors by 5-1. Trevor Ford scored a brilliant hat-trick.

As I understand it, there is no such thing as a professional player in Belgium, and all our opponents had jobs outside football. Centre-forward Joe Mermans, for instance, was a clerk, goalkeeper Meert a hairdresser, and right-back Aernaudts a butcher. They each received an "expenses fee" of about seventy shillings for this match.

Joe Mermanns, "Belgium's Tommy Lawton", was the player who impressed me most. He was dangerous with both feet, and with his head. The other Belgians – little chaps mostly – were clever enough. They had the knack of making us go the wrong way, but they had a habit of beating us too soon, leaving ample time for us to recover.

The influence of their trainer-coach Billy Gormilie, formerly Blackburn Rovers' goalkeeper (who was born in Wales), was apparent in a very useful move that the Belgians employed. This was the long winger-to-winger pass that Gordon Smith was to use with even greater effect against Wales when he represented the Rest of the United Kingdom in the 1951 anniversary match.

During, and following the 1949-50 campaign, Arsenal played a number of international club matches.

On November 1st, 1949, a week before the Wales v Scotland match at Hampden Park, the Gunners met the Racing Club in Paris and we beat them in this annual fixture for the first time since the war by 2-1. Joe Mercer, who had crossed the channel by boat, because he does not like to fly after September, had the distinction of scoring his first goal in Arsenal's colour in this match. He didn't score his first league goal until Arsenal's match at Blackpool in February 1953! The star performer in the

Paris team was none other than our old friend and former colleague, Albert Gudmundsson.

My enjoyment of this game was spoiled by the fact that my old leg injury was giving me a bit of trouble.

Our opponents were constantly exploiting the open space, but I say this with my tongue in my cheek because at Arsenal we tend to create open spaces on our opponents' behalf. As long as they use the open spaces *that we have created*, we know just where they are!

A month later, we received a visit from the A.I.K. team from Stockholm, who were not nearly as poor as the 8-0 score in Arsenal's favour suggests. I didn't play in this match, but it marked the successful return of Laurie Scott following his second cartilage operation.

At season's end we flew to Dublin where, on May 17th, we had another enjoyable encounter at Dalymount Park against a team of Irishmen known as "Bohemians Selected", which we won 5-2.

Two days later we took the famous "Enterprise" train non-stop from Dublin to Belfast, where we were to play an evening fixture against the Glentoran Irish League side strengthened by three guest players, one of who was Danny Blanchflower, of Barnsley, who I have since seen give outstanding displays for Ireland and Aston Villa.

The pitch on which we played was one of the worst I have ever encountered. Below sea level, it had been flooded for a number of years, and had had a soaking just before we arrived, drying out, uneven, dusty and bone-hard, hardly the type of surface we were used to. However, we managed to win 4-2.

After a short rest at home in London, Arsenal flew to Geneva to play the first of two matches against leading Swiss teams.

We spent a few days in the lap of luxury at our hotel on the shores of lovely Lake Geneva, before taking on the Servette team on a hot Monday evening at the Parc de Sports. From this ground the snow-capped peak of Mont Blanc is clearly visible.

Having watched Servette play a league match on the previous day, we had come to the conclusion that they were not likely to prove troublesome. As a result, we were in danger of suffering another "Oporto" until we pulled up our socks in the second half. We were lucky to win 3-1.

Part-time professionals, the Swiss were quick and nippy, playing the short-passing game with commendable precision. Their chief fault was a reluctance to shoot. Had they been more willing to have a go in the first half, Arsenal might easily have faced a three- or four-goal deficit.

The morning after this game we travelled by electric train through the beautiful scenery of the Bernese Oberland. We visited the Jungfrau at Wengen and spent a night at Interlaken before going through to Zurich. Here we were supposed to meet the Grasshoppers Club of Zurich, but found instead that the team to be fielded against us would be a representative Swiss side, and the one which would, in all probability, represent Switzerland in the World Cup.

"Someone's pulling a fast one on us," decided George Swindin, who was acting as skipper in the absence of Joe Mercer and Laurie Scott (Joe had his grocery business to attend to, while Laurie was on his way to Rio with the England team). Not that George was daunted at the idea of meeting the Swiss international team, any more than the rest of us were. Indeed, we were raring to have a go.

But English clubs are not normally allowed to play matches against representative sides of this kind, so Mr. Whittaker was compelled to wire a protest to the F.A., hoping, as we all were, that the F.A. would overlook the irregularity and allow us to play the match. We were all delighted when the boss told us that since the matter had gone so far, the match would be played as arranged, and I'm proud to say that we licked the Swiss World Cup team by 4-2!

The Arsenal team was the one which finished the match at Geneva after substitutions had been made at half-time, i.e.: Swindin (capt.); Barnes; L. Smith; Macaulay; Daniel; Shaw; McPherson; Logie; Goring; Lishman and Roper.

The match started in daylight and was played in floodlight in the second half. We took the lead after twelve minutes through a sizzling header by Lishman. Two minutes later Archie Macaulay drove home a second, and when Lishman added a third in the twentieth minute, we were able to settle down and play exhibition football which delighted the crowd. It was unfortunate that, during the second half, one of the lighting pylons at our end fused, making it rather difficult for us to see what was going on.

I enjoyed this trip to Switzerland very much, and was very pleased to be able to make a return visit with Arsenal in 1952. On this second occasion I was strictly a passenger. My injury, suffered in the 1952 Cup Final, prevented me from playing in any of the games, but I tried to make myself useful by helping Billy Milne pack the skips, stud the boots, and prepare the playing-kit. I also took it upon myself to sweep out the dressing-room before the players came back at half-time and full-time.

Apart from its beautiful scenery and the green grass pitches (greener than anywhere outside the British Isles) we all liked Switzerland for its immaculate cleanliness, and the Swiss people for their friendliness and hospitality.

We found the sun deceptively strong, and on the second trip Joe Mercer got an unpleasant dose of sunstroke after a round of golf at Lausanne where, strangely enough, the golf club secretary turned out to be Colonel Anderson, who had been the O.C. of the barracks at Aberdeen where Joe and I had stayed on a wartime Army tour.

Joe felt a bit dodgy for a couple of days, and when we made a coach tour round Lake Lucerne, he sat in the back seat covered up with blankets. Invited to join the rest of us on a shopping expedition, he shook his head glumly.

As players returned to the coach with cuckoo clocks and musical-boxes they showed them to Joe to try and cheer him up, but he showed little interest. Then I produced my own unusual purchase. At once he threw off his blankets, sat straight up and roared with laughter. Joe was cured!

The novelty purchase that worked the miracle? It was a musical toilet roll!

Chapter Twenty-One

The poor goalie seldom gets a second chance!

Playing in an international match for the first time is an ordeal for any player, but for a goalkeeper it can be a particularly terrifying experience. Others can make nervous mistakes in the opening stages and get away with them, but the man in goal dare not commit the slightest error in handling or judgement for fear of losing the game for his side.

I felt very sorry for young John Parry, of Swansea Town, who played his first match in goal for Wales on October 21st, 1950 (Trafalgar Day), against Scotland at Cardiff. John was only too eager to do his duty well, but the occasion proved too much for him and he made tragic slips that proved disastrous.

After twenty-three minutes play, following a throw-in near our right-hand corner flag, Lawrie Reilly put over a speculative shot. Parry appeared to have it well covered, but then, to our horror, we saw that he had completely misjudged the ball, letting it pass under his body and into the net to give Scotland the lead with the "softest" goal imaginable.

It was too much to expect that John would settle down to normal club form after this, but early in the second half he made another costly mistake – one which he must still have nightmares about. This time Billy Steel hit a centre across the goal. Again the goalkeeper appeared to have it well covered, but in the face of the aggressive Reilly, John appeared to panic, merely pushing the ball forward so that it rebounded from the knee of the oncoming centre-forward into the goal.

Aubrey Powell, a last minute replacement for the injured George Edwards, converted a centre by Roy Clarke to score a goal that momentarily raised our hopes, but almost immediately Billy Liddell headed a third and clinching goal for Scotland.

This wasn't a very satisfactory game from anyone's point of view. Even the Scots, on top though they were, earned a slating from skipper George Young at half-time. It's difficult to explain why two good teams, playing an important match under perfect conditions, in front of a large crowd, should give such poor value in soccer entertainment. On this occasion both teams were highly strung; perhaps they were trying *too* hard?

Despite those unfortunate lapses on Parry's part, our defense was satisfactory, with versatile Roy Paul making a success of the unfamiliar centre-half role. It was our forwards who let us down, and for once Trevor Ford had an off-day. This was understandable for, at the time, he was the centre of a blaze of publicity that would have put the most apathetic player off his stride; and Trevor is far from being insensitive in these matters.

One could hardly pick up a newspaper without seeing Trevor's name featured in the headlines. The story had leaked out that the famous centre-forward wanted to leave Aston Villa, and every day his name was coupled with that of a different club anxious to make a high bid for his services.

"What's it all about?" I asked Trevor before the match.

"I don't know, Walley," said the worried Trevor. "I certainly didn't expect all this fuss and bother. The plain truth is that I do want to find another club. I've been happy at Villa Park for three and a half years, but I don't think I'm doing the team or myself any good now because I just can't get goals like I used to. A change of club might bring me a change of luck. But when I asked for a transfer, the last thing I expected or wanted was to become the centre of a manhunt!"

The following Friday night it was reported that Trevor had been transferred to Sunderland for a fee of nearly £30,000, and the change of club did seem to bring him the change of luck he needed, because he did the hat-trick on his first appearance at Roker Park as a Sunderland player.

I think I've said enough about the Wales v Scotland match – it wasn't one that either Welsh or Scottish supporters would wish me to dwell on.

Although we did badly against Scotland, and season's end again found us disputing possession of the wooden spoon with Ireland, it soon became apparent that our form was better than that of the previous season and that we were beginning to mould into a useful side.

Team talks were now left more or less in my hands, with Doc Hughes and trainer Walter Robbins sitting-in to give us the benefit of their valuable experience. In addition I was helped in my general approach to problems by the wise counsel and philosophy of Mr. Bill Dodman.

"Play your football like I used to train Basham," Bill told me before our match with England on November 15th, 1950, at Sunderland. "Get in there and take your opponents out of their stride before they can settle down."

That's exactly what we planned to do. Only bad luck robbed the plan of success.

Before I go any further, however, I'd like to remind you of the line-up for this important match, because both teams included new names of special significance:

WALES: Hughes (Luton Town); Barnes (Arsenal) capt.; Sherwood (Cardiff); Paul (Manchester City); Daniel (Arsenal); Lucas (Swansea): Griffiths (Leicester City); Allen (Coventry City); Ford (Sunderland); Allchurch (Swansea) and Clarke (Manchester City).

ENGLAND: Williams (Wolves); Ramsey (Spurs) capt.; L. Smith (Arsenal); Watson (Sunderland); L. Compton (Arsenal); Dickinson (Portsmouth); Finney (Preston North End); Mannion (Middlesbrough), Milburn (Newcastle United) Baily (Spurs) and Medley (Spurs).

When he heard that Arsenal were to supply both centre-halves, surely a remarkable record, and that Lionel Smith had been honoured for the first time by England, Tom Whittaker declared, "I couldn't be more delighted if I was picked to play myself." And we were all pleased that big Leslie, at thirty-eight years of age, had at last been rewarded with the full cap that his consistent ability had undoubtedly deserved.

Ray Daniel, who had done well on Arsenal's South American tour but had actually played only seven senior league games, had his pleasure of selection increased by the knowledge that his former Swansea school friend, Ivor Allchurch, would also be making a first appearance in the Welsh jersey. Iowerth Hughes was another newcomer to our ranks. For a long time his brilliant goalkeeping had kept English international Bernard Streten out of the Luton side and our only worry about him was whether he would be fit in time. Luckily he made the grade in a final test and took his place to play a really good game. We were less lucky in getting Ronnie Burgess's swollen calf down to normal proportions, and although his place was kept open until the last second, it was filled ultimately, and brilliantly, by Billy Lucas.

My opposite number as captain this time was the quietly-spoken, gentlemanly character, Alf Ramsey, who stood in for Billy Wright, another casualty. Although captaining our countries, neither Alf nor I were club captains, but there were at least half a dozen club captains in the ranks!

In Billy's place at right-half was Willie Watson, an Army chum of mine, enjoying a bit of luck for a change. By accompanying the England World Cup team to Rio during the summer, Willie had forfeited his chance of selection for the M.C.C. on their cricket tour of Australia, so imagine Willie's chagrin when he failed to get a single game in Rio!

At our Newcastle hotel I tried to give the Welsh team the lowdown on how to beat my Arsenal mates.

A potential English defensive weakness, as I saw it, lay in the differing styles of Alf Ramsey and Leslie Compton. I knew Alf liked to play square, right out with the winger, while big Les seldom strayed from the middle of the pitch. Clearly if these key

209

men stuck to their normal club styles a gap would be left that we could exploit.

Of course I didn't mention this to big Les or Lionel, when I visited them in the English dressing-room before the kick-off.

"I suppose it's all right to talk to this foreigner?" big Les asked his skipper mischievously, remembering, no doubt, the time he had been ticked-off for fraternizing with me during a wartime international.

The game hadn't been in progress very long before the suspected England gap created by the positioning of Ramsey and Compton, was exposed, and we kept putting long balls between them for Roy Clarke to run on to. Alas, Roy was not nearly so quick on the uptake as usual, and he let a number of chances go begging, until Trevor Ford presented him with a gilt-edged opening and then Roy banged the ball into the net.

It looked a perfectly good goal to me, and nearly to everyone else too, but the referee gave Clarke offside. "How could Roy have been offside with Lionel Smith standing alongside Williams on the goal-line?" that frustrated spectator, Ronnie Burgess, wanted to know afterwards. I don't know the answer, Ronnie. What I do know is that this unfortunate decision was the turning-point of the whole game.

In the thirtieth minute Lionel Smith brought the ball up-field on his own and took a good look round before placing a pass to Eddie Baily, which the Spurs' forward collected on the eighteen-yard line. Baily had his back to our goal as he killed the ball with his right foot. Then he swung round and hit a shot with his left that gave the acrobatic Hughes no chance whatsoever.

But the goal should never have happened. Mal Griffiths should have tackled Lionel Smith when Lionel was two yards away from him on the halfway line, and Mal was wrong to assume that the full-back was not his responsibility in this particular movement. It brings home the lesson that a winger should play just as much part in defense as a full-back should play in attack.

Baily scored a second goal five minutes before the interval.

Three minutes after the restart, Mal made amends for his previous lapse by putting across a perfect centre from which Trevor Ford scored. Now we were back in the game with a vengeance, launching attack after attack on the England goal.

But Ramsey and Compton had tumbled to our ruse and were playing closer together. Try as they did, the Welsh forwards could not find a way through, and it was England, after a Mannion breakaway, who actually scored the next goal.

Although 3-1 down we tried all the harder, and in the seventy-fourth minute Trevor Ford again reduced England's lead with a fast low shot from Mal Griffiths's pass.

It was a grand, exciting game, packed with good football, and the result was in the balance until thirty seconds from the end when Jackie Milburn finally broke clear of Ray Daniel and scored from an acute angle.

Ray had no need to blame himself for this goal in any way. He had an excellent match, while his school chum Ivor Allchurch showed all the hallmarks of a class player. Both youngsters did more than enough to retain their places against Ireland later in the year. In fact we kept the same team except that Ronnie Burgess was fit, so he naturally returned to left-half, and new chum Noel Kinsey, then with Norwich City, was capped at inside-right.

Six days before the match against Ireland, I played for the Football Combination in Paris, and Ray Daniel and Noel Kinsey were also members of the Combination team. My full-back partner was none other than Alf Ramsey!

I was impressed with the scheming ability of twenty-five-year-old Kinsey on this occasion. Playing inside to Jack Froggatt, he had a prominent hand in the two goals scored by Charlie Vaughan that gave us victory.

But the Paris game was played on an iron-hard pitch. The muddy conditions at Windsor Park, Belfast, did not suit Noel's style nearly so well. His own modest assumption that he was "out of his class" was not entirely justified. Few of the other players were able to hit top form on this bitter, rainy day.

Quite the best thing in the Wales v Ireland game was the winning goal, in the last three minutes, made for Roy Clarke by Trevor Ford.

Ray Daniel stopped a spirited Irish attack and cleared to Roy Paul, who moved the ball on to Ford. Trevor beat two men before teeing the ball up for Clarke to have a go at it, and Roy cracked a beauty into the top of the net.

Bill Dickson, one of five new caps in the Irish team, gave the first of many sterling performances for his country.

On May 12th, with an unchanged team, we beat Portugal 2-1 in a special Festival of Britain match at Cardiff, thus gaining revenge for a defeat Wales had sustained at the National Stadium, Lisbon, two years previously.

I had not played against the Portuguese national side before, though some of the players were familiar to me as a result of Arsenal's tour. The Portuguese left-half and captain, Ferriera, for example, had given a good display against my club when playing for Benfica, and he again impressed me as did Jose Travacos the dark little inside-left who kept his fellow forwards well supplied with passes. I liked Ben David, the young centre-forward who, I believe, was once a fine high-jumper. He certainly showed ability in heading duels.

The Welsh team were in top gear and gave their best display of the season. Like so many Continental teams, our opponents were inclined to make two passes where one would do. They were more than a little foxed because this time our venturesome wing-halves did a 100 per cent job in defense, closing gaps that the Portuguese had exploited to good effect in the previous encounter.

An interesting innovation in this international match was that, at the request of our visitors, it was agreed to permit the substitution of two players for men injured up to the forty-fourth minute, and a substitute for the goalkeeper at any time during the match.

So Billy Shortt, Billy Lucas and Glyn Williams stood by as substitutes for Wales.

I don't want to see our game follow American football, or ice hockey, and have complete teams standing by on the side-lines ready to be thrown into the fray at a strategic moment, but I can see no reason why substitutes should not be allowed for injured players in international football as they were in our Festival of Britain match.

What of Arsenal in 1950-51? We made a good start, and were top of the league and heading for the championship when suddenly we cracked. Not only did we fail to win a single point over Christmas, but Duggie Lishman, our leading marksman and best forward, cracked a bone in his leg on Christmas day, and Alex Forbes, Jimmy Logie and George Swindin were all hurt. In the end we limped home fifth in the league.

Our dreams of reaching Wembley for the second year in succession were dispelled fourteen days after the Northampton game when we travelled to Manchester. United knocked us out by the only goal in a drab game.

Indeed, our display in this fifth-round tie was almost on a par with that given by Arsenal against Blackpool in the 1952-53 competition. Need I say more?

By far the best game of the 1950-51 season, in my opinion, was Arsenal's league match against Blackpool at Highbury on December 9th. From a spectator's point of view this had everything to be desired – a sparkling display by Stan Matthews at his best; speed, thrills, good football and eight exciting goals.

The match fell distinctly into two halves. In the first, playing in a way that justified our position at the top of the league, we led by 3-1. Young Mudie put Withers through to score he opening goal for Blackpool in the fourth minute, but then, in a blaze of Arsenal glory, Lishman, Forbes and Goring in turn rammed the ball into the Blackpool net.

Came the second half and Stanley Matthews matched our craft with his own special brand of magic, which cracked our defense wide open. With those bewildering runs and two-way body swerves of his, he flummoxed three or four of us at a time, opening the way for two equalizing goals.

I thought I had seen it all before, but it was brought home to me that we shall all have grown long beards before we find a reliable way of outwitting the maestro.

True, after the first goal, Lionel Smith hurt his knee and had to change places with Don Roper, but Hapgood, Male, Crompton and Pennington rolled into one would have made little impression against Stanley on this particular afternoon, so the match had little significance.

With the score at 3-3 we were doing our best to hold on to a point if we could, but nerves were taut; anything could happen, and when it did it had to happen to me! Harry Johnston put a high ball into our goal area that was probably not nearly as dangerous as I supposed, but I felt it necessary to make a desperate attempt to clear the ball, although facing my own goal, and in doing so only succeeded in diverting it into the net. Was my face red!

What a strange game soccer is, though. Less than two minutes later, with the Blackpool goal scarcely in danger, an opponent had a similar attack of jitters and brought Duggie Lishman down in the area. I took the spot-kick and scored to draw the match.

I've already given some ideas on "how to score goals from penalty kicks". Now I'll tell you how to save them.

Playing in goal for Arsenal in a charity match against Joe Mercer's old club, Ellesmere Port Town, at the end of the season, I was twice called upon to face a penalty. Both times I prevented the ball from entering the net.

In saving the first shot I beat the pistol by about five seconds (don't tell the ref!). From the second spot kick the ball went one way and I went the other. Miraculously, however, my flying legs got in the way of the ball and diverted it over the bar!

214

The most surprised men on the York Road ground that day were Ray Daniel and Lionel Smith. When they learned that I was to wear the goalkeeper's jersey, since neither George Swindin nor Ted Platt was available, they had worked out a plot to bring about my downfall. One of their ideas, I discovered afterwards, was to call me out of goal and then put a long punt over my head into the net.

I suspect that the two penalties given away to our Cheshire County League opponents were also part of the plot against me. Under the circumstances, I think I can fairly claim to have countered it and turned the joke against my colleagues. They no longer laugh when I sit down to save goals.

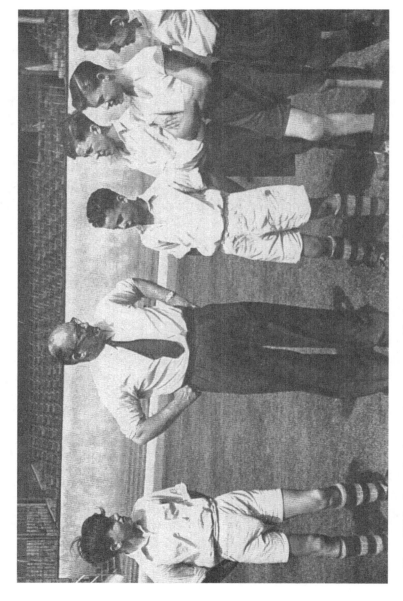

Tom Whittaker, the Arsenal manager, will always make time to help the "stars of tomorrow".

Walley Barnes leaving the Royal Northern Hospital, London, in November, 1952, following his cartilage operation. He is accompanied by his wife, Joan, and daughter, Sandra.

Chapter Twenty-Two

It was one of the proudest moments of my life when I led the Sons of Wales on to the field at Ninian Park, Cardiff, on Wednesday December 5th, 1951, to meet the pick of England, Scotland and Ireland in a special Welsh anniversary international match. Despite the strength of the opposition we were determined to win.

I had travelled from Paddington in the company of Eddie Baily and Les Medley, of the Spurs, and of the five Scots who were to figure amongst the opposition. I suffered a good deal of good-humoured barracking, particularly from that cheerful "Cockney sparrow" Eddie Baily, when I forecast a Welsh victory; obviously my travelling companions did not share my opinion. However, although I failed to convince them that Wales produced the world's finest footballers, I did manage to persuade Gordon Smith that the "Walley Barnes' football boot" was in a class of its own! As a result of this I later received an order from the Hibernian Club for twenty pairs of my special boots!

As for the game, it may have been a showpiece, and a birthday occasion, but the atmosphere on the field of play was far from light-hearted.

"What *is* this?" Eddie Baily demanded to know, after he had been vigorously tackled by Roy Paul in the opening stages. "Anyone would think it's the Cup Final and Rugby League Final rolled into one!"

"This is one match were going to win," answered Roy grimly as he belted the ball up-field.

The Welsh team was magnificent, full of brilliant football, teamwork and *Hwyl* – our own special brand of national spirit – and our tactics of "striking while the iron's hot" paid handsome dividends. Within six minutes we were two goals in the lead, thanks to Ivor Allchurch, who headed home after a brilliant run by

Ronnie Burgess, and to Trevor Ford, who calmly drew Cowan out of goal and then put the ball past him.

Soon after half-time, Billy Morris hit the post with his header from a Ronnie Burgess pass and then Ivor Allchurch scored a third goal for Wales.

But don't run away with the idea that the Rest of the U.K. were letting us off lightly. I can assure you that they tried as hard as they knew how to win, and they fought to the last whistle, scoring two goals in the last twenty minutes and putting enough pressure on our defense to test it to the utmost.

Gordon Smith really showed his paces in the second half – I've never known him so dangerous. He was playing deep and hitting cross-field passes to Medley which kept us at full stretch and partially open in defense.

And I've seldom seen a more powerful shot than the one which Charlie Flemming, the East Fife inside-right, drove into our net from thirty yards. It was there almost before Billy Shortt could move to it.

Then, with about a quarter of an hour to go, Les Medley collected a pass from Eddie Baily and put over a spinner that deceived us all. It hit the far post and went into the net.

These were both inspired goals, but it would have taken all the magic of Merlin to outwit us in our determination to win. And what a splendid victory it was!

Just take a look at the team that was opposing us, and judge its strength:

Cowan (Scotland); Young (Scotland); McMichael (Ireland); Docherty (Scotland); Vernon (Ireland) capt.; Wright (England); Smith (Scotland); Fleming (Scotland); Lofthouse (England); Baily (England) and Medley (England).

"I'm glad we don't have to play as hard as that every week," said big George Young to me as we made our way wearily

219

to the dressing–room. "Still, I'm really pleased and proud to have taken part."

It would be invidious to select one member of the Welsh side for special praise because my colleagues were all good, and it was a team victory, but I must say that this was the best of many brilliant games that I have seen Ronnie Burgess play, both in defense and attack, while Roy Paul had a field-day against the England left-wing triangle.

Two months earlier, at Cardiff, Wales had begun her anniversary season in stirring fashion. Three and a half minutes after the kick-off against England we scored, and the man who did the trick was little Billy Foulkes *with his first kick in international football.*

Quick-thinking Roy Paul took an indirect free-kick and hit the ball just as the whistle sounded. Between ourselves, he was lucky to get away with it because the ball was still rolling when he hit it! Anyway, it nearly caught Billy Foulkes unawares, but full marks to Billy for his lightening reaction – he took the ball in his stride and crashed it into the net from close range. Not strictly a fair goal – but why look a gift-horse in the mouth?

Soon afterwards Les Medley put over a crafty centre which Eddie Baily converted with a header for the equalizer. It was the end of the scoring in this match, but we missed two gilt-edged opportunities of going ahead later in the first half, and were so much on top throughout the rest of the game that, looking back, it seems incredible to me that we did not win by several clear goals. Certainly, as it was generally agreed, and despite the nature of the goal we did score, the moral victory was ours.

At the start of this game I tried a little experiment in tactics, asking Ivor Allchurch to stay back and forage for the other forwards in Brazilian style, but we abandoned the scheme in the second half because by then it was obvious that it wasn't working as I intended.

These were the teams:

WALES: Shortt; Barnes (capt.); Sherwood; Paul; Daniel; Burgess; Foulkes; Kinsey; Ford; Allchurch and Clarke.

ENGLAND: Williams; Ramsey; L. Smith; Wright (capt.); Barrass; Dickinson; Finney; Thompson; Lofthouse; Baily and Medley.

England had made six changes in the team which drew 2-2 with France at Highbury a fortnight previously, and I think I can say we gave the English selectors an even bigger headache as a result of our showing against their new combination. They made three further changes for their next match against Ireland.

Wales, on the other hand, made only one change for the next match against Scotland, Billy Morris replacing Noel Kinsey at inside-right, and that is the team we stuck to for the rest of the campaign.

While England were beating Ireland 2-0 at Villa Park, we gained a 1-0 victory at Glasgow, and the Scots were saying that this was the best Welsh team they had ever seen.

But what a near thing it was! Instead of starting the game with a goal in the opening minutes as we had done against England, there were only ninety seconds left to play when Ivor Allchurch headed in the winning goal.

Once more, Billy Foulkes was the hero, because with Roy Paul he engineered the match-winner, ably supported by Roy Clarke and Trevor Ford.

Billy worked the ball through to the centre on his own, then stabbed the ball through to Trevor who squared to Roy. The winger sent over a pin-point centre which Ivor hit hard and true into the net with his head.

This was the Scottish team:

Cowan; Young; Cox; Docherty; Woodburn; Forbes; Waddell; Orr; Reilly; Steel and Liddell.

221

In this match I was again struck by the poor form of Billy Steel, whose passes were continually going astray. Billy never seems to show his real ability against Wales – perhaps Roy Paul is his "hoodoo" man?

In March, we came to the match against Ireland, a special one for at least two reasons. Firstly, it was played at Swansea, and it was the first time for twenty-five years that Vetch Field had staged an international, although this was the ground where such grand players as Ivor Allchurch, Roy Paul, Ray Daniel and Trevor Ford had begun their illustrious careers. Secondly, we knew that by beating Ireland we would ensure at least sharing the championship honours, with a chance to win the tournament outright if England failed to beat Scotland at Hampden.

Red-headed Alf McMichael, who was to be my opposite number in the Cup Final, and who had already played for the Rest of the U.K. against Wales that season, was Irish skipper for the first time, while Seamus D'Arcy, then with Chelsea, was honoured for the first time. Bill Dickson, the then Chelsea wing-half, was rather surprisingly played in the centre-half position, but what a grand performance he gave. Not many centre-halves can claim to have played Trevor Ford out of the game, but in this match Bill got as near to doing so as anyone else has ever done.

Although we won decisively by 3-0, in all honesty we were not as superior as the result would indicate, and Mr. Powell and myself had to give the team a pep-talk at half-time to prevent the development of a false sense of security. One reason for the poor standard of play from both teams was the difficult surface – a hard crust had formed over mud, making ball control very tricky. The only really satisfactory goal was our second, scored by Swansea's Ivor Allchurch from a corner six minutes from the end.

Up to then we led by a penalty goal, which I scored early in the second half. Bill Dickson brought Trevor Ford down, and Cup Final referee Arthur Ellis pointed to the penalty-spot.

In my opinion Trevor Ford *was* fouled, but outside the area. Indeed the slide marks finished at least three yards outside.

222

But the referee was quite adamant in his decision. What should I do? Place my penalty-kick playfully past the post, or into the goalkeeper's hands?

No! That would be ridiculous. My own opinion of this decision did not matter in the least. It was plainly my duty to score for my side if I could, and score I did. I felt no scruples in doing this, and I'd do the same again.

Fortunately, however, Ivor scored that second goal towards the end – and there was no doubt about it being fair – and in the last minute Roy Clarke put in a third, a rather "flukey" one from the touch-line. At the banquet afterwards, Alf McMichael was called upon to make a speech. He got to his feet, and the first words he used were, "I still think it wasn't a penalty…!"

Naturally, we would all have preferred to finish the campaign in a blaze of glory, instead of in this somewhat unconvincing fashion, but I won't allow this match to detract from the honour which the Welsh team won in 1951-52. If we had a little luck here, we certainly didn't have it against England and, of course, ultimately we only shared top of the table position with England because they went on to win at Hampden.

Our success in the international championship was all the more remarkable when it is borne in mind that Wales used only twelve players in her three international matches.

The last time Wales had shared the championship was in the triple tie with England and Scotland in 1938-39, having last won it outright in 1936-37. This is how we finished:

	P	W	D	L	Goals	Pts
Wales	3	2	1	0	5-1	5
England	3	2	1	0	5-2	5
Scotland	3	1	0	2	4-3	2
Ireland	3	0	0	3	0-8	0

Chapter Twenty-Three

"How does it feel now, Walley?"

"Not so good."

Billy Milne sighed and shook his head.

"Well, that's it I'm afraid. Better make up your mind that you've had it this time."

The scene was the dressing-room at Wembley Stadium: the subject of conversation – my right knee, injured during the first twenty minutes of the 1952 Cup Final.

There was no doubt that trainer Billy Milne was right. I couldn't stand up without pain, let alone resume my place on the field where ten men of Arsenal were fighting their grim, never-say-die battle against Newcastle United.

Thirty minutes earlier I had taken the field to play in my second Final, sharing my team-mate's hope and determination to make this match a fitting climax to our most memorable season.

And what a season it had been! Helped by "new chums" Cliff Holton and Arthur Milton, we had maintained steady form in the league championship from the start. In the Cup we blasted our way through to the semi-finals, beating Barnsley (at home), and Norwich City, Leyton Orient and Luton Town (away) in convincing style.

Our semi-final opponents were Arsenal's great Cup rivals, Chelsea. A violent snowstorm on Boat Race Saturday caused the tie to be postponed and this, I believe, created something of a record, besides causing a mix-up in our league fixtures and robbing Alex Forbes of a cap, for which he would have been due on the revised date.

When the postponed semi-final tie resulted in a 1-1 draw, our fixture list grew even more crowded. It seems that ninety minutes' play is never long enough for us to get the better of our doughty opponents from South London. In the replay, however, Freddie Cox again did his stuff to help put us into the Final. We

224

remained in a favourable position in the League, so what price the Cup and League double?

The price was high. Played to a standstill through our heavy programme, crippled by injuries to almost every member of the team, we stood level on points with Manchester United with two games to go before the Cup Final.

Hard-hit by injuries, our team at West Bromwich included six reserves, and we lost 3-1, which meant that we had to beat Manchester United 7-0 at Old Trafford to win the title. It just wasn't possible, and in fact, after that grand team man Arthur Shaw broke his wrist in the first ten minutes, we were well and truly beaten 6-1. So much for the double.

But there was still the Cup and, thanks to a last-minute dispensation by Lady Luck, all our injured players were happily restored to the ranks. This is how we took the field:

ARSENAL: Swindin; Barnes; Smith; Forbes; Daniel; Mercer; Cox; Logie; Holton; Lishman and Roper.

NEWCASTLE UNITED: Simpson; Cowell; McMichael; Harvey; Brennan; E. Robledo; Walker; Foulkes; Milburn; G. Robledo and Mitchell.

For the first fifteen minutes of the game we were on top – no doubt about that. Doug Lishman, fresh from his hospital bed, missed scoring by a hair's breadth with an overhead shot in the fourth minute. Soon after, Jimmy Logie, also a hospital patient four days earlier with an injured thigh, went through on his own and nearly netted.

I thought it could only be a matter of time before we took the lead. But this optimism was ill-founded: Lady Luck had only been having a jest at our expense. In the nineteenth minute Jackie Milburn appeared on the left-wing. He attempted to back-heel the ball to Mitchell and I tried to whip it away from him. Changing direction, I felt a stab of pain in my leg as the studs of my right boot stuck in the turf and the full weight of my body was borne by the ligaments of my right knee. The knee couldn't take the strain and I collapsed.

Billy Milne ran on to the pitch and strapped my knee up then and there. "Can you carry on, Walley?" Joe Mercer asked anxiously. I tested my leg and it made me wince. But I nodded quickly. "I'll carry on," I told Joe.

A few minutes later, however, I had to make a "giant-stride" tackle in order to dispossess George Robledo, who was coming through with the ball on the edge of the penalty area. In making the tackle, the full weight of my body was thrown on to my injured knee; and this time I'd really bought it. I had to leave the field altogether.

I sat on the trainer's bench alongside Mr. Whittaker while Billy Milne restrapped my injured knee. Meantime, Don Roper had moved into my place at right-back, and was giving his usual, capable performance.

As soon as I found I could stand up and hobble I told Mr. Whittaker that I wanted to return to the pitch. "If I can hang on, then I might at least have a nuisance value," I suggested.

"All right, Walley, it's up to you," said the boss. "If you think you can manage it take over the outside-right position." So I stood on the touchline and waited for the ball to go out of play so that I could fill the vacancy on the wing. Freddie Cox had switched to outside-left.

Soon after I returned I found myself within eight yards of goal, and I thought, "If only Freddie Cox could get the ball across I could push it in," but a defender headed the ball away before it could reach me. Otherwise I might have forestalled Eric Bell, of Bolton, the "cripple" who scored under similar circumstances the following year.

Then, after twenty-five minutes' play, George Swindin made a long clearance. The ball came towards me and, in attempting to head it, I was challenged by Alf McMichael. I stumbled, collided with the half-way touch-flag, and the flag snapped in half like a carrot under my weight as I fell.

That was the end of the 1952 Cup Final for me. Billy Milne helped me off the field and into the dressing-room, and the thought uppermost in my mind was that I had let the rest of the lads down. How could they possibly avoid defeat now, with only ten men and an hour still to play?

I didn't mind so much for myself – well, I'd already got a winners' medal. But I knew how much it meant to Lionel Smith, Ray Daniel, Cliff Holton, Doug Lishman and Don Roper, who had not been in the 1950 team. They were the chaps I was thinking of at that moment.

Later, as I lay on the table in the dressing-room with Billy Milne to comfort me, messages from the field of play bolstered our hopes slightly. And when there were only seven minutes left to play, and still no score, we even started to think that the boys might after all achieve the "impossible" – hold out and force a replay.

Then we heard a roar from the crowd, and Billy and I exchanged a glance. There was something awfully conclusive about that cheer.

We heard slow, hesitant footsteps approaching down the tunnel and, after a pause, the door opened to reveal the figure of a very dejected-looking dressing-room attendant. He seemed at a loss for words to tell his news.

At length, "We're one down," he said. Quite unconsciously he had employed the personal pronoun.

That dressing-room attendant must have seen dozens of Cup Finals and big, international matches. Great dramas were everyday events in his life, and one team was like another. But obviously this match was affecting him like no other had done: all his emotion had become entangled in it, and there was no doubt which side his sympathy lay.

I believe that the dressing-room attendant was just one of many new friends that Arsenal's "gallant ten" won on 1952 Cup Final day.

Newcastle boss Stan Seymour visited our dressing-room after the match and he told us, "We've won the Cup, but you've won the glory." To this statement I added a hearty "Hear, hear" when I saw the film of the match. All credit to Newcastle United – it takes a great team to win the Cup two years in succession – but I belonged to Arsenal, and I was made prouder of that knowledge than I had ever been before.

There is no doubt that season 1951-52 was the most memorable of my career. Wales shared the international championship and beat the Rest of Britain in the special anniversary match, and Arsenal came nearer to achieving the Cup and League double than any club during the century.

I played fifty-eight games altogether, including the Cup Final. The only league match I missed was the one against Charlton, and that was due to the fact that I was captaining Wales against England. I had forty-one league games, and on December 15th at Huddersfield I captained Arsenal for the first time. I also had the honour of leading my club in three subsequent league matches, against Wolves (with my old England rival Billy Wright opposing me), West Bromwich Albion and Portsmouth.

And, after all that, in the last and most important club game of all, I had to suffer another leg injury, serious enough to put me out of action for the whole of the following season.

After accompanying Arsenal to Switzerland in May I spent the rest of the summer having remedial treatment for my knee, and doing light training. My knee didn't make the progress that I hoped for. August ball practice revealed that the knee was still rocking either way and fluid remained on the joint. It was a bit of a mystery. As time went on we began to suspect that there was a foreign body there, and after a meeting with the boss and the club surgeon, towards the end of September, it was decided that I should enter the Royal Northern Hospital to have an operation.

When the knee was opened up the surgeon did not find a foreign body, but he did discover that my cartilage was split. It looked like a haricot bean split long-ways! The cartilage was duly removed and within a few days I was busy exercising my leg muscles while in bed to keep them in tone. I found that I could lift my leg without pain and had great hopes of playing again as early as November. My greatest wish, of course, was to be fit to take my place in the Welsh team against England at Wembley, probably the most important fixture my country ever had, and I knew that it was possible to start playing again six weeks after a cartilage operation.

Unfortunately, however, although I got down to tentative training within a fortnight of my release from hospital, and received daily treatment from Billy Milne and Bert Owen, it soon became obvious that I had been over-optimistic. At thirty-three years of age, recovery from a serious injury can be a tedious business, and I just had to be patient and let time act as the healer.

During those long weeks out of the game I couldn't help remembering the words of the Newcastle United specialist who examined my knee immediately after the Cup Final.

"Your cartilage has gone," he told me at once.

I didn't believe him: didn't want to, I suppose. If only I'd been able to act on his advice at once, however, I might have been spared months of frustration. My job is to play football – not to watch. I hate watching my own team. Kicking imaginary footballs is much more exhausting than kicking real ones!

At this stage I must express my appreciation to all those people who helped me during my long lay-off. I want to thank the staff of the Royal Northern Hospital, for whose skilful treatment and thoughtful attention I and my Arsenal mates have had so much reason to be grateful.

Next I must mention the members of the Press, who continued to write nice things about me, helping me to keep my pecker up.

I've always tried my best to help the Press boys to do their job, and I must say I've had more than a square deal from them as a result. They haven't always praised my play of course – often they've given me a kick in the pants, and I've deserved it! But nearly always their criticism has been helpful and constructive, and I've yet to meet the sports' writer who did not respect a confidence. That may surprise you, but it's a fact.

Among my Press friends I must mention Dowey Lewis (*Western Mail*), John Graydon (*Kemsley Newspapers*), Desmond Hackett and John Thompson (*Daily Express*), Roy Peskett (*Daily Mail*), Bob Ferrier (*Daily Mirror*), Scottie Hall and Jack Milligan (*Daily Sketch*), Clifford Webb (*Daily Herald*), Charles Buchan (*News Chronicle*), Frank Coles (*Daily Telegraph*), Frank Butler and Harry Ditton (*News of the World*), Alan Hoby (*Sunday Express*), Ivan Sharpe (*Sunday Chronicle*), Pat Reekie (*Sunday Dispatch*), Maurice Smith (*People*), Gilroy (*Sunday Graphic*), Capell Kirby (*Empire News*), Bernard Joy (*Star*), Bill McGowran and John Orange (*Evening News*), Harold Palmer (*Evening Standard*), Archie Quick (*Army Newspapers*) and, of course, my friend Ken Wheeler (*Kenneth Wheeler Ltd*), who has helped me to compile this book, all of whom have given me more than a fair crack of the whip for many years.

Finally, I want to thank my club. How can I ever repay them for all they did for me? Not only did they provide the finest medical attention and advice, but they kept me on full wages all the time.

Don't tell me that clubs are out to exploit the professional footballer! As you can see, my own experience makes nonsense of such an idea.

Of course, I speak as an Arsenal player, and players from other clubs have told me that this makes a difference.

When a famous English international player visited Highbury recently he told me that he would give a year's wages to have the honour of playing for Arsenal! Another famous player, and a loyal member of a Northern club, admitted: "Of course, we all know that there's only one club in football. We'd all want to play for the Arsenal if we had the choice."

It makes you think!

Speaking as a one-club professional player I've been completely happy at Highbury, and the idea of moving to another club has never entered my head. I think that goes for most of us. It's all part of what I can only call the Arsenal family spirit. From the Chairman of Directors to Len Taylor, the commissionaire; from Tom Whittaker to Danny who "fetches the tea"; from Bob Wall to the youngest player on the staff we're like a band of brothers – squabbling often enough, arguing and losing our tempers in everyday conversation on every subject except one: the Arsenal. Where the well-being of our club is concerned we all pull together.

For instance, off the field, Jimmy Logie and I haven't always seen eye to eye: probably it's been a clash of personalities. But when we're both wearing the red shirt it's different. I'd give my last breath to see that Jimmy is properly backed-up, and I know that he'd do the same for me. In action no differences exist between us.

Sometimes I have openly disagreed with the boss's selection of a player I considered "not ready" or "off form". Having had my say, however, in the game itself I have found myself going out of my way to help that player to do well, hoping against hope that the boss would prove right, and I wrong! I know that this is also the attitude of my colleagues.

The 1952 Arsenal team to which I was so proud to belong, was not perhaps a great one compared with the side of twenty years earlier. We had no outstanding personalities like Alex James or Eddie Hapgood. But we got good results, and since other teams have not deteriorated I can only conclude that we must have had

231

our fair share or team spirit, guts and determination to get where we did.

Undoubtedly each member of the team gave his utmost of strength and endurance in the fight for the "double".

Yet we failed, and I'm not going to suggest that "the double" is impossible in modern times.

Some people seem to think that a team should concentrate exclusively on one target – the Cup, the League title, or on avoiding relegation. I don't subscribe to that opinion. In my view, any team worth its salt will play is hardest every game no matter what else is at stake.

Adopting this attitude, a team CAN achieve the "double", I feel sure.

Because of the injury bugbear, I think we play enough football at present – but not too much. Physically, two hard ninety-minute games every week should not make the slightest difference to the player who is fit. Mentally, with league points and the Cup in the balance, there is a good deal of strain which only team spirit built on a solid foundation can overcome.

Pursuing the subject of physical fitness for a moment, I do not think that all British footballers train hard enough. Often there are signs of flagging in the last twenty minutes of a hard game.

You will find players who do their full whack of training, and those who do less. But soccer is a team game, and every member of the team must be capable of giving his maximum effort for the full ninety minutes.

If Britain is to retain supremacy in world soccer this is a particularly important point. The whole business or training must be seriously investigated. Not only must we train more rigorously, but we must consider revising our methods. Let's get out of the habit of assuming that because we taught the world to play soccer that our traditional methods must always remain the ideal. We should study the way that other countries prepare, and where they hit on a successful idea we should consider adopting it. Why not?

Uruguay are present holders of the World Cup. They won the championship with a very young team who trained together for nearly two years before the Rio competition. According to all the expert Brazilian coaches, their success was due not so much to outstanding ability as to really superb fitness.

I hesitate to recommend that we should slavishly copy the Uruguayan methods. It would mean pilfering league clubs of their most promising young stars, and isolating those players from league football so that they might be welded into a world-beating national team. I think it's the answer, but I wonder if it would be fair to the clubs, or to the British public who naturally want to see those young stars develop with their own team.

Certainly it would mean a sacrifice. Are they prepared to make it in order that Britain should have the best possible chance of winning the highest world honours?

Apart from the international aspect I feel that the club training should be more rigorous. Let's at least put in a full day's training *every* day – like the Brazilians, with lapping in the mornings and ball practice in the afternoons. I'm sure the standard of play would improve as a result. It's full of difficulties, of course; the older players like me, who, rightly I believe, are permitted to run businesses and hold outside jobs, would find plenty of snags. But none that can't be overcome. Ask Jim Peters about that. The British marathon champion does forty training runs every month, totalling nearly 300 miles AND he spends eight hours at his optician's shop each day.

This business of trotting round the track for a couple of hours five mornings a week and spending the rest of the time chatting in cafes is no good for young players. Let them consider their own future in the game. Why is it that players like Stanley Matthews, Sam Bartram and Joe Mercer are still in the front rank although nearly forty years of age? Superb physical fitness, the result of years of hard training and self-denial is their background, and that's the answer. They know you cannot take anything out of sport without putting something into it, and they have reaped the benefit of their wisdom.

Chapter Twenty-Four

What do I do with myself when I'm not playing football? Plenty! I've already made it clear that I believe in doing a full day's training, in addition to which, in case you didn't know, I devote a considerable amount of time to the running of my sports outfitting business, which is situated opposite Harringay Stadium, London.

In 1950 I left my job as soccer coach at the Royal Military Academy and started in business with my friend and partner, Raymond Slayton. We soon realized that it was not just a case of putting up a sign with my name on it, and then sitting back to await results. In business, as in football, it's maximum effort that reaps rewards, and Raymond and I have gone all out to make our business a success. Our aim is to ensure that the customer is really satisfied; not to sell him something whether he wants it or not. With that principle we seem to have hit on a happy formula.

Playing football and running a sports shop represent a formidable working combination, but I've got plenty of other interests too. I enjoy a full and industrious family life at my Southgate home, with quite a large garden to look after, and with my fair share of Joan's housework and Sandra's homework to do! Sandra, of course, is my eleven-year-old daughter.

Friends are always popping in to chat, or to see the television, and sometimes Joe and Norah Mercer are able to get away from their grocery business near Liverpool to come and stay with us for a few days.

As you can imagine, sport is our main topic of conversation and on this subject Joan and Sandra, who see most of Arsenal's home matches, are perfectly capable of holding their own. Young Sandra is rather reserved, but knows her own mind and expresses opinions quite forcibly when moved to do so. She likes sport, and already shows quite an aptitude for skating, rounders and golf.

Golf is one of my favourite pastimes, by the way, and Mr. Whittaker has encouraged me to play more and more recently, in order to take my mind off my "knee", and to strengthen the ligaments at the same time. I don't claim to be in the same class as Arthur Milton, or Leslie Compton, but I can hold my own with most of the boys.

Among my other hobbies are motoring – Joan, Sandra and I often pop down to Gosport at weekends to see the folks – and reading. On train trips to away matches you'll usually find me in a corner with a good book, rather than in the solo and bridge schools.

Quite often there are official functions to attend, and I'm always glad to meet the members of the Arsenal Supporters' Club who, though not officially recognized, are one hundred per cent behind our team. They are probably the outstanding example of a supporters' club whose idea is to help, not hinder. It is particularly pleasing to find so many of our supporters at away matches, and they make all their own arrangements about tickets and travel. Much of the success of Arsenal Supporters' Club is due, I feel sure, to the enthusiastic and skilful organization of Mr. R. V. Jones, the secretary, and his wife. Although Mr. Jones is a Highbury season ticket holder, and I have often asked him to be my guest in the stand at away matches, he always insists on standing among the crowd on the terraces to be with the majority of his club members.

I'm a great believer in supporters' clubs: most of them do a grand job. At the same time, I can appreciate a club's reluctance to give them official recognition, because it might make supporters feel entitled to interfere in team policy, and that would never do.

Occasionally I have had the thrill of appearing on B.B.C. radio and television programmes, such as "Know Your Partner" (with George Swindin), and "Kaleidoscope". Recently, at the suggestion of Gordon Ross, my good friend who edits the Arsenal programme and makes it such a good job, I have become a member of the panel in a brand-new quiz game called "Owzat". This entertainment seems to be causing quite a lot of interest.

Besides all this activity, I frequently go along to youth clubs, amateur football clubs, and to factories, to talk about basic tactics and to answer questions about the game. In all these talks I emphasize that, while it is necessary for every player to master the individual skills of the game (such as kicking, heading, tackling and ball control), soccer is first and foremost a *team* game. I try to make my talks simple and straightforward, because that's what I think soccer tactics should be. They are mostly a matter of common sense, and I've no time for all the "fancy talk" and technical theory. Rather I am in sympathy with the attitude of such level-headed practical coaches as Bill Bowes, who is said to have told fast bowler Freddie Trueman: "Forget all this fancy stuff. Just bowl *blooming* fast." Full-backs? Learn all the individual skills of the game – practice hard – learn to fit in with your team – and use your loaf. That's my recipe for success.

However, no doubt my younger readers will expect me to give them some advice about full-back play in this book, so here goes.

First you must realize that while forwards are famous for their success, defenders are usually noticed for their mistakes, so in a sense the best defenders are those who make the fewest mistakes! However, a good defender can also start attacks.

Contrary to popular belief, you needn't be a big, beefy bloke to make a full-back. Indeed, if you are hefty, you may find yourself at a disadvantage, for the modern defender has to be every bit as quick as everyone else, and he must be particularly quick on the turn.

His is a combination of several jobs, the first and most important of which, in my opinion, is to cover the centre-half and the centre of the pitch at all times.

The reason that I put this first is because most goals are scored from a position in between the lines from which the goalie takes his goal-kicks, and those scored from an angle are

237

comparatively few. Thus the centre of the goal area is the door that has to be shut at all costs.

Many full-backs have the impression that their main job is to stop the winger from scoring, or even crossing the ball into the centre. This is wrong, to my mind, because by concentrating exclusively on this task a full-back is playing purely for himself, and not for his team. He may even prove a liability to his side in this way.

As I see it, you should always be thinking about your colleagues; play from their point of view, and fit your ability to suit theirs – don't expect everyone else to alter their style to suit yours.

From the full-back's point of view the golden rule is: never be caught square across the pitch with your partner. I know that some club pairs play "square" to each other, and they play the offside game, but in my opinion this denotes a general weakness – not just in defense but in the whole team, because the defense is part of the attack, and the attack is part of the defense. Attack and defense are not two separate units on the playing-pitch.

For instance, when the ball is in that area of the field which is occupied by your outside-left and your opponent's right full-back, then you, as a right-back, should position yourself well towards the centre of the pitch and at least five yards behind your own centre-half on a diagonal line. With the play on the other side of the pitch, you are thus covering the middle of the field in the event of a counter-attack.

You should position yourself similarly when facing a goal-kick, or a free-kick taken from the opposing right flank and for corners which are taken by your own outside-left.

I know that this method will leave the wingman you are marking well out on his own. But in order to travel from the opposing right full-back to his left winger, the ball has to cover fifty or sixty yards, and while it is doing so you will have plenty of time to get across and force your man down the wing.

A notorious example of bad covering of the middle of the pitch occurred in the 1951 Cup Final between Blackpool and Newcastle United.

Right from the start Blackpool defense adopted offside tactics. There were nine hair's breadth offside decisions given against the Newcastle forwards in the first half.

Five minutes after the restart, Jack Milburn put Newcastle ahead with a dramatic goal, receiving the ball in midfield and going through on his own to score from fifteen yards out. In its progress from Newcastle's penalty area to the Blackpool goal, the ball was only touched by three players, and one of them was George Farm who recovered it from the back of the net.

On this occasion the Blackpool full-backs were as wide open as the old barn door, so that when Milburn had rounded the centre-half with the ball at his toe, he had the field clear to do whatever he pleased. If both, or even one of the Blackpool backs had been obeying the fundamental rule of positional play, Milburn would not have had a free cut at goal and the result of the 1951 Final might have been quite different.

In this case, with Milburn coming through in the centre, both full-backs should have closed in on him, leaving the wingers to do their worst. They were a long way from the danger area.

With regard to marking the winger my advice is, "Don't lose any sleep over his reputation." You can easily get the wind-up if you let your mind dwell on his ability shown in previous performances while actually, on the day, he may be doing everything wrong, while it will be your turn to do everything right.

If you are opposed by a clever ball player, my advice is to let him keep possession of the ball and try to keep him on the touch-line. The longer he has the ball, the tighter your defense becomes and the better they will be placed to start an attack when the ball comes into their possession.

Of course, to play this way you must have a good understanding with the rest of your team, but it is a method that has stood me in good stead in my duels with many famous First Division wingers, and I recommend it to you.

In order to become a complete team player it is most important that you should ask yourself, "What are my limitations?" And don't kid yourself – we've all got some sort of weakness in our play. You should always be prepared to have those limitations criticized and discussed by your colleagues for the good of the team.

In a match against Preston North End in February 1952, I made a mistake that cost a league point, and perhaps the runners'-up position in the league table. I called for a short goal-kick from George Swindin, but even as I did so I saw Charlie Wayman, the little Preston centre-forward, coming up very fast, so I decided to return the ball at once to George for safety. In doing this, with half and eye for Wayman, I committed the cardinal error of taking my eye off the ball for an instant. The result was that I miskicked – allowing Wayman to intercept and put the ball into our net.

This was an example of lack of understanding in the defense, and I take full blame for not ensuring that George was fully prepared for me to pass back to him.

Not that I would condemn the practice of passing back to the goalkeeper. Done at the right time – and not overdone – it can be a very useful move, and sometimes it is essential. For instance, when you are facing your own goal-line it is much better to tap the ball back for your goalie to clear than to attempt an unnatural clearance yourself.

I've talked about defending, now what about the full-back in attack? One means of starting an attack, to which I have already referred in this book, is by means of the cross-field pass.

Imagine that you are playing at right-back and you have just taken the ball from the opposing outside-left. You take the ball forward for two or three paces then hit it across the field to your own outside-left who, if he has been thinking from the team's point of view, will have retreated well into his own half and away from the opposing right-back.

This pass enables you to achieve three things. You can clear your lines, start an attack and cause your opponents to open their defense momentarily.

The great thing to remember is that you should never kick the ball back to the place it has come from. This is bad tactics because the place the ball has come from is where the players are congregated in strength. Clearances of this kind usually cost goals.

It's just a matter of common sense, isn't it? "Do the simple thing, and do it quickly," is another good rule to remember, whether you are attacking or defending.

For example, never hesitate to give away a corner in order to relieve pressure. An emergency is no occasion for fancy stuff. Over the line with the ball then. That's the safe thing to do: it gives your team time to reform, and time is the important factor when the opposition are in your danger area.

Finally, here are a few more of my golden rules for full-backs, and I think they explain themselves:

1. *Prevention is better than cure.* Try to check the danger before it starts by intercepting passes to the winger.
2. *Let "Safety First" be your motto when defending.* Don't dribble close to goal, play the way you are facing, don't clear across the goal, always head away towards the wings.
3. *Be prepared for all defensive emergencies.* Have a close understanding with your colleagues. Don't unsight your goalie. Work to an agreed plan, and don't be drawn out of position unless you are absolutely certain of getting the ball.
4. *Always try to drive the man with the ball outwards.* Keep your body between the ball and the centre of your own goal.
5. *It's not the big kick that means a good clearance, but the good pass.* Try to place the ball just over the heads of intervening opponents but don't over-kick your own forwards. Having cleared your lines, follow up in formation.
6. *And, last but not least, play for the team* – not for yourself.

At one time or another, I should imagine, everyone connected with soccer has been persuaded to select the "best team of all time" from the players he has known. I've always refused to do it, because I've never been able to see how once can make comparisons between players of different teams, different generations and different styles. Hughie Gallacher, Tommy Lawton, Trevor Ford – all great centre-forwards in different ways with different teams at different times. How can one possibly say which of them is *best*?

No, I'm not going to stick my neck out in that way. Besides, I'm all against building up individual personalities in this game of ours. Throughout this book I have tried to emphasize my opinion that it is the team that matters.

So what I will do is to select a team of "team men" – the ten men I would most like to have playing with me assuming that each one is at his peak, not necessarily because they are the best players I've ever seen in each position, but because I know them to be one hundred per cent good triers and good troopers.

Here goes then:

In goal I should want *George Swindin*, and I'd choose *Laurie Scott* for my full-back partner. Half-backs? *Joe Mercer*, *Tommy Jones* and *Ronnie Burgess* pick themselves straight away, and with no argument as far as I'm concerned. On the right-wing I'd have *Billy Elliott*, who used to play for West Bromwich Albion, and who played in a Victory International for England, with the one and only *Jimmy Logie* as his partner. Centre-forward? Trevor Ford, of course, but it's a pity I can't have Tommy Lawton too! *Peter Doherty* is my choice for inside-left but for outside-left I can't choose between *Leslie Smith*, who was the best natural two-footed left winger I've played against, and *Denis Compton* who was, to my mind, as great a natural footballer as he is a great natural cricketer.

There now – I've done it! So please don't write and tell me about all the fine team men I have left out. I know!

Chapter Twenty-Five

Soccer is my sport, and I play it today with as much enjoyment as I did as a schoolboy, and kick-about amateur. But it's also my trade. From a purely practical point of view I look upon myself as a skilled tradesman in a major industry; and there's no doubt about it, professional football is very big business indeed.

From humble beginnings, the game of football has grown into the most popular game in the world. Now it is so much more than a game.

On any Saturday afternoon between mid-August and May, a million people watch a thousand young men play football for less than a hundred professional league clubs. For this entertainment they pay, between them, £7million in gate money every season.

Nine million people fill in the football pool coupons each year, investing £60million, each hoping to win a prize of up to £75,000 any week for a correct forecast.

Twenty-five thousand people are employed by the pool magnates to mark the coupons and to see "fair play". Sports journalists are present at the matches to tell the world the results, and the story of the games. Directors, managers, trainers and coaches, sit back in their seats and try to relax. The week's preparations completed, now it's up to the twenty-two men on the field of play.

And as the ball sails towards goal, propelled by the foot of a player whose talent may be worth more than £30,000 in the football market, spectators, listeners and viewers hold their breath....

If that ball enters the net you may find yourself rich tomorrow. If it doesn't, then maybe your neighbour will be lucky. The fate of many people is pinned to the accuracy of that shot: dependent on the skill and agility of the goalkeeper.

But the player kicking the ball, and his opponent – trying to stop it from entering the net: how do *they* stand? How much does it mean to them in hard cash?

As a "craftsman" I am on the maximum rate of pay – that is to say that I receive £15 a week during the playing season and £12 in the summer, subject to tax. In addition, when I am a member of Arsenal's wining team, I receive a bonus of £2; I get £1 for a draw. In each case the bonus is subject to tax.

Our club contract says that after five years service' we *may* receive a benefit of up to £750. By the time the tax man had finished with my benefit, in 1948, I received £470.

What about international matches? The fee we have received in recent years is £30 a match – which is worth about fifteen guineas after tax has been deducted, though it's since been increased to £50 gross.

Like other international players, I have the opportunity to make a little extra money by writing for the Press, sponsoring advertiser's products and so on. In this way, in a reasonably good year, my football income amounts to £1,000, less tax.

I don't think it's enough.

Let's get it straight: I'm not complaining personally. I've always had a straight deal from my club, my country; from the spectator, the Press and from the game as a whole. Like many others I play football because I love it: I'd play whether I was paid or not, so long as I could afford to do so.

But bearing in mind the amount of money brought into the game by the efforts of the players at the top of the profession, I consider they are grossly underpaid.

Mind you, I don't advocate that wages should be as fantastically high as those paid to sportsmen in some other countries; and I'm against the payment of "star" money to individuals – that, to my mind, would destroy team spirit. I agree that it is necessary to fax a minimum and maximum basic wage.

But what I would like to see is a higher basic wage for the skilled tradesmen and, in addition, a more imaginative system of payment by results.

How can this be achieved? It's a very complicated question I know, and better brains than mine have wrestled with it in an attempt to find the ideal solution.

The scheme that I favour most is the one that Tom Whittaker has put forward. "Let the players share the profits," is his theme. He believes that players should be made shareholders in their club.

A similar idea has been successfully worked in the theatre business; artists naturally spare no effort to ensure that their production is a successful one because of the promise of rich individual rewards.

How would it work out in football? Well, in 1952, after tax had been paid, Arsenal showed a profit of over £20,000. Under Mr. Whittaker's scheme, at the season's end, each player on the staff would receive a shareholder's dividend from this money in proportion to his number of team appearances and his length of service.

Now hold it, chums! I know what you're going to say! It's all very well for the Arsenal, and for other clubs that draw big gates, but what about the unfashionable teams – those that have to struggle along, often with no profit margin at all?

All right! My answer to that is: "Arsenal were not always fashionable. They did not always draw big gates."

And under Mr. Whittaker's scheme, what an incentive the "working shareholders" of unfashionable teams would have to play winning football – the kind that would draw the crowds and thus create a profit margin.

It's a good scheme and I'm all for it.

But I do realize that a number of clubs are in immediate need. It isn't an incentive *they* need, but a lifeline.

Well, there's nothing very extraordinary about that position. All big businesses need money from time to time. They find it by encouraging investment.

Why shouldn't the Pools put money back into soccer to help the struggling clubs? Just after the war, I remember reading a statement that the Pools Promoters Association would be willing to consider cooperating with the F.A. in a scheme designed to benefit players and the game generally. So they should in my opinion. Why was nothing done about it?

Finally, what about the money that is allowed to go out of the professional game and into the coffers of the amateur clubs via the F.A. Cup? Now that the amateurs have their own Wembley Cup Final, and bearing in mind that Mr. Butler has freed them from paying entertainment tax, I feel that the time has come to bar amateurs from the F.A. Cup competition.

The Cup is the salvation of many small professional clubs. They rely on a good share of the big third-round gates to keep them going. So when they see an amateur club advance to a late stage at the expense of the professionals, taking a huge slice of the kitty to bolster amateur club funds, can you blame them if their cheers are somewhat faint?

In 1953, for instance, Walthamstow Avenue took £5,000 from their tie and replay with Manchester United alone. I'm not saying that they didn't earn it – their brave and courageous display captured the sympathy and support of all football followers. But Avenue are not in the game for financial reward, and the professional game, with its many financial problems, cannot afford the luxury of permitting amateur giant-killers to steal such plums.

And with the amateurs out of the F.A. Cup, you'd still have your romantic giant-killers from the Third Division and non-league professional clubs, and if amateur associations forfeited their allocation of Wembley tickets, genuine supporters might even get the chance of seeing the Cup Final!

Incidentally, I've heard rumours that there is a class of player about who calls himself an amateur, but who actually makes quite a lot of money out of the game. If those rumours are true, and if there is such a person as a sham-amateur, then he is a creature I despise. Why can't he come out in the open? If he wants to be paid to play, let him earn his money in the professional ranks where he rightly belongs, instead of acting the spiv among true-blue amateurs, the type we all admire.

After spending a whole season as a soccer spectator, I now find myself looking at our game from the point of view of the man on the terraces, as well as from the player's angle, and I can no longer let my love of the game blind me to its faults.

Brighter soccer did you say? Yes, I'm all for it. Let's start a campaign.

But *my* way of achieving brighter soccer may be different from yours. You say, some of you, let's have some changes in the game and its organization. You want to tighten up the rules – change the promotion and relegation system – alter the league points system. I'm all against that. I think the game's all right as it is – it's an improvement in the standard of play that I'm after; an improvement that I'm sure would lead to brighter soccer.

Let's take some of your points first. You ask for timekeepers and goal judges? I'm against it. There are enough officials already. If you have your way the players will become no more than puppets, controlled and hampered with supervision at every move.

You want kick-ins instead of throw-ins? I don't. There's enough time wasted now with throw-ins – free-kicks would take more time in my opinion. And if the object is to "keep the ball on the island", then I'd say that a kick is not as dangerous as a well-organized throw-in.

You don't agree? Then you couldn't have seen Cliff Britton's and Jimmy Hagan's system at work. Playing for Aldershot they never failed to use a throw-in to advantage. It requires study, but with practice and cooperation any team can achieve similar results, and their opponents would be loth to give them the opportunity.

You want to cut out the indirect free-kick inside the box? No, I say: I regard this as a necessary evil. There are offences committed inside the penalty-box (such as obstruction, and the goalkeeper taking more than four paces with the ball), and they do not rate a penalty. The indirect free-kick is the fairest way of dealing with them. The trouble with this rule is that so few have taken the trouble to learn it.

A few years ago, at a luncheon in Bristol, I was asked, "Why do players so often commit the blunder of anticipating the referee's whistle?"

My reply was, "The reason is that not more than twenty per cent of our players know the rules of the game." I added, "Most clubs need to tighten up training and discipline, especially for younger footballers who are inclined to think they know all the answers and all the moves after six months in professional soccer."

That is still my opinion. The average player should know more about that rules of the game than he does now, and the clubs should do something about it. One afternoon every week could be usefully spent in discussing the rules and their interpretation. It would cut out a whole lot of argument and gesturing on the field of play.

Change the rules? No – learn the present ones, I say. If the laws are tightened any more there will be no loophole for the human element, and one of the reasons the average spectator enjoys a football match is that it provides an outlet for his feelings. It's his privilege to cheer and boo: to agree and disagree as he wishes. Take away all the doubts and controversies and what is there left? A very orderly and dull entertainment indeed.

For ninety minutes on a Saturday afternoon the professional footballer is the property of the spectator, and generally speaking the British fan gives him the treatment he deserves. When he plays well he earns a big hand: when he fails

248

to please he earns a boo. And I say that players are not big enough for the game. To me, the leather-lunged fan is as much a part of the game as are the ball and the goalposts. Take away the fan's opportunity, and his right to boo, and you are depriving the game of part of its character.

Another of the spectator's traditional targets for criticism is the referee, and from what I have seen recently, many refs deserve the treatment they receive. The standard of refereeing is not as high as it should be, and the shortage of top-class officials is serious.

One way of overcoming this would be to encourage selected professional players to take the referee's examination and to qualify during their playing days. Properly trained ex-professional players make first-class referees in my opinion. George Reeder, the former Southampton pro, is a shining example. I consider him to be the best referee of modern times.

Of course I am aware of the age difficulty. An ex-player retiring from the game at thirty-three, cannot qualify in less than seven years, by which time he is too old to go on the league list. That is why I suggest that players should be trained during their playing days. It would help them, and help the game too. A better all-round standard of refereeing would cut out unnecessary rough play, time-wasting and petty infringements, all of which spoil the game as a spectacle.

All right then, I've gone out of my way to try and destroy some of your pet ideas; now, you're entitled to ask for my recipe for brighter soccer.

Well, here it is in a nutshell:

Leave the game as it is, but improve the efficiency of its players by paying them better wages and offering the financial incentives that will encourage talented youngsters to make football their career. Tighten up on club discipline: insist that players train harder to maintain the high standard of craftsmanship for which they are being paid.

249

What of the future? To most soccer folk the future is summed-up in one word – floodlight. All over the country the lights are going on in an attempt to cash-in on the new spectacle and to attract a vast new public of Saturday afternoon workers to soccer as an entertainment .

No doubt about it – floodlight football opens up tremendous possibilities. In the near future I'm sure we shall see big clubs forming local Floodlit Leagues in different parts of the country, and making night soccer a regular entertainment. Not only that, it can be used to boost reserve team games, and to allow part-time players to train after office hours.

Before long, I'm sure, *all* clubs will have installed floodlighting equipment, and then I can foresee normal league games being played under floodlight as well as under daylight conditions. There's no reason why they shouldn't be, providing both home and away matches between the same two clubs take place under the same conditions.

Then there is the International Tournament. At present, international fixtures drain clubs of their best players when representative matches and vital club matches coincide, and the international programme must necessarily be curtailed. But now that football can successfully be played at night, there is no reason why the international programme should not be extended, with a number of showpiece games being played by floodlight.

It means more matches and harder work for the players, with an added risk of injury. Well, why not, providing the players are allowed to share in the extra profits? And as for injury, why, a player faces a hazard potentially as dangerous while crossing the road to go to the cinema. He might get knocked down by a bike!

Let's get soccer lit up by all means. It's the one sure way of brightening up the game.

Now I've told my story and I've had my say. I'd like to add; thanks for listening. It's been fun going back over the years and recapturing the laughs, the thrills and the proud moments that soccer has given me, and I've been glad to have the opportunity of getting a few things off my chest.

"There are easier ways of making a living than by playing football. The job's got glamour all right – plenty of it while you're on top. But make one mistake – run into a spot of bad luck – and you're liable to find yourself on the slippery slope. Fail them once, and the chaps who praised you last week will be the first to abuse you, and they won't be slow to remind you of the youngster ready and eager to step into your shoes."

With this warning, bitterly spoken to me by a once famous player, I entered the ranks of professional football ten years ago. I was prepared for the worst, but the worst never happened. Not for an instant have I regretted my choice of career.

Twice, I nearly had to quit because of serious injury; but each time loyalty and understanding on the part of my colleagues helped me to fight my way back. Now I've started on another come-back, and once more I'm reminded of that warning. This time, perhaps, it'll be different.

But I've got the answer. It's this. So what? Soccer's been good to me, and it doesn't owe me a thing. If I want to take more out of the game, I've got to put more into it, and if my best is no longer good enough, then let that youngster have my place in the team and good luck to him.

I'm back where I started; all the honours and medals count for nothing. If I'm going to keep my place in the red shirt, it's up to me!

Also available from GCR Books:

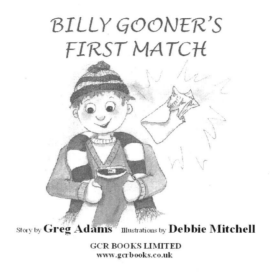

BILLY GOONER'S FIRST MATCH

Story by **Greg Adams**   Illustrations by **Debbie Mitchell**

GCR BOOKS LIMITED
www.gcrbooks.co.uk

Billy Gooner's First Match is a story about a special occasion for all Arsenal supporters; going to watch the team play for the very first time.

It's 1976 and Billy Gooner celebrates his seventh birthday with an unexpected trip to Highbury with his Dad to watch Arsenal play West Ham United.

Billy's day is filled with highs and lows and lots of goals and ends with a birthday surprise he'll treasure forever.

Visit **www.gcrbooks.co.uk** for details.